Coulon de Villiers

Coulon de Villiers

An Elite Military Family of New France

FEATURING THE TRANSLATED WORKS OF
AMÉDÉE EDMOND GOSSELIN,
PIERRE-GEORGES ROY, AND AEGIDIUS FAUTEUX
WITH ADDITIONAL APPENDICES

TRANSLATED AND EDITED BY
COL. SAMUEL L. RUSSELL, U.S. ARMY, RETIRED

Russell Martial Research

SAVANAH, GA.
2018

Also by Samuel L. Russell
Sting of the Bee: A Day-by-Day Account of Wounded Knee and the Sioux Outbreak of 1890-1891 as Recorded in the 'Omaha Bee' (Carlisle, Pa., 2016)

Cover art: Sketch art of François Coulon de Villiers and three medalions of the Royal and Military Order of the Knights of Saint-Louis representing the three brothers who were so knighted.

Russell, Samuel Lawrence, 1966 -
Coulon de Villiers: An Elite Military Family of New France, featuring the translated works of Amédée Edmond Gosselin (1863-1941), Pierre-Georges Roy (1870-1953), and Aegidius Fauteux (1876-1941) with additional appendices / edited and translated with a preface and notes by Samuel L. Russell.

ISBN-13: 978-1546388463
ISBN-10: 154638846X

Library of Congress Control Number: 2018943156

First Edition: June 2018

Copyright © Russell Martial Research. All rights reserved. No part of this book may be reproduced in any manner without the express written consent of the publisher, except in the case of brief excerpts in critical reviews or articles. All inquiries should be addressed to Russell Martial Research at info@RussellMartialResearch.com.

Russell Martial Research books may be purchased in bulk at exclusive discounts for sales promotion, corporate gifts, fundraising, or educational purposes, and signed copies may be available on request. For details, contact Russell Martial Research at info@RussellMartialResearch.com.

To the Order of the Indian Wars

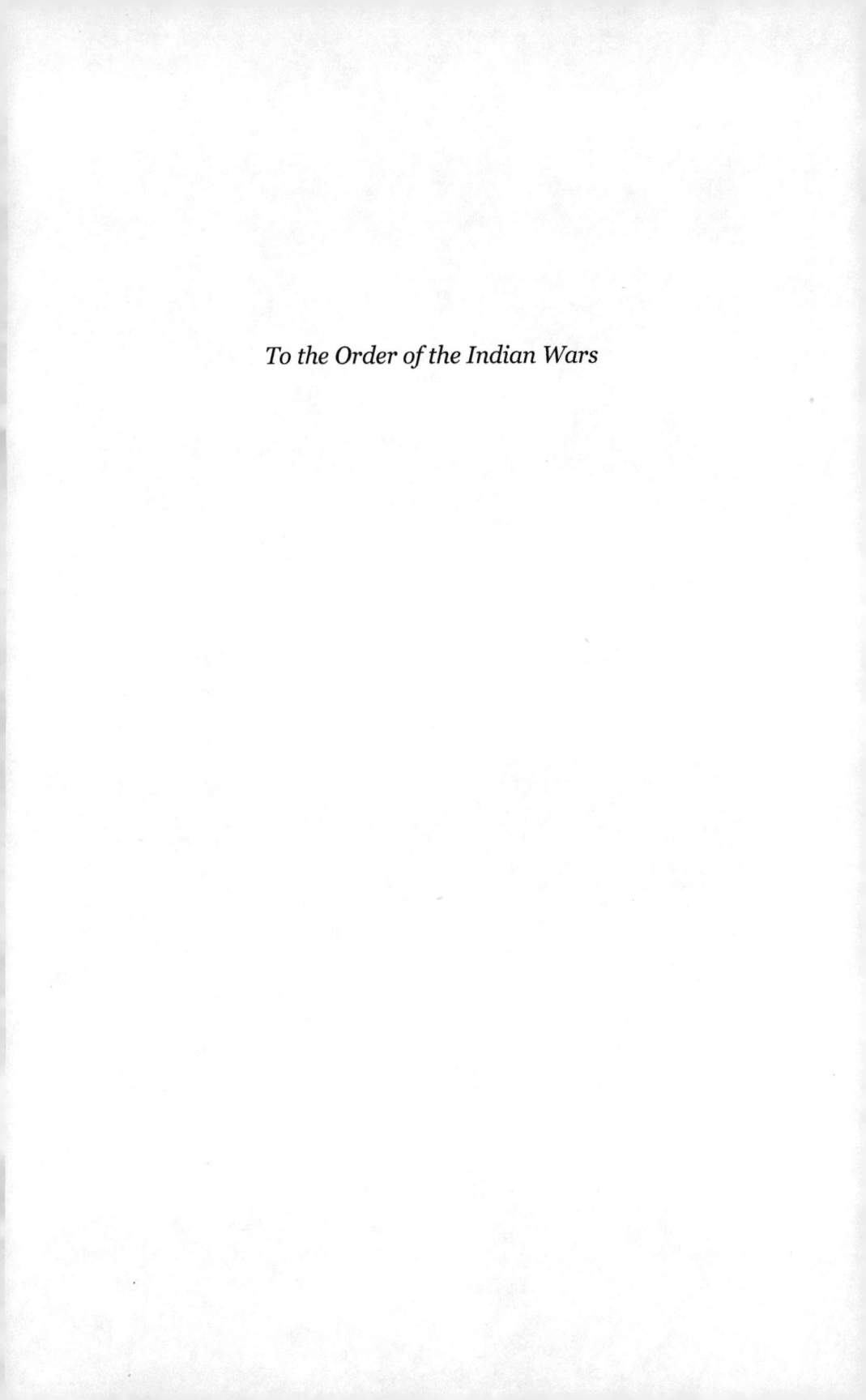

Table of Contents

Table of Illustrations ix
Preface xi
Gosselin's Introduction 1
I. Head of the Family: Nicolas-Ant. Coulon de Villiers 3
I-A. The Nobility of Coulon de Villiers 11
II. Children of Nicolas-Antoine Coulon de Villiers 14
III. Nicolas-Antoine Coulon de Villiers, the son 21
IV. Joseph Coulon de Villiers, Sieur de Jumonville 33
IV-A. The Descendants of Coulon de Jumonville 44
V. Louis Coulon de Villiers known as le Grand Villiers 47
VI. François Coulon de Villiers, known as le Chevalier 69
VII. The Damsels de Villiers 85

Appendices

A. 1730 De Villiers Report of Destruction of the Fox 92
B. 1733 Beauharnois-Hocquart Letter of de Villiers's Death 97
C. 1734 Beauharnois Letter of Captain de Villiers's Death 101
D. Grignon Reminiscence of Captain de Villiers' Death 105
E. French Account of the Battle of Les Mines 108
F. Contrecoeur's Summons Borne by Jumonville 112
G. Captain Contrecoeur's Order to Jumonville 115
H. 1754 Journal of Louis Coulon de Villiers 117
I. Villiers Seeks the Cross of Saint-Louis 132
J. The "Jumonville" of Thomas and Washington 134
K. Portrait of Le Chevalier de Villiers 141
L. 1777 Petition to the King of Spain 142
M. Genealogy of Chevalier de Villiers 148
N. The Knights of Saint-Louis in Canada 151

Endnotes 175
Bibliography 207
Index 215

Table of Illustrations

1. Amédée Edmond Gosselin 2
2. Signature of Nicolas-Antoine Coulon de Villiers 6
3. Signature of Pierre Lespiney de Villiers 18
4. Signature of Nicolas-Antoine Coulon de Villiers, the son 23
5. Signature of Joseph Coulon de Villiers, sieur de Jumonville 35
6. Signature of Le Chevalier François Coulon de Villiers 66
7. Signature of Louis Coulon de Villiers 67
8. Signature of Le Grand Villiers 67
9. Signatures from the capitulation of Fort Necessity 68
10. Occidental part of New France or Canada 89
11. Battle of Grand-Pré 111
12. Assassination of Jumonville at the fort of necessity 114
13. Washington Surrenders 131
14. Portrait of Le Chevalier de Villiers 141
15. Grand Cross sash badge of the Order of Saint-Louis 156

Preface

Lord of Verchères, Destroyer of the Renards, Victor at Les Mines, Vanquisher of Colonel Noble, Major of Three Rivers, Capturer of Fort Granville, Survivor of Iroquois and British Captivity, Alcalde Ordinario of New Orleans, Knight of Saint-Louis, and, most famously, Avenger of Jumonville, Victor at Fort Necessity, and Vanquisher of Colonel Washington. These are among the formal and informal titles bestowed by peers and historians upon the officers Coulon de Villiers comprising a father and his six sons. All were killed, wounded, or died of disease in the service of their King. Their military exploits ranged along the St. Lawrence River from Acadia to Quebec and Montreal to Niagara; across the frozen lands of the upper country from Lake Ontario to Lake Michigan, Lake Erie to Lake Huron, and from Lake Superior to Green Bay; through the Illinois country down the Illinois River and the mighty Mississippi, to the Gulf of Mexico; along the Belle-Riviere down the Allegheny and Ohio Rivers and up the Monongahela; along the Red River from Natchitoches to New Orleans; and throughout the vast expanse of 18th Century French colonies in North Amercia that were the territories of Acadia, Canada, Illinois, and Louisiana. Among the sons, three were knighted into the Royal and Military Order of Saint-Louis. Truly they were among the elite military families of New France.

Yet despite their renown, or perhaps because of it, the accomplishments of these seven men have been overlooked, ignored, misunderstood, or misconstrued by historians spanning more than two and a half centuries. It was this confusion that inspired Monsiegnor Amédée Edmond Gosselin at the beginning of the 20th Century to mine the Canadian archives and distinguish father from sons and brother from brother. His 1906 work, *Notes sur la famille Coulon de Villiers*, did much to correct the record and properly attribute to each their own accomplishments. However, his work has never been translated into English, and, despite it being oft cited, the Coulons de Villiers continue to be misrepresented by American historians and authors.[1] Gosselin's work is thorough, but not infallible. Access today to a far richer vein of archival records provides additional clarity. It is for these reasons that I have undertaken this work to translate and "correct and complement."

I have supplemented Gosselin's landmark *Notes* with translations of several other French-Canadian works on the subject, those of Pierre-Georges Roy and Aegidius Fauteux, so as to provide a more complete record of the Coulons de Villiers and the officers with whom they served. In addition to the Monseignor's four original appendicies, I have included nine more that provide important primary sources written by or related to the Coulons de Villiers and the more noteworthy events in their lives. These include the previous translations and editorial works of Reuben G. Thwaites, James Chattin, Joseph L. Peyser, Henry B. Dawson, and Dr. Gilbert C. Din.

Where I have come across mistakes, I have corrected the record; my notes are [*bracketed and italicized*]. I have sought out Gosselin's original sources in order to provide a more complete description listed in the bibliography, and I have expanded it to provide a more thorough list of works that touch on or delve into the Coulon de Villiers family. Finally, I have presented the footnotes of Gosselin, Roy, and Fauteux as originally published, denoted by-Roman numerals, and have added, for correction or complement, my own endnotes, annotated with Arabaic numerals.

Gosselin believed his work was important to historians who study and document the old Candain families. Far more reaching, I believe his work, and that of the others presented in this book, are important to any who would study and record the origins of the American Revolution that was the French and Indian War. Like Gosselin, I do not pretend to be infallible, and can only hope that these translations of Gosselin, Roy, and Fauteux's works will assist future scholars in providing a more accurate and thorough account of the exploits of the officers Coulon de Villiers.

COL. SAMUEL L. RUSSELL, U.S. Army, retired

Gosselin's Introduction - Notes for the Coulon de Villiers Family

Among the families that distinguished themselves in Canada during the last years of French domination, there are few more remarkable than that of the Coulons de Villiers, who are not as well-known as they ought to be.

Two of its members, Jumonville and his avenger, have more easily escaped oblivion. The reason for this is very simple: the Coulons de Villiers are rarely identified in the documents by their Christian names, and historians, without devoting too much attention to giving each one the credit that belongs to him, have attributed to one of them—the avenger of Jumonville—the acts and gestures of two of his brothers.

The absence of the Christian names and the confusion resulting therefrom have therefore caused some members of this interesting family to remain in the shadows, and they have not been accorded all the justice to which they are entitled.

Despite all the difficulties, we have tried to shed some light on this issue. We do not flatter ourselves with having succeeded, but we can at least give testimony of having spared neither time nor research. Let those who are better informed than we, correct and complement us.

The title we give to our work indicates enough that we do not intend to write a detailed history of Coulon de Villiers. Our aim is simply to make known the different members of this family, to give each one their rightful share, to present the pros and cons in the debated questions, and finally to collect materials for the future historian.

As to the facts already known, which belong to the general history of Canada, we give only just what is necessary to show the part taken by those of whom we speak; for the other details, we take the liberty of referring to the historians who have dealt with these questions. These pages will appear dry to many; nevertheless, they may have some interest to those who deal with the history of our old Canadian families, and this is what commits us to publish them.

We would like to thank those who have helped us in our work; We cannot name them all, but we would think we were wanting in the strictest duties of gratitude if we did not mention the name of one of the descendants of the family de Villiers, Mssr. J.-W. Cruzat, of New Orleans, who has provided us with several precious documents on his ancestor.

❧

Ill. 1. Amédée Edmond Gosselin

[*Catholic priest, professor at the Petit Séminaire de Québec, archivist at the Séminaire de Québec from 1904 to 1936, superior of the Séminaire and rector of Université Laval from 1909 to 1915. Born on September 30, 1863, in Saint-Charles de Bellechasse, son of Eugène Gosselin, farmer, and d'Arthémise Fournier; died at Quebec on December 20, 1941.[2]*]

I. HEAD OF THE FAMILY: NICOLAS-ANT. COULON DE VILLIERS

It has been said and repeated that the Coulon de Villiers brothers originated in France.[i] That is a mistake. All were born in Canada. But the head of this family came from France, and it is advisable to make known the father before dicussing the children.

Nicolas-Antoine Colon (sic) de Villiers seems to have arrived in Canada at the end of the 17th century. In fact, on October 16 of that year, Mssr. de Callière,[3] writing to the minister, informed him that, according to the King's letters, he had received the Sieurs Duplessis, sons, Fournier de Belleval and de Villiers.[ii]

A note in the catalog of officers of Canada,[iii] for 1701, states the said originating in Nantes [*sic: Mantes*] and aged 19 years.[iv] In 1703, he was found in a garrison at Montreal. Appointed as a witness at a trial, he wrote down his names and surnames: "Nicolas-Antoine Colon de Villiers, squire, lord of the place, ensign in the company of Longueuil,[4] aged about 20 years and now being garrisoned in this city."[v]

---

[i] Cf. Thomas: *Poème de Jumonville*, 1759. Sargent: *The History of an Expedition Against Fort DuQuesne in 1755*.

[ii] Official correspondence of the governors, VI, 21. (Copy in the archives of the Seminary of Quebec.)

[iii] Archives of the Seminary.

[iv] Abbé Casgrain in the biography of Mssr. de Gaspé, whose maternal grandmother was a Coulon, said he was allied with the grand master of the Order of Malta, Villiers de l'Ile Adam. We could not verify this statement.

Daniel, (*Histoire des grands familles, supplement*, pp. 417), speaking of the Coulon de Villiers, asserts that a family of this name still exists in France; His arms are: "*Azure with the chevron of gold, accompanied, in chief, of two stars, and in point of a stag, all the same.*"

L'Annuaire de la noblesse, of which Mssr. P.-G. Roy has kindly provided us with numerous extracts, mentions several families de Villiers still living in France and Guadeloupe in recent years; But there is no question of Coulon de Villiers.

[v] We owe this note and several others to the kindness of Mssr. Ph. Gagnon.

He was still in Montreal in 1706, at least in passing. In fact, on July 17, he appears as a witness to an act of donation made by Philibert Roy to the Ladies of the Congregation.[i]

We do not wish to state that Mssr. de Villiers habitually resided in Montreal. In his capacity as a soldier, he was not to remain in the same place for long. He did not, however, move far from the Montreal area, and lived several years at Verchères, where the King maintained troops. It was at least there that he went to seek a wife, and where most, if not all, of his children were born.

The marriage record, which would have been so useful to us to know the precise place of their birth, the names of the parents, father and mother, no longer exists. The years 1704, 1705, and 1706 are missing from the registers of Contrecoeur, where all the marriages, baptisms, and burials of the surrounding parishes took place.[ii]

However, we know roughly the date of the marriage of Mssr. de Villiers. According to the register of insinuations,[5] in Montreal, the contract was passed, before the notary Abel Michon, on December 7, 1705. Unfortunately, this book contains only what one might call the financial part of the contract.[iii]

If the register of insinuations is correct, Mssr. de Villiers married at the end of 1705 or at the beginning of 1706.[iv]

He married Angélique Jarret de Verchères, daughter of François and Marie Perrot and sister of the heroine of that name.[v]

---

[i] Registry of Adhémar, Montreal.

[ii] We are indebted for this note of several extracts of baptisms to the Abbe Ducharme, curator of Contrecoeur.

[iii] In sending us this information, Mssr. Leandre Lamontagne pointed out to us that Michon's office is at Montmagny. The research that we made there done by a friend has resulted in nothing. Abel Michon who would have notarized this record in 1705 received his commission of notary only on June 17, 1706. How to explain this?

[iv] As a general rule, the contract took place a few days, sometimes a few weeks before the marriage was celebrated; there are cases where the contract was made afterwards, but these examples are rare.

[v] Madeleine de Verchères is well known for her beautiful defense against the Iroquois in October 1696: only our heroine, who gave herself 14 years at the time, was actually 18½ years old, having been baptized on

This alliance, one of the most brilliant at that time, shows that Mssr. de Villiers was himself to belong to a good family, and, moreover, to have personal qualities.

From this union were born several children, whom we shall later make known.

The documents tell us little about the life of Mssr. Villiers from 1706 to 1725; It must be remembered that the country, under the good governance of Mssr. de Vaudreuil,[6] enjoyed an almost complete peace, and that opportunities of self-identification were relatively rare. Mssr. de Villiers therefore, like many others, had to lead the rather monotonous life of the garrisons, either in Montreal or in the surrounding region, but more particularly at Verchères, where his family lived.

In 1714, most of the troops of Canada and that of Three Rivers were vacant by the death of their holders. Two promotions of captains to these posts left two companies and, consequently, two lieutenants. Mssr. de Villiers asked for one of these lieutenancies, for it seems to us that it is to him that the following note relates to the table of advances: "Des Villiers, French, nephew of the Sieur De la Fausse, valet of the King's wardrobe, who asks for his advancement—has been an ensign since 1700—is a good officer."[i]

On March 14, 1715, the minister wrote to the Princess of Nesmond that he would propose to the King the advancement of Mssr. Coulon de Villiers.[ii]

Thanks to this certificate of "good officer," thanks also perhaps to the recommendation of his uncle, and to the patronage of the Princess of Nesmond, Villiers obtained his promotion. It was announced in a memorial of the King to Mssr. de Ramezay,[7] on July 10, 1715.[iii]

April 17, 1678. A happy time that when young, their age was already forgotten! Cf. Report of Richard, 1899. [*Canadian histories date the attack to October 22, 1692, when Madeleine was 14 years old.*]

[i] Official correspondence of Governors quoted by Mssr. J. E. Roy, *Bul. R. H.*, II, p. 117.

[ii] Report of Richard, 1899, p. 475.

[iii] Ibid, p. 115.

Three days later, on July 13, Mssr. de Pontchartrain[8] wrote to Mssr. de Villiers himself to inform him that the King had granted him a lieutenancy.[i]

Again, there was silence on the part of Mssr. de Villiers, and it was not until 1725 that he was found, commander for the royal post at the St. Joseph River of Illinois, where he seems to have replaced Mssr. de Villedonné.[9]

On August 26, 1725, the name of Mssr. de Villiers appears for the first time in the register of the fort. It is to a record of baptism, in which the godfather is Nicolas-Antoine Coulon de Villiers, "son of Mssr. de Villiers, commander."[ii]

Mssr. de Villiers, the father, was himself a godfather on November 30, 1726, and the registry said, "of present commander for the King in this post."

On November 25, 1730, he again had a child on the baptismal font. This time the missionary, Fr. Mésaiger, S. J., wrote: "Mssr. Coulon de Villiers, squire, lord of Verchères and commander for the King in this post."[iii]

Finally, on January 31, 1731, a record of baptism in the same post again gives him the title of commander.

At the bottom of almost all these records which we have just mentioned, Mssr. de Villiers signed with a good and fairly beautiful handwriting:

Ill. 2. Signature of Nicolas-Antoine Coulon de Villiers.

We have just said that on November 25 Mssr. de Villiers is called in the register: lord of Verchères. This seigniory, which Mssr.

---

[i] Ibid, p. 482.
[ii] Registry St. Joseph of Illinois—Archives of the Seminary.
[iii] Ibid.

de Verchères had acquired in 1672 and increased in 1673 and 1678,[i] was, by his death, passed to his wife. It would appear from a record under the seal of François Raimbault, seigneur de Saint-Blin, that Madame de Verchères conceded it in whole or in part to Mssr. de Villiers. In this record of August 22, 1733, Saint-Blin declared himself authorized by Mssr. de Villiers to grant land in the seigniory he had acquired from Madame de Verchères.[ii]

Madame de Verchères had died at the end of September 1728,[iii] and it may happen that Madame de Villiers, her daughter, had received part of the seigniory.[10]

Be that as it may, the records of faith and tribute do not mention this transfer of property.

The last years that Mssr. de Villiers passed through the upper country [*Great Lakes region*], were rather turbulent. It was the time when the Meskwaki or Fox tribe, whom they [*the French*] had thought were destroyed in 1712, reappeared more insolent and more dangerous than ever. Abandoned by the Kickapoo and the Mascouten, their former allies, they nevertheless continued to evoke terror among the surrounding nations.

In May 1730, they had taken some prisoners near le Rocher on the St. Joseph River in the Illinois. Mssr. de St. Ange,[11] who then commanded the Fort de Chartres, assembled four hundred Indians and a hundred Frenchmen, and attacked them in the fort which they had built near le Rocher.[12] It was August 17; two days later the Fox asked to parley, but they did not want to listen to them, and they continued to shoot at them. A few days afterwards Mssr. de Villiers arrived with five hundred Indians and fifty or sixty Frenchmen. On his side, Mssr. de Noyelles[13] brought two hundred Miamis. Against such considerable forces one might have thought that the Foxes could not resist for an extended time; yet the siege was longer than expected. Famine prevailed on both sides.[iv] In the report which he left of this expedition, Mssr. de Villiers said: "The siege of their

---

[i] *Doc. sur la Tenure seigneuriale*, Quebec, 1852, pp. 6, 7, 8.
[ii] Montfortqué Registry, Montreal.
[iii] Tanguay, *Dictionnaire*, IV, p. 588.
[iv] Ferland, *Cours d'Histoire*, II, pp. 437 and next.

fort lasted 23 days, they were reduced to eating the leather, and we were scarcely better." Then he relates how, in the midst of a storm, and in the favor of the night, the Foxes had escaped, how they had been pursued, joined, and massacred, etc.[i]

This affair was in the month of September, and despite the advanced season, Mssr. de Villiers had to hasten to send news to the governor. He commissioned one of his sons, probably the eldest, Nicolas-Antoine. Parkman writes[ii] that "Late in the autumn of 1730 young Coulon de Villiers, who twenty-four years later defeated [*Colonel George*] Washington at Fort Necessity, appeared at Quebec with news that Sieur de Villiers, his father, who commanded the post on the St. Joseph, had struck the Meskwaki a deadly blow and killed two hundred of their warriors [*besides six hundred of their women and children*]."

If this young Coulon is the eldest son of Mssr. de Villiers, as we think, Parkman is mistaken in saying that it was the same who took the fort of Necessity in 1754.

As to the date of this journey, it must be correct, since, as early as May 1731, Mssr. de Beauharnois[14] had the news. That day he wrote to Mssr. de Maurepas[15] about the Meskwaki: "This is a nation humiliated to such an extent that it will no longer trouble the earth."

There is something here that we admit we do not understand. Mssr. de Montigny,[16] wrote from Fort Michilimackinac, to Mssr. de Saint-Pierre,[17] on June 18, 1731: "Mssr. de Villiers passed a few days ago to conduct the Fox to Montreal, to request mercy of life from the General, accompanied by a few persons from every nation near the St. Joseph River; I do not know what the intention of the two is."[iii]

Which Mssr. de Villiers? Is it still young Coulon? Had he had the time since the previous fall to go up to St. Joseph River and set out for Quebec City on June 18? This is possible, but we do not believe that this is the young Coulon, but Mssr. de Villiers, the father.

---

[i] Report of Richard, 1899, p. 133. [*See appendix A for Nicholas-Antoine's report.*]

[ii] *A half century of conflict*, I, p. 328.

[iii] Original letter; Archives of the Seminary.

The Head of the Family

And it was probably on this trip to Quebec that he received his appointment as commander at the post of La Baye [*at present day Green Bay, Wisconsin*].

He was certainly appointed to this post in 1731. On April 22, 1732, in a memorial addressed to Mssrs. de Beauharnois and Hocquart,[18] the king approved that they had sent the Sieur de Villiers to reestablish the post of La Baye.[i]

This news could not have been sent to the Court until the previous year.

Ferland relates[ii] that in 1732 a number of Christian Iroquois and Hurons wished to carry a last strike against the Foxes; three hundred people were killed or taken. The few who escaped went to Mssr. de Villiers, who then commanded the fort at La Baye.

Despite their repeated defeats, the Foxes did not consider themselves beaten; they had ended up with the Sauk and had taken refuge in their own home at the bottom of La Baye. Mssr. de Villiers undertook to go and dislodge them. On September 16 (1733), he arrived at the post. He summoned the Sauk chiefs, and told them that the governor was ready to pardon them, provided they went to Montreal, and he added that if, at such a time that he indicated, the Foxes were not before him, he would go and fetch them. They did not budge. Mssr. de Villiers, with Mssr. de Repentigny[19] and a few Frenchmen, went towards the enemy. There, without paying any attention to the warnings of the Sauk, he set about striking the gate. At this moment, a gunshot fired by a Sauk, killed the son of Mssr. de Villiers. A general discharge followed, and Mssr. de Villiers himself was killed with Mssrs. Repentigny, Duplessis-Faber and several French.[iii]

Mssr. de Villiers had shown great courage, but he had been wanting in caution, and was reproached for it. The President of the Marine Council wrote to Mssr. de Beauharnois on April 12, 1735: "It appears that in the La Baye affair it was the imprudent and reckless

---

[i] Report of Richard, 1904, p. 157.
[ii] *Cours d'Histoire*, II, p. 439.
[iii] Ferland II, p. 440.

conduct of the Sieur de Villiers that contributed most to what happened."[i]

At his death, Mssr. de Villiers was a captain. On April 13, 1732, the President of the Marine Council had written to him that, in order to reward him for his services and conduct in the [1730] fight against the Foxes, the King had "granted him the expectation of a company and his son who was part of the expedition an ensign *en second.*"[ii]

Mssr. de Villiers did not wait long for his rank as captain; he was appointed to the promotion on April 1, 1733.[iii] He scarcely had the news; In any case, we have seen that he did not enjoy it for long.

On April 13, 1734, the Marine Council announced to Madame de Villiers that a pension of 300 livres had been granted to her.[iv] It was very little when one considers that she remained a widow with several children, some of whom were still not very advanced in age. However, she received only the first payment of this pension, for she died the same year. She was buried in Montreal on December 30, 1734.[v]

This family now without a leader was dispersed; the boys were already in the service, and the youngest girls went to some relative's house, perhaps to their elder sisters who were already married.

---

[i] Report of Richard, 1904, p. 209.
[ii] Report of Richard, 1904, p. 155.
[iii] Archives of the Seminary.
[iv] Report of Richard, 1904, p. 193.
[v] Tanguay, IV, p. 588.

I-A. THE NOBILITY OF COULON DE VILLIERS

[Inserted here is an essay by Pierre-Georges Roy, "La Noblesse des Coulon de Villiers," in which he details the ancestry of the Coulon de Villiers family in France.[20] Gosselin's Notes sur la famille Coulon de Villiers continues immediately following with chapter II.]

Mssr. Aubert de Gaspé, and after him the Abbe H.-R. Casgrain wrote that the Coulons de Villiers were of the same family or at least allies of the great master of the order of Malta, Villiers of the Isle-Adam. It is known that the maternal grandmother of the author of the *Ancients Canadiens* and the *Mémoires* was a Coulon de Villiers. It was perhaps from his venerable ancestor that he kept this information. All the same, after having consulted many nobiliaries, we are led to believe that there was no relation of kinship between the Villiers of the Isle-Adam and the Coulons de Villiers.

It is certain, however, that the Coulons de Villiers belonged to the nobility.

Msgr. Tanguay, in his *Dictionnaire généalogique*, does not give Nicolas-Antoine Coulon de Villiers's original place in France, the first of this family who moved to New France. It was on April 26, 1700, that Mssr. Coulon de Villiers received from the King an expectation of ensign for the troops of Canada. He was to arrive at Quebec in the summer of 1700, for on October 16 of this year the governor of Callières informed the minister that, according to the King's letters, he had received the Sieur de Villiers.

A catalog of the officers of Canada for 1701, quoted by Msgr. Amédee Gosselin in his *Notes sur la famille Coulon de Villiers*, says "Coulon de Villiers, a native of Nantes, nineteen years of age." There is a mistake or an error of a copyist: Mssr. Coulon de Villiers was born not in Nantes but in Mantes, a small town situated on the left bank of the Seine, 42 kilometers from Versailles. Nicolas-Antoine Coulon de Villiers was baptized in the church of Saint-Etienne de Mantes on March 20, 1683. So, he was not yet eighteen years old when he came here [*New France*].

Coulon de Villiers

As early as 1594, Nicolas Coulon, Sieur de Chahagny and Méhéron, was mentioned as the royal provost at Mantes.[i] According to the records of the Chamber of Accounts of Paris, Nicolas Coulon was ennobled as early as 1590.

The filiation of our Coulon de Villiers is established perfectly and most likely from the early years of the seventeenth century.

On September 6, 1609, Fieffé and Tolleron, notaries at the Chatelet in Paris, received the contract of marriage of nobleman Nicolas Coulon, lawyer in Parliament, son of nobleman and wise master Nicolas Coulon, Lord of Chahagny and Boutainville, King, provost, ordinario civil and criminal judge of the city of Mantes, with Miss Marie Leber, daughter of nobleman Simon Leber, Sieur de Malassis, and young lady Rachelle Midorge.

From the marriage of Nicolas Coulon and Marie Leber was born a son, Guillaume, who was baptized in the parish of Sainte-Croix, erected in the royal and collegial church of Notre-Dame de Mantes, October 30, 1616. This Guillaume Coulon married, in turn, May 21, 1650, Ms. Elisabeth Le Couturier, daughter of Philippe Le Couturier, councilor secretary to the King, house and crown of France and his finances, and Anne Laubois. The marriage contract received before Besancon, a notary in the bailiwick of Mantes, described Guillaume Coulon as "squire, sieur de Chanteraine, counselor to the King, his procurator at the bailiwick, and the presidia seat of Mantes." It is this same Guillaume Coulon, Sieur de Villiers and Chanterenne, president of the presidia of Mantes, who, on June 8, 1669, obtained a judgment of the Council of State which kept him in his nobility.

Of this last marriage, among other children, there was Raoul-Guillaume Coulon who married at the parish church of Beaumont-sur-Oise, on July 4, 1677, young lady Louise de La Fosse, daughter of nobleman Antoine de La Fosse, Sieur de Valpantant, and of young lady Louise Le Grand. The marriage certificate, signed by Msgr. Vignon, parish priest of Beaumont, says of Raoul-Guillaume Coulon that he was Sieur de Villiers.

---

[i] E. Grave, *Supplément au nobiliaire et armorial du comté de Montfort l'Amaury*, p. 59.

It was from this last marriage that our Nicolas-Antoine Coulon de Villiers was born, baptized at the royal and parish church of Saint-Etienne de Mantes-la-Ville, diocese of Chartres, March 20, 1683.[i]

In a document dated February 17, 1762, Louis-Pierre d'Hozier, the chief judge of the nobility of France, describes the arms of Coulon de Villiers: "Azure, a gold fess charged with three letters sable, on a bend argent."

---

[i] Nicolas-Antoine Coulon de Villiers was orphaned of father and mother when he moved to New France.

II. Children of
Nicolas-Antoine Coulon de Villiers

In the catalog of officers quoted earlier, it is said, at the date of 1732, that Mssr. de Villiers had eleven children.

Ferland, after having related the death of Mssr. de Villiers (1733), adds that he left ten children.[i]

This note agrees with the first, since Mssr. de Villiers had a son killed with him in 1733.

Now one of the children had died in infancy, which would bring the number of these children to twelve. And if we admit that Therese, of whom no one mentions, is from the family, we must count thirteen children from Nicolas-Antoine Coulon de Villiers. According to us, seven sons and six daughters.

Reconstructing this family is not easy; we shall try it, however, with the help of the *Dictionnaire Généalogique des Familles Canadiennes* of Msgr. Tanguay, which we will correct quite often,[ii] and with the notes we have been able to collect.

The author of the *Dictionnaire*, in the two articles[iii] he has devoted to Nicolas-Antoine de Villiers and his family, identifies eight or nine of the children, yet in fact, he lists two with the eldest son, Nicolas-Antoine.

The family had to consist of at least twelve children, perhaps even thirteen.

We give them here in the order we think ought to belong to them, but we may be mistaken.

I and II.-- Marie and Madeleine, twins, born at the end of 1706 or the beginning of 1707. Tanguay clearly states that the first was born in 1706 and the second in 1707, but he gives these dates approximately because he has not seen the records. We have not seen them ourselves, since they have disappeared, but we rely on a note found in the archives of the Ursuline Dames of Quebec, which

---

[i] *Cours d'Histoire*, II, p. 440.

[ii] We recognize, nevertheless, the merit of the Abbe Tanguay: the *Dictionnaire* is a colossal work in which errors could and must have slipped; that is why it is always good to confirm it whenever possible.

[iii] I, p. 144; III, p. 167.

The Children

says that in 1720 the two young ladies de Villiers, aged 14, were admitted.[i] We should not understand that the two sisters had been given the same age if they were really of different ages.

III.-- NICOLAS-ANTOINE, born on June 25 and baptized on August 26, 1708.[ii] Tanguay denotes two sons of this one child: Antoine, baptized in 1708 and Nicolas, in 1709. The record of baptism that we shall quote further on proves that it is one and the same individual.

IV.-- LOUIS, born on August 10, 1710, baptized on November 13, according to the record. On the margin, the missionary wrote: Baptism of Louis Coulon this 13th of August of 1710. But the November 13 has not been corrected.

V.-- FRANÇOIS. He was later known under the name of Chevalier de Villiers. Tanguay does not name him, but tradition in the family indicates he was born in 1712, and in Montreal. The record of baptism is not to be found in the registers of Notre-Dame de Montreal, which we have had compiled. We think that François, like his brothers and sisters, was born at Verchères and that it was between 1712 and 1715; Unfortunately, the years 1712, 1713, 1714, are completely wanting in the registers of Contrecoeur,[iii] and we cannot affirm anything.

VI.-- _____ Immediately before or after François we would place that of his brother who was killed with their good-father in 1733, and whose name we do not know. [*François, in a 1777 letter, provided the name* DAMONVILLE *for his brother who was killed with their father in 1733. Likely, this was a surname taken later in life, much like Sieur de Jumonville. The Sieur de Damonville was between 18 and 23 years old when killed.*[21]]

VII.-- JOSEPH, surnamed de Jumonville, born September 8, 1718, baptized the next day.

---

[i] We have this information from Rev. Mother Marie of the Assumption, assistant archivist at monastery of the Ursulines Dames of Quebec.

[ii] All the baptismal records which we are about to quote are in the registers of the parish of Contrecoeur, where the missionary resided. The Abbe Ducharme, current curator of Contrecoeur, has kindly sent us the certified extracts of these records

[iii] Letter from the Abbe Ducharme to the late Abbe Rhéaume, December 9, 1901. (Archives of the Seminary)

VIII.-- PIERRE, born May 4, 1720, baptized the next day.

IX.-- CHARLES-FRANÇOIS, born June 14, 1721, baptized the 22nd of the same month and died on November 4 of the same year.

X.-- MARIE-ANNE, baptized on September 6, 1722.

XI.-- THERESE? We place here this young lady de Villiers, of whom no one mentions, because in the census of Quebec in 1744 she gave herself as 22 years of age, which would place her birth in 1722. Was she a twin of Marie-Anne?[i] Was she actually wrong in giving her age, or is she even a member of the family? What makes us believe she was part of this family is that she lived with Nicolas-Antoine in 1744.

XII.-- MADELEINE-ANGÉLIQUE, and not *Marie*-Angélique, baptized January 31, 1726, born eleven days earlier according to the record.

XIII.-- MARGUERITE, whose record of baptism and the record of her marriage with Pierre de Gannes Falaise, have not been discovered, is only known by the burial of her daughter, buried at Pointe-du-Lac, September 27, 1757.

This list, if it is accurate, identifies thirteen children: seven boys and six girls.

In a certificate dated 1784, Mssr. de Beauharnois said that Mssr. de Villiers, a captain killed in action against the Sauk and the Foxes, had six children and two sons-in-law.[ii] Although the governor did not say that Mssr. de Villiers had six children with him at St. Joseph's River, it seems to us that we cannot read this sentence otherwise: for it was probably he who, in 1732, had informed The Court that Mssr. de Villiers had eleven children.[iii]

These sons were Nicolas-Antoine, Louis, François, Joseph, Pierre, and another whose name we did not find [*Damonville*[22]], and who was killed with his father.[iv]

---

[i] Would not she have been baptized with Marie-Anne?

[ii] Note of Mssr. Villiers at the strike from Mssr. J.-W. Cruzat.

[iii] Officers' Catalog of Canada. (Archives of the Seminary)

[iv] Cf. Registry St. Joseph of Illinois and service statement of Jumonville.

The Children

The two sons-in-law of whom Mssr. de Beauharnois speaks were Mssr. Duplessis-Faber, who was killed in action, and Mssr. Dagneau-Douville.

We have made the family known, as a whole, and now must discuss each of its members in particular; it is not the easiest part of our work.

Hitherto, what has deceived the historians who have occupied themselves with the de Villiers is the uniformity of names, or, if we prefer, the absence of the Christian names. At first sight, it seems that all these brothers, apart from Jumonville, were only known by the name of Mssrs. de Villiers. But an attentive study of the documents leads us to believe that they each had a proper appellation which allowed their contemporaries to distinguish them from one another.

Thus, the elder, Nicolas-Antoine, is most often Mssr. Coulon, simply. Louis was to answer in the name of Mssr. de Villiers, and later that of Captain de Villiers. Joseph, was called and signed Jumonville. François was known as the Chevalier de Villiers. Finally, Pierre seems to have added to his name that of Lespiney. [*Again, the unnamed brother, according to François, was known as Damonville.*[23]]

For clarity, we will follow not the chronological order of their birth but that of their death.

Charles-François having died at an early age, we do not have to speak of him. The same is true of the man who was killed in 1733, and whose Christian name we do not know. [*François wrote in 1777 to the King of Spain the following concerning the death of his father, brother, and brother-in-law, providing perhaps the only known documentation of this brother's name: "In 1733 I returned with my father against the same Indians who had taken refuge in the Sac's fort. In this action, my father was killed when he advanced to set fire to the fort's gate. My brother Damonville and my brother-in-law Duplessis experienced the same fate there."*[24]]

We have just said that Pierre seems to have added to his name de Villiers that of Lespiney. Perhaps we are mistaken, but despite all our inquiries we have not been able to connect him with any other family. LeGardeur de Villiers²⁵ did not leave any son, we believe. The others LeGardeur and L'Espinay do not seem to have had Villiers in their families, and besides, we do not find in their genealogies a single child named Pierre who corresponds, at least in age, to the one in question: we have concluded that Lespiney de Villiers belonged to the Coulon family as Jumonville de Villiers was himself. [*François in his 1777 letter to the King of Spain confirms that Lespiney was his brother when he stated, "My other brother, Lepinay, also died in the same [1747] fight."*²⁶

*The first mention we have found of the use of the name Lespiney, or L'Epinay, is in a document dated July 15, 1740. It only adds to the confusion of this Villiers's name, for it is signed by "Joseph L'Epinay DeVillier," not Pierre. Written below his name is, "Ye Captain of a Marine Detachment and commander of the party returning from the Chickasaw, certify that Mssr. DeVilliers de l'Epinay provided me the supplies listed above to complete the payment of a slave for the replacement owed Raven; made in Montreal July 15, 1740. Signed Céloron."*²⁷]

On March 24, 1742, Lespiney de Villiers was a godfather at St. Joseph's River in Illinois, where Nicolas-Antoine, the eldest of the Coulons, was then commander. The missionary, Fr. Du Jaunay,²⁸ a Jesuit, after writing to the record, Pierre Lespiney de Villiers, erased the word Lespiney, but a little farther on he changed his mind and wrote again Pierre Lespiney de Villiers.

Two years later, in March 1744, he was again a godfather; the record says cadet *à l'aiguillette*.

In the first case the godfather signs in a very neat script:ⁱ

Ill. 3. Signature of Pierre Lespiney de Villiers.

ⁱ Registry of St. Joseph of Illinois.

The Children

In the role of officers and cadets appointed to go with Mssr. de Saint-Pierre[29] and dated October 22, 1745, we find the name de Villiers Lespinay.[i]

Finally, we meet him in 1746 as part of the expedition against the English in Acadia: that is where he died.

In his diary of the 1746 – 1747 campaign in Acadia, Mssr. de Beaujeu[30] stated on December 25, 1746: "Mssr. de Lespinay de Villiers fell quite dangerously ill from the place where he was in winter quarters to hear Mass at Beaubassin."

And January 2 he wrote: "Mssr. Lespiney Villiers died at 3 o'clock in the morning, giving during his illness silent, harsh evidence of great patience and perfect resignation to the will of the Lord, especially when it was announced to him that it was necessary to make the sacrifice of his life. All those who approached him at this last moment were undoubtedly edified by the feelings of religion of which he seemed to be constantly occupied."[ii]

That is all that we know about Pierre Lespinay de Villiers; we are waiting for a researcher to tell us whether he belonged to the Coulon family or not. [*Indeed, we now know that he did belong to this family through the testament of his brother François.*]

We may be asked whether Pierre[-*Joseph*] Neyon de Villiers, who was one of the principal officers of Louisiana at the time of the conquest, was not the same individual; we seek to identify.

O'Callaghan[iii] and some others with him have believed it was him. We admit that we ourselves had not thought otherwise at first. Fortunately, Mssr. Villiers du Terrage in the *Les dernières années de la Louisiane française*[iv] put the matter in order, and the following extract leaves no doubt about it:

Chevalier Pierre Joseph Neyon de Villiers, he said, was born in Lorraine of a family nobler than rich. In 1735, he was ensign in the regiment of Choiseul, 1738, reformed, 1742, lieutenant in Marinville; 1744, aide-major in the Royal-Lorrain (wounded in Weseembourg); 1747, captain (took part in the battle of Land-pest); 1748,

---

[i] Archives of the Seminary.
[ii] *Canada-Français* 1889, doc. unpublished, p. 37.
[iii] *Doc. of New York*, X, p. 1160, note.
[iv] Paris, E. Guilmoto, 1904[, *p. 190*].

Coulon de Villiers

reformed, 1749, attached to the body of Louisiana; 1755, major commanding officer at Fort de Chartres, Illinois; 1759, Knight of Saint-Louis; returning to Paris in 1765, he stayed there until 1772; placed himself at the disposal of Kerlérec to defend him in his trial; 1773, colonel of the regiment of Guadeloupe; brigadier-general in 1775; governor of *Marie-Galante*; died at sea, August 1779.[i]

---

[i] Note to the kindness of Mssr. J.-W. Cruzat.

III. NICOLAS-ANTOINE COULON DE VILLIERS, THE SON

Although the author of the *Dictionnaire généalogique* makes two characters of it, Nicolas and Antoine, we do not hesitate to affirm that the two names belong to the same individual. Let us prove it by citing the record of baptism.

> In the year of Our Lord, one thousand seven hundred and eight, on the twenty-fifth of June, a son—he was given the name Nicolas-Antoine—was born to him of the legitimate marriage of Nicolas-Antoine Coulon de Villiers, ensign from a company of detachment of Marines, and Angélique Jaret de Verchères his wife, and the twenty-sixth of August, I, Louis de la Faye,[31] priest, parish priest of Verchères, supplemented him with the ceremonies of baptism because he was delivered at home by midwife Catherine Cara. The godfather was Joseph Jaret de Verchères[32] and the godmother was marguerite perrau. The godfather declared that he could not sign and the godmother signed with me.[i]
>
> (Signed)   Coulon de Villiers   De la faye,
>   Marguerite perrot
>
> Born June 25, 1708, this child was solemnly baptized on August 26 under the name of Nicolas-Antoine.[ii]

How is it that Msgr. Tanguay, in the first volume of his *Dictionnaire*,[iii] inscribes it only under the name of Antoine, when the record is so clear?[iv] We do not know. But this mistake led him to other errors, and one should not be surprised that he killed Nicolas-Antoine twice: Nicolas in 1750 and Antoine in 1757.

---

[i] Registry of Contrecoeur.

[ii] Baptized two months after his birth; facts of this kind are not rare in our old registers. The missionary was often absent, and it was necessary to wait until his return to carry the child to the churches.

[iii] p. 144.

[iv] In the first volume of the *Dictionnaire*, Tanguay does not speak of Nicolas; on the other hand, in the third volume, there is no question of Antoine but of Nicolas baptized in 1709.

21

Coulon de Villiers

Nicolas-Antoine made his debut, we believe, at the St. Joseph River of the Illinois. It is, at least, in the register of this post that one meets his name for the first time.

On August 26, 1725, he was godfather: "Nicolas-Antoine Coulon, son of Mssr. de Villiers, commanding officer," said the deed. He simply signed Coulon. This is the only time we have seen this signature.

In 1730, it will be remembered, he was deputed by his father to Mssr. de Beauharnois[33] to announce the defeat of the Meskwaki.

He took an active part in the campaign of 1733 against the Sauk. Mssr. de Villiers, father, had sent him, with ten Frenchmen and fifty Indians, at the passage of the little Cascalin, through which the Foxes could escape. It was while he was there that the tragedy of which we have spoken above took place on September 16.

Three days later, the Sauk having abandoned their fort in favor of the night, Coulon de Villiers assembled all the French and Indians, Ottawa, Menominee and Saulteaux,[34] whom he could find, pursued the fugitives, and reached them at eight leagues [*about 28 miles*] from the post. He attacked them, killed twenty-six, and wounded nine mortally.

Villiers, on the other hand, had two Frenchmen killed and some wounded, among whom was his brother, a cadet. The allied Indians also lost some of their own.

Coulon de Villiers remained, by the death of his father, commandant at the post of La Baye. He hastened to send the last news to Mssr. de Beauharnois. His brother (the Chevalier de Villiers) [*sic: Louis Coulon de Villiers*[35]] wounded in the last affair, and Mssr. Douville[36] left for Quebec, where they arrived on the evening of November 11.

On the same day, the governor and the intendant wrote to the minister informing him of the last blow of the Sauk.[i]

Mssrs. de Beauharnois and Hocquart took advantage of the opportunity to remind the minister that the death of Mssr. Villiers, captain, and Repentigny, lieutenant, "two great subjects lost by the

---

[i] Archives of Ottawa—General correspondence, vol. 60, p. 134. All these notes taken from the general correspondence were provided to us by the Rev. Father Odoric, O. F. M., to whom we offer our best thanks.

Nicolas-Antoine, the son

colony," had left two places for Mssrs. de Ramezay[37] and de la Martiniere,[38] and a lieutenancy, two ensigns *en pied*, etc., were still free.

"The sieur de Villiers," they wrote, "who has distinguished himself, who has had his father and brother killed, and another brother, a cadet wounded, deserves the vacant lieutenancy, the final affair having evolved due solely to him."[i]

The minister welcomed this request and Coulon de Villiers was a lieutenant with the promotion of March 30, 1734.[ii]

How long did he remain commanding officer at the St. Joseph River? We cannot say. We see by the register of that place that Mssr. de Muy[39] commanded there in 1735 and Mssr. de Lusignan[40] in 1738.

In 1740, on April 27, the name of Nicolas-Antoine Coulon, commander of this post, reappeared in the St. Joseph Register of Illinois. It is still found there on March 24, 1742. At the bottom of each of these records Coulon signs in beautiful handwriting:

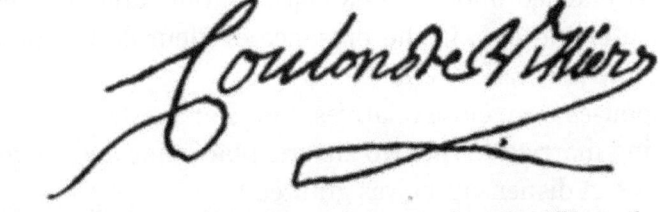

Ill. 4. Signature of Nicolas-Antoine Coulon de Villiers, the son.

[*In 1739 and 1740, there was a series of correspondence, now archived at Archives nationales d'outre-mer (ANOM), France, in which Coulon documented payment owed for supplies provided during the Chickasaw War. Beauharnois wrote to the minister on January 26, 1741, that he had ordered Coulon de Villiers to prevent the French at St. Joseph River from trading at Chikagon and Méolaki (modern day Chicago and Milwaukee) because of the ill effect they were having on the Indians there. Beuaharnois also*

---

[i] General Correspondence, Vol. 59, p. 37. In this letter of November 11, 1733, Mssr. de Beauharnois said that Mssr. de Villiers, father, had *with him* six of his children and two of his sons-in-law. This confirms what we have written above [*p. 16*] about a certificate of this governor.

[ii] Archives of the Seminary.

Coulon de Villiers

provided details of six letters from Coulon in which the latter detailed strikes by the Ottawa and Pottawatomi against Chickasaw and Cahokias against the Sauk, trouble between the Cahokias and the Peoria chief La Babiche, trouble of Illinois of Pimitoui (modern day Peoria) with the Fox, Sauk, and Sioux, and the voyage of the Indians of the St. Joseph River to Fort Chouaguen (modern day Oswego).⁴¹]

On October 30, 1742, Mssr. de Beauharnois asked for a company for Mssr. Coulon.[i]

The following year, on October 20, the governor returned to the charge with the minister in favor of Coulon de Villiers "good officer and very proper for negotiations in the upper country."[ii]

Mssr. Coulon descended from the upper country between March 24, 1742, and October 7, 1743. At the latter date, he married Marie-Anne Tarieu de la Pérade, the widow of Sieur Testu de la Richarderie.[iii] [42]

He was married under the name of Antoine Coulon, Sieur de Villiers, lieutenant, etc., in the presence of Sieur de la Gorgendiere,[43] Mssr. de la Pérade,[44] etc.

The spouses were close relatives, first cousins, their respective fathers being married to the two sisters, Madeleine and Angélique de Verchères. A dispensation was granted.[iv]

In 1744, Mssr. Jacrau[45] made the census of the city of Quebec. He inscribes Mssr. de Villiers under the sole name of Nicolas, says he is 36 years old, and an ensign of troops.[v]

---

[i] General Correspondence, vol. 75, p. 312.

[ii] General Correspondence, vol. 79, p. 233.

[iii] Contract of October 4, Du Laurent, not. (Note from Mssr. Ph. Gagnon).

[iv] Registry of Notre Dame of Quebec (at the registry).—We had first consulted the register of the curator of Quebec. There is no mention of the degree of kinship and the curator does not sign. The copy kept at the registry is complete.

[v] Archives of Notre-Dame of Quebec.

Nicolas-Antoine, the son

See how everything is right! In 1743, Mssr. de Villiers was called Antoine, and he was a lieutenant. This year, his name is Nicolas and is now only an ensign! We can see at once where such data may lead.

And yet this is the same character, since in both cases he has Marie-Anne de la Pérade as his wife.[i]

Nicolas-Antoine Coulon appears to have remained in Quebec until the spring of 1746. We just documented him there on the 1744 census. On April 25, 1745, he was the patron of his nephew, Nicolas-Antoine Tarieu.[ii] In the record, Mssr. de Villiers is said to be a captain, which would put his promotion to the year 1744.

On June 30, 1745, he signed the certificate of marriage of Roch Saint-Ours Deschaillons[46] and the same day to that of his sister Marie-Anne, who married Monsieur de Gaspé.[47]

On April 15, 1746, he was the patron of a daughter of Mssr. de Gaspé.[iii] After this date, the name of Coulon does not reappear in the parish registers. The reason was that he had left Quebec and he was to come back only in passing.

Several historians, among others Casgrain[iv] and Parkman,[v] have claimed that Coulon de Villiers, who took such a handsome part in Les Mines campaign, was the same as the one who avenged Jumonville in 1754. It is a mistake, for the one who led Les Mines campaign was none other than Nicolas-Antoine, who could not avenge his brother in 1754 for the excellent reason that he had been dead for four years.

The expedition which was to end with the Battle of Les Mines left Quebec City in June 1746 and was chiefly commanded by Mssr. de Ramezay.[48] At that time, five Mssrs. de Villiers were alive:

---

[i] Mssr. de Villiers lived on the Lamontagne coast. His neighbor, Louis Levrard, was the brother-in-law of his wife, with whom he was in a lawsuit shortly after his marriage. De Villiers won his case. (Archive of the Seminary).

[ii] Archives of Notre-Dame of Quebec.

[iii] All these records are in the registers of Notre Dame of Quebec City.

[iv] *Une seconde Acadie*, p. 160. In *Relations et Journaux*, collection Lévis, p. 65, note, the Abbe Casgrain attributes to the same de Villiers, the capture of Fort Granville in 1756.

[v] *A Half Century*, etc., II, p. 202.

Pierre, a simple cadet *à l'aiguillette* or at most an ensign, who died at Beaubassin on January 2, 1747, more than a month before Les Mines affair.

Jumonville, who was himself in Acadia [i] with Mssr. de Ramezay, was still only an ensign. It was not he who commanded at Grand-Pré.

Louis, a lieutenant, was at Quebec in November 1746: "The General has sent Monsieur de Villiers, lieutenant of the troops with a hundred Indians of Acadia, who winter in the environs of Quebec, to go to Montreal."[ii]

François, who was a lieutenant, since he was made captain in 1753 [*sic: 1754*], was in the upper country. On July 9, 1746, Mssr. de Beauharnois, in an ordinance to Mssr. De Muy, said: "He will command the party from the upper country, and have under his orders the chevalier de Villiers."[iii]

Finally, Nicolas-Antoine, was the only one who was captain at that date. He was the only one who could command Les Mines since it was not Jumonville, and Louis and François were not then in Acadia.

Let us recall in a few words this campaign which ended in one of the most beautiful feats of arms in Canada. We will take care more particularly of Coulon de Villiers.[iv]

Mssr. de Beaujeu[49] wrote in his diary, June 5, 1746:

> Six vessels destined to transport the detachment of the militia from Canada to Acadia, composed of seven hundred men, including twenty-one troop officers, sail on June 5, 1746, at nine o'clock in the morning, into the harbor of Quebec, under the orders of Mssr. Coulon, captain, second-in-command of the detachment, to go and wait for the Pot-à-l'Eau-de-Vie,[v] the

---

[i] Service Statements.
[ii] Corresp. off. of gov. (Copy to the Archives of the Seminary)
[iii] Archives of the Seminary.
[iv] For more details: Cf. Casgrain, *Une seconde Acadie*; The journal of Mssr. de Beaujeu, and of Lacorne published in *Canada français*. 1889.
[v] This is our Brandy-Pot of today. Why did they not keep the French name? [*Brandy Pot Island lighthouse in the St. Lawrence River near Rivière-du-Loup, Quebec.*]

Nicolas-Antoine, the son

ship the *Tourneur*, in which Mssr. de Ramezay, commander-in-chief, was embarked.

In consequence of circumstances which it would be too long to recount here, this expedition did not at first have all the success expected of it. On August 20, Mssr. de Ramezay was ordered to go back to Quebec with a portion of his troops, after having left five officers and 250 men to Mssr. Coulon, who was then at Les Mines.

The presence of Mssr. Coulon's detachment had been badly seen by the Acadians, and the deputies of Les Mines represented to Mssr. de Ramezay that it was impossible for them to feed so many men during the winter, and that besides this body of troops, far from having a favorable effect, would contribute to putting them worse with the English.

To calm them down, Mssr. de Ramezay replied that he would communicate their representations to the General; which he did, since on September 8 the governor sent orders "to Captain Coulon, who is to command the detachment of 300 Canadians who must winter in Acadia to calm and protect the Acadians from the resentment of the English."[i]

In the meantime, the Duc d'Anville's[50] squadron arrived at Chibouctou [*sic: Richibouctou*]. Despite the repeated orders of the governor, Mssr. de Ramezay, thought he might not return to Quebec at once.

Autumn and a part of the winter passed in marches and counter-marches of the various detachments which were distributed everywhere: at Les Mines, at Beaubassin, at Chibouctou, etc. Mssr. de Ramezay had taken his winter quarters at Beaubassin.

On January 8, 1747, it was learned by an Acadian that 250 Englishmen had returned to Les Mines since December 24.[ii]

At this news Mssr. de Ramezay assembled his officers and proposed to them to attack the English and dislodge them from Grand-Pré. Despite the difficulties of the enterprise all applauded the project.

---

[i] *Doc. relatif à la Nouvelle-France*, III, p. 302.
[ii] Journal of Lacorne, *Canada Français* 1889. p. 11. De Beaujou says on Nov. 24 (Ibid.)

Mssr. de Ramezay, who was suffering from a hurt knee and unable to walk, handed over the command of this detachment to Mssr. Coulon, captain. "This setback," said Casgrain,[i] "was more regrettable for him than for the expedition, for it counted in its ranks.... the Canadian *noblesse* that was braver and more experienced in this kind of war,—Coulon de Villiers was the same, who eight years later was to avenge the death of his brother, the chevalier de Jumonville, at fort Necessity, to beat Washington and make him prisoner," etc.[ii]

On February 9, the little band arrived at Pigiquit, five leagues from Grand-Pré. There it was learned that the English were at Grand-Pré, about six hundred men under the command of Colonel Noble.[51] [*See appendix E for the French report of the battle of Les Mines.*]

Mssr. de Coulon rested his people for a day. On the 10th, at noon, the troops continued their march, and in the evening, at nine o'clock, they camped half a league from Grand-Pré.

When sentinels were placed on the roads, the detachment, which had been divided into ten companies of twenty-eight men, spread to the houses on the other side of the Gaspereau River. They could then rest, dry their clothes, and take some food while gathering information about the English positions.

These were dispersed in 24 houses, one of which, made of stone, was defended by cannon.

Immediately Mssr. Coulon settled his plan of attack; since there were not enough men to attack the 24 houses at the same time it was decided to strike ten of them. Coulon, with 55 men reserved the stone house.

At two o'clock in the morning, everyone went out. Each took his rank, and at a given signal, officers and soldiers knelt while Abbe Maillard[52] gave the general absolution. Then they set off. A heavy downpour that had lasted a few days had rendered the roads difficult, and the guide who had undertaken to lead Mssr. Coulon to the stone house, having lost his way, stopped in front of another to be attacked by Mssr. de Repentigny.[53]

---

[i] *Une seconde Acadie*, p. 160.

[ii] The rest will prove that this is not correct and that Les Mines Commander was not the vanquisher of Washington.

Mssr. Coulon seeing that it was dangerous to ignore, bore down on the house and the whole troop followed him. De Beaujeu killed the sentry. The English, stunned for a moment, recovered themselves, made a general discharge, and Mssr. Coulon fell seriously wounded in the arm. De Beaujeu thought him dead, but, he added, "He withdrew as best he could out of the fight." At the same time Mssr. de Lusignan[54] received two serious wounds.

The battle continued for ten minutes, during which twenty-one Englishmen were killed and three were taken prisoner.

Meanwhile the other houses were attacked, and the English killed or taken prisoner.

"We forced the houses with axe blows," said Lacorne,[55] "and in a very brief time we made ourselves masters of it, and the officers and cadets distinguished themselves in this action, and all our Canadians gave signs of their courage. The enemy had a hundred and forty men killed, among whom were Colonel Noble, his brother, and three others, thirty-eight wounded, and fifty-four prisoners. Their killed were only seven men, including two Indians, and fourteen wounded, among whom were Mssr. Coulon and Mssr. Lusignan."[i]

Although the bulk of the battle lasted only a few minutes, the fire continued, from one house to another, until eleven o'clock in the morning. The English first demanded a cease fire, which they were granted, and then they consented to surrender.

On February 12, the capitulation was signed by the British, and French officers brought it to Mssr. Coulon who in turn signed it.

He had been transported to the Gaspereau River, where the surgeon had given him the first dressings, and then returned to Beaubassin with the detachment.

Mssr. de Villiers had received a wound more serious than was first thought. He suffered horribly. It was necessary to return to Quebec, but the distance was great and the communications difficult. He did not arrive until the evening of June 22: "Mssr. de Coulon arrives from the Baie Verte in his skiff and is still very much troubled by his arm."[ii]

---

[i] Journal of Lacorne, *Canada-Français*--These figures differ slightly from those given by Mssr. de Beaujeu.

[ii] Corresp. off. of gov. June 22, 1747. (Copy in the Seminary)

Coulon de Villiers

On July 10, Msgr. de Pontbriand,[56] writing in favor of Mssr. de Lusignan, said: "Mssr. Coulon, the captain, has sustained his reputation. A wound, which he will feel for a long time, soon put him out of action."[i]

Coulon de Villiers never recovered from this wound. Believing a voyage across the seas might do him good, he obtained permission to proceed to France.

On October 9, 1747, intendant Hocquart ordered Sieur Causse, commanding the French warship *La Gironde*, to take on board a certain number of passengers, to whom "he will be obliged to provide subsistence at his table and at his office during the crossing to France." Among these passengers were: "Mssr. de Coulon, captain, his wife and a servant."[ii]

Mssr. de Villiers went to take the waters at Bareges, a thermal spa in the Pyrenees.[iii] This is at least what we learn from the correspondence of Louisiana for the year 1749.[iv]

As Coulon de Villiers was a man of merit, the Canadian authorities warmly recommended him to the minister. On November 3, 1747, Mssr. de la Galissonnière[57] wrote to the latter: "I have the honor to represent to you that there are officers who by their wounds or by some other form of action deserve the Cross of Saint-Louis, or other rewards, or both, in which case Monsieur Coulon de Villiers is in the latter case, and the journey which he is obliged to make in France for his wound will entirely disturb his fortune if you have not the goodness to assist him liberally."[v]

This recommendation had its effect. A list of promotions for 1748 tells us that Coulon de Villiers was appointed Major of Three Rivers and a Knight of Saint-Louis.[vi]

---

[i] *Canada Français*, 1889. Doc. unpublished, p. 77.

[ii] General correspondence, vol. 89, p. 15.

[iii] Sulphurous thermal waters, famous especially for the healing of gunshot wounds. (Bouillet.)

[iv] Ministry of the Colonies—Note from Mssr. J.-W. Cruzat, supplied to him by Mssr. Villiers du Terrage.

[v] General correspondence, vol. 87 bis, p. 218.

[vi] Archives of the Seminary.

Nicolas-Antoine, the son

The cross to reward him for his bravery and the government to permit him, while remaining in service, to spare his injured arm. What more could one desire?

Mssr. de Villiers spent two years in Europe. On his return, he took possession of his office as Major of Three Rivers. On October 23, 1749, he attended the marriage of his sister Angélique, who married Charles de Gannes de Falaise. The deed identifies Mssr. de Villiers as Knight of Saint-Louis and Major of Three Rivers.[i]

After this date, nothing can be found about him in the registers of this parish.

He died the following spring "in Montreal, after having had his arm amputated, which was wounded and of which he could no longer bear the pain," wrote La Jonquière[58] and Bigot,[59] October 2, 1750. He was buried in this town on April 4, 1750.[ii] The record stated, "Nicolas Coulon, squire, Sieur de Villiers, Major of Three Rivers, at the age of 41, buried in the chapel St-Amable."[iii]

On October 2, 1750, the governor and the intendant asked the minister for a pension for the widow of the Major of Three Rivers:

> He left, they said, a widow to whom there is not enough to live on. She has consumed a portion of her property during the two years she has lived with him in France for the cure of his wound.—We beseech you, my lord, to procure her a pension which may help her subsist. We flatter ourselves that you will have regard to our request, which seems to us well founded, the death of Mssr. Coulon, from the wound he suffered at the action of Les Mines in which he commanded.[iv]

The inventory of the property of the late Mssr. Coulon and his widow Dame de la Perade took place on February 2, 3, and 4, 1752.[v]

---

[i] Registry of Three Rivers —We are indebted to a copy of this record to the Rev. Father Odoric. O. F. M., who was kind enough to compile a part of these registers for us.

[ii] General correspondence, vol. 95, p. 40.

[iii] Registry of Notre Dame of Montreal.

[iv] General correspondence, vol. 95, p. 40.

[v] Sanguinet and Du Laurent, notaries.

Coulon de Villiers

A few weeks later, on March 12, Madame de Villiers married Jean François Gaultier,[60] his Majesty's physician, counselor, etc.[i]

We do not know of any children born from this marriage with Mssr. de Villiers. According to the Abbe Daniel,[ii] she died about 1776, leaving no posterity.

The documents we have provided clearly demonstrate that Nicolas-Antoine is one of the brothers Coulon de Villiers, who commanded at Les Mines in 1747, and died of his wounds in 1750. There can be no question of him at the capture of the fort of Necessity in 1754, and still less that of Fort Granville in 1756. It will be easier now for us to present the part of those who remain.

⚜

---

[i] The contract entered into before Du Laurent was March 2, 1752.
[ii] *Histoire des grandes familles*, p. 457.

IV. JOSEPH COULON DE VILLIERS, SIEUR DE JUMONVILLE

Joseph Coulon de Villiers was born at Verchères on September 8, 1718, and was baptized the following day under the name of Joseph and not Joseph-Louis, as has been said a few times.

His godfather was Joseph de Verchères[61] and for godmother Marie-Anne Déjourdy.[i]

Jumonville's military career, however, was relatively short. It is also better known than that of his brothers, for, besides the fact that Jumonville's name prevents his being confounded with the other de Villiers, his *Etats de services*, enable us to follow him quite surely.

This *statement of services*, made to be presented to Mssr. Rouillé,[62] minister and Secretary of State of the Navy, span from 1733 to 1749 inclusive.[ii] We give them here, if not in form at least in substance.

In 1733, only 15 years old, Jumonville was in the fort at La Baye, under the orders of his father [*at the time that his father, brother, and brother-in-law were killed*].

What did Jumonville do from 1733 to 1739? He does not mention it. Perhaps he stayed at St. Joseph's in the Illinois? In 1739, he took part in the expedition against the Chickasaw, who, as is well known, were defeated and forced to make peace.[iii] [*In the report of Mssr. Edouard Richard, he details an account of the cadets* à l'aiguillette, *"Villiers-de-Jumonville—A very steady youth and eager to excel. Has been out against the Chicachas. A most promising officer."*[63]]

During the winter of 1745, he was found in Acadia under the command of Mssr. Marin,[64] and informed us that he spent the winter traversing the woods on snowshoes.

---

[i] Registry of Contrecoeur.

[ii] Archives of the Seminary.—An ancient copy brought from Europe by the Abbe Holmes in 1837.

[iii] Volume 44 of the Moreau St-Méry collection (Archives of the Marine), contains several accounts of this expedition. We find the names of Mssr. de Villiers and of the Chevalier de Villiers. (Richard's Report, 1899, 32)

Coulon de Villiers

The following year he was still in Acadia, but under Mssr. de Ramezay.[65] It is possible that he took part in the battle of Les Mines, although his name is not mentioned.

In 1747, he was sent to Riviere-aux-Sables, at the head of a party of French and Indians to oppose the Mohawks' incursions. The same year, he again campaigned against Corlar,[66] under the orders of Mssr. de Lacorne,[67] the elder.

Jumonville had the command of a party of the French and Indians raised in 1748 to go against the English. He left Montreal at the beginning of June, and on the 26th of the same month he was back. He had killed fourteen or fifteen enemy.[i] [*According to O'Callaghan, "The party, commanded by Sieur Villiers de Jumonville, has returned to Montreal with 5 English scalps; it had not time to remove those of 9 @ 10 other Englishmen, who were also killed. He attacked, between 3 forts, a party of the enemy, who made a gallant resistance. Two of our Iroquois and Sieur Hertel, the younger, have been killed."[68]*]

Finally, in 1749, Mssr. de la Galissonnière[69] entrusted him with the mission of going to put in order the post "disturbed, which he succeeded perfectly." [*This was the post at Nipigon on the north inlet from Lake Nipigon to Lake Superior.[70]*]

After recalling that his brother Coulon had died because of the gunshot he had received in Acadia, Jumonville ended his *Etats de services*:

> The supplicant hopes, my lord, that by virtue of the above services in which he holds the certificates, you will not refuse him your powerful protection for one of the three vacant lieutenancies in Canada, and he begs Your Highness not to lose sight of the death of his father, two of his brothers, and a brother-in-law killed in the service, and his gratitude will equal the sincerity of his wishes for your preservation.

---

[i] E. B. O'Callaghan, *Documents relative to the colonial history of the state of New York*, vol. X, p. 168.

Joseph, Sieur de Jumonville

This document must have been written after April 4, 1750, since Jumonville spoke of the death of Coulon who died on that date.

This plea so well motivated, however, was not heard and Jumonville died an ensign.

And again, this rank of ensign he had long awaited to receive. On October 20, 1743, Beauharnois[71] proposed Jumonville as ensign *en second*.[i]

The following year, on October 30, the governor returned to the charge and remarked that the ensigns *en second* would be filled by Srs. Villiers de Jumonville and Rigauville[72] who have the first expectations of this year.[ii]

Finally, on November 8, 1745, Beauharnois wrote to the minister that he could provide for one ensign, Villiers de Jumonville.[iii] Was he heard this time? We like to believe it.

It is difficult to say what Jumonville did from 1750 to 1754. Only the inventory of his brother Nicolas-Antoine's property, made in 1752, tells us that he was then garrisoned in Montreal. He gives his proxy and signs:

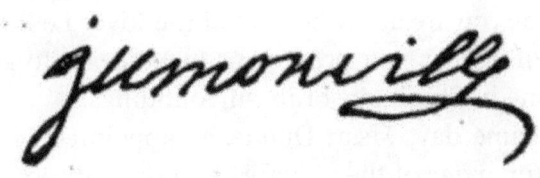

Ill. 5. Signature of Joseph Coulon de Villiers, sieur de Jumonville.

[*Peyser writes that in May of 1752 Jumonville "was sent to France by Acting Governor General Charles LeMoyne de Longueuil[73] to report on rebel Indians in New France, the assignment reflecting considerable trust and confidence in the officer."[74]*]

Then we come to the fact that has made his name famous not only in Canada but in a part of Europe.

What we have rightly or wrongly called the assassination of Jumonville is well known. Historians of both French and Canadian,

---

[i] General correspondence, vol. 79, p. 233.
[ii] Ibid., vol. 81, bis, p. 282.
[iii] Ibid., vol. 83, p. 221.

English and American have dealt with this subject at length so that it is not necessary to go into all the details.

However, we believe that it will be useful to give an overview of the facts.

Everyone knows that the French and the English were fighting for possession of the valley of the Ohio, called the Belle-Riviere.[75]

Shortly after his arrival in the country, Mssr. Duquesne[76] wrote to Mssr. de Contrecoeur,[77] the commanding officer at Niagara, to inform him that he was about to send a detachment of 2,200 men to occupy the disputed territory.[i]

Unavoidable delays prevented the governor from putting his plan into effect at once.

On January 27, 1754, he wrote to Mssr. de Contrecoeur, whom he had appointed on December 25, 1753,[ii] commanding the River Le Boeuf [*now French Creek*] and dependencies, to go with 600 men to take possession of the Belle-Riviere. "Although," he said, "I have no reason to suppose that the English or the Indians have any inclination to oppose an open force to the taking possession of land which belongs to us. It is prudent, and from the wise precaution, that as soon as you are at the bottom of the River Le Boeuf with the last convoy of effects, you press your movements to go and build Fort Duquesne in Chiningué or its surroundings."[iii]

On the same day, Mssr. Duquesne appointed Mssr. de Contrecoeur commander of the new fort and the entirety of the Belle-Riviere.[iv]

The governor deceived himself into thinking that the English would not oppose their taking possession of the Ohio valley.

Before he had written the above, towards the end of 1763, Dinwiddie,[78] governor of Virginia, had sent Washington to summon Mssr. de Saint-Pierre[79] to abandon the territory he occupied. The latter had replied that he could do nothing without the consent of his General and that in the meantime he would keep his post.

---

[i] Letter of Oct. 28, 1752.—Archives of the Seminary.
[ii] Archives of the Seminary.
[iii] Ibid.
[iv] Ibid.

Joseph, Sieur de Jumonville

Informed of the fact, Duquesne immediately wrote to Mssr. de Contrecoeur:

> I have just received a dispatch from the Sieur de Saint-Pierre, who has sent me expressly a letter from the Governor of Virginia, in which he claims that Belle-Riviere belongs to them and summoning the commander of the detachment to retire peacefully.
>
> As the governor does not write directly to me, I will confine myself to ordering you, that in case he should again summon you, you must inform him that in your instructions it is asserted that the Belle-Riviere and its dependencies belong to His Most Christian King incontestably. That regarding the insults made against the law of nations he cannot attribute any of them, and that if the English who come to treat on our ground are arrested, it is because we are entitled to do so because we do not go to them. That, furthermore, the King, my master, only asks for his right; he has no intention of disturbing the good harmony and friendship which prevails between his Majesty and the King of Great Britain.
>
> The General of Canada can give proofs as he concurs in maintaining the perfect union between two friendly princes, for having learned that the Iroquois and Nipissing of the Lake of the Two Mountains had struck and destroyed an English family on the Caroline side, barred the way and forced them to give him a little boy from this family who was the only one living and whom Mssr. Werich (sic) who was negotiating in Montreal brought back to Boston.
>
> Moreover, he has forbidden all the Indians not to exercise their ordinary cruelties upon the English with whom we are friends.
>
> This, sir, is the answer you will have to make to this governor and even to the others in case of a new deputation. That of Mssr. de Saint-Pierre, which he will

undoubtedly have communicated to you, is struck with great dignity, firmness, and politeness.[i]

Although somewhat long, we wanted to provide this quotation because it shows the ideas of the Governor General of Canada.

Shortly afterwards, Duquesne sent the Chevalier le Mercier[80] to the Belle-Riviere with the best officers and cadets then in Montreal.

Mssr. de Contrecoeur soon learned that the English were building a fort at the junction of Monongahela and Ohio.

He thought it was time to make use of Duquesne's answer to the Governor of Virginia. He entrusted this mission to Mssr. le Mercier.

We have before us a fine copy of the summons made by this officer; It is of April 16, 1754, "last Easter feast" and signed Contrecoeur.[ii]

This step had a beneficial effect. The English abandoned their labors and fled. There was no disorder, and Duquesne wrote on May 11: "It is to be hoped that nothing has happened in your conduct that approaches the act of hostility."[iii]

Washington was soon informed of the blow the French had just delivered to their establishment. On May 1, 1754, he left Will's Creek, went to the Great Meadows, and built a fort there.[iv] [81]

Meanwhile, Mssr. de Contrecoeur, who foresaw that the English would not be discouraged for so little, had charged Jumonville to go to the expedition. He informed the Governor, who replied on June 20: "I have learned with pleasure that you are making use of the Srs. de Jumonville and Druillon[82] to assure you of the rumors that the Englishman is marching openly."[v]

On leaving, Mssr. de Jumonville had received from Mssr. de Contrecoeur a summons which he was to read to the English if he

---

[i] Duquesne to Contrecoeur, Jan. 30, 1754 - Archives of the Seminary.

[ii] Archives of the Seminary. At this summons, Mssr. de Contrecoeur added "Words for the Indians who are with the English at their establishment."

[iii] Archives of the Seminary.

[iv] Ferland, II, p. 506.

[v] Archives of the Seminary.

Joseph, Sieur de Jumonville

met them. We have a copy of that document. It is signed by the hand of Mssr. de Contrecoeur, who wrote on the reverse: "This last summons to the English, if Mssr. de Jumonville finds them in his exploration, of May 23, 1754." Later and in another ink, Mssr. de Contrecoeur wrote: "He found them, and they killed him when read."[i]

In fact, Mssr. de Jumonville, with an escort of thirty-four men, was surrounded by Washington's detachment on the night of the 27th to the 28th of May. The French, seeing themselves surrounded, seized their arms. "Fire," shouted Washington, and discharged his gun. A second discharge closely followed the first. But Jumonville, by an interpreter, cautioned that he had something to communicate. The fire ceased, and while Jumonville had the summons read, he received a bullet in the head, which killed him. The English threw themselves upon the little troop. There were ten Canadians killed, one wounded and twenty-one prisoners. Two Canadians[83] were able to escape and brought the news.[ii]

Mssr. de Contrecoeur hastened to inform Mssr. Duquesne of the circumstances of this affair. The latter replied on June 24: "I did not expect the sudden change, sir, that you informed me by your letter of the two events, and that the English had pushed cruelty to the assassin (sic) of an officer in charge of my orders: yes, this murder is unique, and can only be washed by a shedding of blood, if the English are not in a hurry to press the murderers as proof of his disavowal, which he ought to do on the spot where the murder was committed. While waiting for him to give you satisfaction, lay hands on all that is to be found in this nation."[iii]

We see that Duquesne spoke of nothing less than an assassination. Thus, the outrage was extreme not only in Canada but also in France. The authorities narrated and commented on the details of the case and the future academician Thomas began to work on a long poem dedicated to the memory of Jumonville.[iv]

---

[i] Ibid.—appendix [G].
[ii] Ferland, II, 506.
[iii] Archives of the Seminary.
[iv] This poem was published in 1759. [*an 1862 analysis of the poem from an American perspective along with select verses translated in English are listed in appendix J.*]

The English, on the other hand, explained their conduct, and asserted that there had been no ambush, no assassination, but an act of just war, adding that Mssr. de Jumonville had been imprudent, and that it was he who brought on the attack that had just occurred.

Washington wrote in his diary that the prisoners "informed me that they had been sent with a summons to order me to depart," and he added: "a plausible pretense to discover our Camp, and to obtain the Knowledge of our Forces and our Situation!" And further on: "They say that they called to us as soon as they had discovered us; which is an absolute Falsehood, for I was then marching at the Head of the Company going towards them, and can positively affirm, that, when they first saw us, they ran to their Arms, without calling; as I must have heard them, had they so done."[i] [84]

All these assertions, so contrary to those of the French, are not made to clarify the affair. If, as Washington said, it was the prisoners who informed him that they were carrying a summons, it would have to be concluded that Jumonville had not read the summons and then it would be explained that the commander did not see an ambassador in the person of the French officer.

But it remains unclear if things occurred thusly.

[*Lieutenant Chaussegros de Léry*[85] *was a 31-year-old engineer posted at Chadakoin along the Lake Erie –Chautauqua Lake portage in June 1754. He kept a detailed journal that year, and recorded the following information concerning news received at his post on June 19 detailing the death of Jumonville:*

> *They asserted that Thaninhison*[86] *was with the English, and chief of a party of savages who are serving them. This Thaninhison is a Teste Plate; he had been taken when very young by the Sonnonthouons who adopted him. He is highly regarded among the nations of the Belle-Rivière and is absolutely devoted to the English. It was he who came last year to Riviere au Boeuf. He talked there very boldly, and the report spread that he had killed Mssr. de Jumonville. who*

---

[i] Cf. Memoir of the Duke of Choiseul, p. 127.

Joseph, Sieur de Jumonville

was wounded, saying, "You are not yet dead, my father," and striking him several times with his tomahawk.[87]

It has been said that the apology which Washington makes of himself and his conduct in his diary shows that he feels the need to justify himself.

That was his right. Nevertheless, it seems to us that he pretends a little too much not to believe in an embassage. But was it such a rare thing? The wind was in the summons. Dinwiddie himself had sent one to Mssr. de Saint-Pierre in October 1753, and the officer [*the same George Washington*] in charge of handing it over to him had been received with all possible politeness. The previous April 16 (1754) Mssr. de Contrecoeur had summoned the English to retire from the confluence of the Ohio and the Monongahela, and things had gone well.

Was it surprising that Mssr. de Contrecoeur, informed that the English were still advancing, had sent a new summons? And this new summons, though Washington claimed otherwise, was not so insolent and did not smack of braggadocio. It was only the counterpart of that which Mssr. le Mercier had served the English a few weeks before, and of which no one had complained.

Finally, Washington seems to exaggerate when he says that the party that accompanied Jumonville would have been worthy of a prince who would have been an ambassador while he was only a French officer.

In London, Paris, or Boston, the thing might have seemed so, but through the woods, in the middle of the forest, exposed to encountering savage enemies, a prince or a manager would have been mad to leave with only a few men. [*Washington's assertion that the large detachment under Jumonville portended more than a mere embassage is perhaps understandable when it is recalled that Washington delivered his message the previous December to the French at Fort Le Boeuf accompanied only by a guide and a few Indian allies.*]

Again, all is not clear in this matter and it will always be difficult to allot the responsibilities that belong to each.

Coulon de Villiers

If we admit that Washington had too much nobility of character for having wished to take advantage of a trap, we must also admit that Duquesne, Contrecoeur, and Jumonville were too gentlemanly to have had the intentions that Washington attributes to them. The excerpts we have given above prove enough to what extent the French sought to avoid war.

Let us say, if you will, that there has been some misunderstanding, haste, even imprudence, but let us leave to each of the commanders the benefit of the doubt and let us not turn to whitewash one over another.

On October 10, 1754, Duquesne wrote to the minister: "The life of Sieur Villiers de Jumonville, an ensign who was a most distinguished subject in his rank, merits commiseration."[i]

On October 11, 1746, Mssr. de Jumonville married Marie-Anne-Marguerite Soumande, daughter of Jean-Pascal Soumande and Ursule LeVerrier. From this union five children were born: Joseph born and died in 1746; Joseph born in 1748; Hippolyte-Etienne born in 1749; Marie-Anne-Catherine born on June 12, 1752, and buried the following August 8th at Montreal;[ii] finally Charlotte-Amable baptized on August 16, 1754, and born probably after the death of her father.[iii]

Charlotte-Amable was still living in 1760.

On December 15, 1756, Madame de Jumonville married Pierre Bachoie, sieur de Barrante,[88] knight, captain in the Régiment of Béarn.[89]

On May 21, 1760, Madame de Barrante became a widow a second time, and the following June 28 the Marquis de Lévis[90] wrote to the Minister Berryer:[91]

> I join my solicitations to those of the Marquis de Vaudreuil [92] in favor of Madame Barrante [*sic: Baraute*[93]], former widow of Mssr. de Jumonville, an officer of the colony, killed at the commencement of the

---

[i] General correspondence, vol. 99, p. 275.
[ii] Tanguay does not mention this girl.
[iii] Registry of Notre Dame of Montreal.

war, with whom she has a daughter, and who had subsequently married Barrante, the first captain of the régiment of Béarn, a man of status with whom she has a daughter.[i] He has just died of his wounds, and this widow is destitute, responsible for her two daughters: I shall be particularly obliged to you for what you will do for her, and to procure her a pension and position at St. Cyr for her daughters.[ii]

The same day he wrote in much the same terms to the marshal of Belle-Isle, only he added: "She is a little girl to the Mssr. Marquis de Vaudreuil."[iii]

Did Madame de Jumonville obtain a pension for herself and positions at St. Cyr for her daughters? We do not know.

We cannot even say where or when she died. What we know is that the name Jumonville, so famous in Canada, was not there for long.

⚜

---

[i] Louise-Charlotte, baptized Dec. 15, 1756, in Montreal—Mssr. de Montcalm was her godfather.—Registry of Montreal.

[ii] *Lettres du Lévis.*—Collection Lévis, p. 365.

[iii] She was a little daughter of Vaudreuil, by marriage: Madame de Jumonville's maternal grandmother, [*Jeanne-*]Charlotte Fleury d'Eschambault, had married the Marquis de Vaudreuil in a second marriage.

IV-A. THE DESCENDANTS OF COULON DE JUMONVILLE

[Inserted here for further clarification of the progeny of Joseph Coulon de Villier, sieur de Jumonville, is a translation of Pierre-Georges Roy's article "La Descendance de Coulon de Jumonville."[94] The translation of Gosselin's Notes sur la famille Coulon de Villiers *continues immediately following with chapter V.]*

It is not in the poem dedicated to Coulon de Jumonville by the celebrated poet Thomas that one can know the history of this hero. Thomas, in his verses, has widely used the licenses allowed to poets. He was not at all concerned with historical truth.

Msgr. Amédée Gosselin, in his *Notes sur la famille Coulon de Villiers*, told us all about the too short career of Coulon de Jumonville. We just want to ask a question: did the Canadian hero killed in his encounter with the Washington troop, the future founder of the United States, leave descendants?

Joseph Coulon de Jumonville had married Marie-Anne-Marguerite Soumande, daughter of Jean-Paschal Soumande and Ursule LeVerrier, in Montreal on October 2, 1745.

Five children were born of this union:
(1) Joseph Coulon de Jumonville, born in Montreal on August 21, 1746, and died at the same place on August 26, 1746.
(2) Joseph Coulon de Jumonville born in Montreal on March 6, 1748, and died before May 21, 1760.
(3) Hypolite-Etienne Coulon de Jumonville born in Montreal on July 5, 1749, and died before May 21, 1760.
(4) Marie-Anne-Catherine Coulon de Jumonville born in Montreal on June 12, 1752, and died at the same place on August 30, 1752.
(5) Charlotte-Amable Coulon de Jumonville born in Montreal on August 16, 1754.

The widow of Coulon de Jumonville remarried in Montreal, December 15, 1755, to Jean-Pierre Bachoie de Barraute, captain of the Béarn regiment. This officer took part in the battles of the Plains of Abraham and Sainte-Foy. On May 12, 1760, in a skirmish, he was wounded in the head by a bomb. He was transferred to the General Hospital of Quebec and died there on May 20, 1760.

Descendants of Jumonville

On June 28, 1760, the Chevalier de Lévis wrote to Minister Berryer:

> I join my solicitations to those of the Marquis de Vaudreuil in favor of Madame Baraute,[95] former widow of Mssr. de Jumonville, an officer of the colony, killed at the commencement of the war, with whom she has a daughter, and who had subsequently married Baraute, the first captain of the régiment of Béarn, a man of status with whom she has a daughter.[i] He has just died of his wounds, and this widow is destitute, responsible for her two daughters: I shall be particularly obliged to you for what you will do for her, and to procure her a pension and position at St. Cyr for her daughters.[ii]

It is therefore a certainty that on May 21, 1760, there remained only one daughter of the Jumonville—Soumande marriage: Charlotte-Amable.

Saint-Cyr was the house founded by Madame de Maintenon in 1680 and established in the park of Versailles to receive and instruct 250 noble and poor daughters free of charge.

Did Charlotte-Amable Coulon de Jumonville receive her entrance into this celebrated house?

We have before us the certificate of Mssr. d'Hozier, a judge of arms of the nobility of France, for the entrance of the young girl to Saint-Cyr.

Mssr. d'Hozier declared:

> I Louis-Philippe d'Hozier, knight, judge-at-arms of the nobility of France, councilor of the King in his councils and commissioner of His Majesty to certify to him the nobility of the young ladies raised in the Royal House of St. Louis to Saint-Cyr.
>
> Let the King know that Charlotte-Amable Coulon de Jumonville has the nobility necessary to be admitted to the number of young ladies whom His Majesty has brought up in the Royal House of St. Louis, founded at

---

[i] Louise-Charlotte, baptized Dec. 15, 1756, in Montreal—Mssr. de Montcalm was her godfather.—Registry of Montreal.

[ii] *Lettres du Chevalier de Lévis*, p. 365.

Saint-Cyr in the park of Versailles, as he is justified by the acts enunciated in this proof which we have verified and drawn up at Paris, on Wednesday, the seventeenth of February, one thousand seven hundred and sixty-two.

Charlotte-Amable Coulon de Jumonville entered Saint-Cyr at the end of 1762 and left it on July 22, 1774. She had chosen religious life and shut herself up in a convent of Benedictines. The King, on September 14, 1774, had been kind enough to pay her dowry to enable her to enter the cloister.

The last descendant of Joseph Coulon de Jumonville then died in France after 1774.

[*By looking at the later work of Aegidius Fauteux, we can provide a few more details of the widow of Jumonville and her only surviving child of that marriage. Fauteux writes, "The widow of Barraute, undeterred by the tragic death of her first two husbands, had remarried to Gallifet." Fauteux goes on to provide the full title of this third husband, "High and mighty Lord Louis de Gallifet, Knight, Viscount of Gallifet, lord of Lacour, Lavau, and other places, knight of the royal and military order of Saint-Louis, former major of the regiment of Queen's cavalry, residing in his Chateau de la Cour, parish of Cherry, near Orleans, and of lady Anne-Marguerite Soumande, damsel his wife."*96

*Indeed, in the Centre des archives d'outre-mer (France) vol. 388, we find a letter dated August 12, 1775, in which Mssr. Gallifet writes, "The Keeper of the Seals has just sent me the ordinance of a gratuity of 600 livres which you have had the honor of having granted by the Majesty to Mademoiselle de Jumonville, my daughter, of whom I sincerely thank you." He goes on to state that Jumoville's only daughter entered the religious life with the Benedictines of Villarceaux in the Priory of Saint Mary Magdalene of Villarceaux. Fauteux confirms that Charlotte-Amable Coulon de Jumonville made her religious profession on October 15, 1776.*97]

⚜

V. Louis Coulon de Villiers
known as le Grand Villiers

The death of Jumonville in 1754, leaves only two survivors of the brothers Coulon de Villiers: Louis and François. Both have been noted for the number and importance of the services they have rendered to the colony. It is only necessary to give each one the credit that belongs to him and it is, in our opinion, the important part of our work.

Jumonville was avenged by one of his brothers: Louis or François, obviously, since they were the only ones who survived him; But which of the two?

Some historians have presented, it is true, that Nicolas-Antoine had been the avenger of Jumonville, but we have proved in this venue that this assertion is incorrect, and we shall not return to it.

Others, such as Dussieux,[i] Thwaites,[ii] Mssr. E. Mallet,[iii] etc., affirm that it was Louis. Finally, a respectable tradition preserved in the family of François attributes to the latter the honor of this memorable vengeance.

If, in our turn, we are permitted to give our opinion, we shall say, without, however, pretending to infallibility, that Louis, surnamed le Grand Villiers, was the true avenger of Jumonville, who took Fort Necessity in 1754.

Some very clear and categorical documents would have settled the question: it would have sufficed if a good old paper had borne in full the name of Louis or that of François, in connection with the taking of Fort Necessity. Unfortunately, the gentlemen de Villiers were not lavish with their Christian names and the authorities of the time did not care either. [*François's 1777 petition to the King of Spain (appendix L) is just such a document.*]

We will therefore content ourselves with less affirmative documents, but all of which, we believe, does not fail to prove our progress.

---

[i] *Le Canada sous la domination française*, p. 123, note.
[ii] *The Jesuit Relations and Allied Documents,* Burrows Edition, vol. 70.
[iii] "Washington et Coulon de Villiers," (*Bulletin de la Société historique Franco-Américaine*, Boston 1906.)

Coulon de Villiers

The surest means is to give the *curriculum vitae* of Louis, to disengage him, so to speak, from those nearly which have made him so easily confounded with his brother, le Chevalier François.

A remark before going further. The numerous manuscripts and prints which we have consulted, with some exceptions, have enabled us to observe that Louis was generally known by the name of Mssr. de Villiers, captain or officer of the colony, while François was always or almost always called le Chevalier de Villiers. Let us add, moreover, that Louis was more particularly employed in the country of the Great Lakes, or in the region of Montreal, while François, who was an officer in Louisiana, lived there most frequently.

[*It is here that Gosselin has fallen into the same trap as other historians and genealogists before him. His research has led him to assume that only François was referred to in records as le Chevalier, but access to a multitude of primary sources through the Library and Archives Canada shows that Louis was at times also recorded as le Chevalier. The November 1751 Franches Marine roll for Canada includes companies at Quebec, Montreal, and Three Rivers. The first company listed for Montreal shows "Ch^{ev} de Villiers" as a lieutenant. The fourth company for Montreal shows "Villiers de Jumonville" as an ensign. These are the only two Villiers listed on the roll. There were three Villiers brothers in uniform in 1751: Louis, François, and Joseph. François was serving in the Illinois district, part of Louisiana, which would account for why only two Villiers are listed on the Canadian rolls. That would also indicate that Louis was documented with the surname Chevalier. Additionally, on the October 1754 roll for Canada, we find only one Villiers. Listed as a captain is the name "le Ch^{ev} de Villiers." Joseph had been killed earlier that year at the end of May, and François was still serving in the Illinois district. We know that Louis was at that time a captain in Montreal. Moreover, the roll shows that Captain Villiers's ensign en second was "De Bailleul canut,[98]" who is also referred to in the 1754 Journal of Coulon de Villiers. So, again we see Louis documented with the name le Chevalier de Villiers. Gosselin's error has caused him to at times confuse the two brothers.[99]*]

Louis, le Grand Villiers

Louis was born at Verchères on August 10, 1710. He had as godfather Louis Audet Sieur de Bailleul[100] and for godmother Marguerite de Verchères.[i]

Like his brothers, he entered the service young and followed his father to the post of St. Joseph River of the Illinois. On March 7, 1729, he was godfather: "Louis Coulon de Villiers *fils*," said the record. On January 26, 1731, he again held a child on the font. He was then cadet *à l'aiguillette* and simply signed Villiers.[ii]

He was made an ensign *en second* with his promotion in 1732, which gave his father an expectation of company "Villiers *fils* cadet," stated the list.[iii] [*Nicholas-Antoine was the brother promoted to ensign in 1732, at the same time that his father was promoted to captain, both in recognition of their services during the 1730 Fox War, see note ii on page 10.*]

We cannot say with certainty what became of him after that date; perhaps he remained several years in the upper country. [*Louis remained at La Baye with his father and was wounded in the pursuit following the 1733 affair in which his father, brother, and brother-in-law were killed. Gosselin, like so many other historians, confuses Louis with his brother François, and attributes this action to the latter Villiers brother rather than to Louis. His promotion to ensign* en second *came in 1733, not 1732, following the fight with the Sauk and Meskwaki. Louis confirms his being wounded during the 1733 La Baye affair in a 1754 letter he sent to the Minster of Marine following his victory at Fort Necessity, writing, "It is I who Was shot in the arm during The attack of the Foxes."* [101] *Moreover, Peyser provides a copy of the certificate of the surgeon who treated the wounded Villiers, dated June 10, 1734:*

> *I, the undersigned surgeon major of the troops in this country, certify that Mssr. Louis Coulon de Villiers a cadet with the troops stated, has been wounded by a shot in his left arm which penetrated the front of the middle part of the arm, and exited from the inner part*

---

[i] Registry of Contrecoeur.

[ii] Registry St. Joseph of Illinois.

[iii] Archives of the Seminary. The elder was already an ensign at that date, and François was not an ensign until after 1733.

> *of the lower arm, which has so badly injured the muscles that the whole forearm has withered and has caused so great a disability that he can make almost no use of it at all, and that he will remain crippled by it, in witness whereof I have given him the present certificate to be used and be valid for legitimate purposes."*[102]

Beauharnois[103] and Hocquart[104] recognized the bravery of the young Louis in the action against the Sauk and Meskwaki and requested on October 18, 1734, a pension for his crippling wound: *"We are also Attaching an Attestation by S*^{r} *Benoist, Surgeon Major at Montreal from which you will see that S*^{r} *Coulon de Villiers, who Was appointed as Ensign this Year, was shot so badly in the left arm that he is crippled from it, and We beg you, My Lord, to grant this Young man, who has demonstrated great strength during the conseqences of his father's action, a Disability pension which will put him in a Position with his salary to provide for his needs."*[105] The crippling wound was not severe enough to end Louis's military career, as the young ensign served another 23 years.]

A list of officers for 1739 mentions a Coulon de Villiers ensign *en second*, which affirms.[i] Would it not be Louis?

Several accounts of 1740 on the affair against the Chickasaw indicate the names of the Chevalier de Villiers and de Villiers;[ii] the latter leaves us still uncertain as to the Sieur de Villiers who is at Fort St. Frédéric from 1741 to 1744.[iii] In both cases, however, we are led to believe that it is Louis.

In November 1746, the general sent "Mssr. de Villiers, lieutenant of the troops, with a hundred Indians of Acadia, who wintered

---

[i] The Abbe Daniel, *Famille De Léry*, p. 202.
[ii] Report of Richard, 1899, p. 32.
[iii] U. Baudry, *Un vieux fort français*, Reports of the Royal Society, V, p. 97.

in the vicinity of Quebec, to go to Montreal, and thence to be distributed in the different garrisons established on the ridges towards Fort St. Frédéric."[i]

This must be Louis, since in the month of July preceding, Mssr. de Beauharnois had appointed le Chevalier to serve under the orders of Mssr. De Muy[106] in the upper country,[ii] and that Nicolas-Antoine and Jumonville were in Acadia.

On April 12, 1747, Mssr. de Villiers, an officer, eight cadets and 100 habitants left Montreal for Chateaugué on several trails which the Iroquois had assured them they had seen. They returned without finding anything.[iii]

Mssr. de Villiers was often in Montreal, where he remained at the return of his expeditions.

On February 10, 1749, he witnessed a marriage "Coulon de Villiers, lieutenant in the troops," signed "de Villiers."[iv]

[*It was likely Louis who accompanied Céloron*[107] *on his 1749 expedition of the Belle-Riviere. Céloron recorded de Villiers's role early in the expedition: "The 16th, at noon, I arrived at the portage of Chatakuin. As soon as all my canoes were loaded, I despatched Mssr. de Villiers and Mssr. le Borgne*[108] *with fifty men to go clear a road."*[109]]

On June 7, 1750, he was a godfather and a lieutenant; he simply signed: "Villiers."[v]

Soon after, he took command of the post of the Miamis.

His instructions, signed by La Jonquière,[110] are dated from Montreal, July 10, 1750: "for Sieur de Villiers, lieutenant of infantry, commanding officer at the post of the Miamis."

After having ordered him to go immediately in a canoe of the king with two soldiers to the post of the Miamis with the convoy of Mssr. de Céloron going to Detroit, the governor added: "We have informed him of the less advantageous dispositions of the nations of the said post for the French, and he knows that we have resolved

---

[i] Corresp off. of the gov.— Copy to the Archives of the Seminary.
[ii] Archives of the Seminary.
[iii] *Doc. relatif à la Nouvelle-France*, III, p. 332.
[iv] Registry of Montréal.
[v] Ibid.

Coulon de Villiers

to give him the command of it, on the credit he has acquired among these nations, his capacity, and his zeal for the service of the French. So, he must do his utmost to respond to the confidence we have in him in such an important command in the present circumstances."[i]

Mssr. de la Jonquière then enters into a multitude of details which it would be too long to relate here, but which may be summed up thus: granting a general amnesty to the Miamis, detaching them from the English alliance and making them friends of the French. He concludes by ordering Mssr. de Villiers to report to him what will happen in his post on every possible occasion, and to send him express only for extraordinary and pressing cases. "Besides," said he, "we refer to the wisdom, prudence, and experience of the said Sieur de Villiers for all the other cases which we have not been able to foresee in this instruction."[ii]

We may wonder whether this Mssr. de Villiers is indeed Louis. We find the answer to this question in the inventory of Nicolas-Antoine's property, made in 1752. The notary mentioning the absence writes: "Louis Coulon, Squire Sieur de Villiers, lieutenant in the troops, currently in the upper country, and le Chevalier de Villiers, lieutenant at Mississippi."[iii]

It was Louis de Villiers who commanded the Miamis. He remained there until the autumn of 1753. In the month of July of the same year, Mssr. de Courtemanche [111] wrote to Mssr. de Contrecoeur:[112] "I do not doubt, as a friend of Mssr. de Villiers, that you would not take charge of his parcels that Mssr. Chabert[113] must hand over to you at Niagara."[iv]

[*Indeed, it was Louis who commanded the Miamis. Writing to the Minister of Marine in 1754, Louis elaborated on his duties with the Miamis:*

> *In 1750 I had the honor of Being detached by Monsr the Marquis de la Jonquière to go bring the miamis back to reason. I succeeded, and I believe I rendered a*

---

[i] Archives of Ottawa. North America. Canada. Establishment of various posts, vol. 13, p. 285.

[ii] Loco cit.

[iii] Du Laurent, not.—Greffe de Quebec.

[iv] Archives of the Seminary.

great service to this Colony, since they Were Slaughtering the French wherever they found them, and they even Killed two of my Soldiers about one thousand feet from my fort, and by dint of Negotiating with this Nation I had them come back to their senses. This was the key to the other Nations: the hurons, Pianguichias, and ouyatanons Came back As Soon as they saw the miamis Surrender.[114]

There is additional proof that it was Louis who commanded at Miami in the form of a contract signed by him on July 13, 1750, in which he gives his names and titles, "Louis Coulon, esquire, Sieur de Villiers, lieutenant of a company of infantry and commandant for the king at the post of the Miamis, on the one part, and François Josué de la Corne, esquire, Sieur Dubreuil,[115] also lieutenant of a company of infantry on the other part, a resident in this city."[116]]

And on October 31 Duquesne[117] wrote to the minister: "Despite the precaution of the Sieur de Villiers, the rebellious Miamis have raised their hair to the English."[i]

Mssr. de Villiers returned shortly after to Montreal. On December 29, 1753, he was married. The certificate reads: "captain of the troops of this garrison" and is signed: Coulon Villiers.[ii]

Mssr. de Villiers did not live long in Montreal. The governor had been informed by Mssr. de Contrecoeur of the attempts of the English against the establishments of the Belle-Riviere, and he prepared to send him succors and reinforce the posts in the region.

He succeeded in raising numerous Indian Christians of the Sioux, Lake of Two Mountains, and Lorette, and after having placed good officers at their head, he sent them to Belle-Riviere. On June 14, 1754, they arrived at Chadokoin[iii] and the engineer Léry, *fils*,[118]

---

[i] Brymner, 1888, CLXIV.

[ii] Louis de Villiers varied his signatures. We know four or five different ones: Louis de Villiers, Villiers, De Villiers, and Coulon-Villier. The three of which we give the facsimiles farther on resemble absolutely, as written.

[iii] Chadakoin, Chatocoin or Chautauqua, lake located in the county of Chautauqua, state of New York; A few leagues from Lake Erie.—*Cours d'Histoire*, II, p.

who was there, wrote in his journal:[i] "On June 14, at 6 o'clock in the evening, Mssr. de Villiers captain at the head of the Nipissing and Algonquin, Mssr. de Longueuil,[119] ditto, at the head of the Iroquois, Mssr. de Montesson,[120] lieutenant, at the head of the Abanakis, Mssr. de Longueuil[121] ensign *en second*, with the Hurons of Lorette, and all these nations could make the number of 120 to 130 men."

These words of Mssr. de Léry are of significant importance. They prove that Mssr. de Villiers, when he arrived at Fort Duquesne, came neither from the upper country, nor from the Mississippi, but from the region of Montreal.

The Nipissing and the Algonquin, whom he commanded more particularly, had their residence, with a number of Iroquois and Hurons, at the Lake of Two Mountains.[ii]

It is now understandable that de Villiers could have written in his journal that he had arrived at Fort Duquesne "with the different nations of which Mssr. le General had given me the command."

The general, or, if you like, the governor, was in Montreal at that time, and he sent in groups the reinforcements he had promised Mssr. de Contrecoeur.

When the news of the death of Jumonville reached Montreal, Parkman wrote,[iii] "Coulon de Villiers, brother of the slain officer, was sent to the spot [*with a body of Indians from all the tribes in the colony*]."

We read again in *Illinois historical and statistical*, Moses:[iv] "When he learned of the defeat and death of Jumonville, his brother Coulon de Villiers, who had been sent for that purpose from Montreal, left for Fort Duquesne to avenge his death."

That de Villiers had left Montreal or the region, we are convinced of it, but that he was sent, as this author says to avenge Jumonville, is what we cannot admit because when de Villiers left

---

[i] Archives of the Seminary.

[ii] Cf. *Cours d'histoire*, II, p. 458.— A plan of the mission of Lake of Two Mountains indicates the place occupied by the different nations.— Archives of the Seminary.

[iii] *Montcalm and Wolfe*, I, p. 153.

[iv] Vol. I, p. 113.

with the Nations for the Ohio valley the news of the death of Jumonville was not yet known in Montreal. De Villiers was to learn it on the way.

Two days after his arrival at Chadakoin, he departed, and Mssr. de Léry wrote in his diary, June 16: "Mssr. de Villiers and the other officers at the head of the Indians leave for Fort Duquesne by the road to Lake Chadakoin in canoes of bark." Mssr. de Villiers bore to Mssr. de Contrecoeur goods and powder.[i]

[*It seems certain that Mssr. de Villiers knew of his brother's death by the time he left Chadakoin. Léry wrote in his journal on June 15, the day after de Villiers arrived at Chadakoin, "Saturday, at 11 o'clock in the morning Mssr. Péan[122] arrived, and I found him greatly changed; he told us of the betrayal of Mssr. Jumonville." Clearly news of Jumonville's fate arrived at Chadakoin the day after de Villiers arrived there, and a day before he departed. So, it stands to reason that he learned of the death of his brother at Chadakoin while in transit from Montreal to Fort Duquesne.[123]*]

Péan, who was then at Chadakoin, wrote to his uncle, Mssr. de Contrecoeur: "I had great difficulty in getting rid of Mssr. de Carqueville,[124] who is an excellent officer, and he and Mssrs. de Villiers and le Mercier[125] will perfectly assist you; I envy their happiness."[ii]

On the same day, Péan sent to inform the Governor in Montreal of the departure of Mssr. de Villiers for Fort Duquesne.

The intention of Mssr. Duquesne was that Mssr. de Villiers, after carrying provisions to Mssr. de Contrecoeur, should return to continue the tour of the posts, in case Mssr. Péan, who was ill, could not do so.[iii]

However, things did not happen quite so. Mssr. de Villiers had arrived at Fort Duquesne on June 26, at eight o'clock in the morning, "with the different nations of which the Mssr. le General had given me the command," he said in his journal.[iv]

---

[i] Letter of Péan, June 15, 1754.—Archives of the Seminary.
[ii] Péan, loco. cit.
[iii] Duquesne to Contrecoeur, July 1, 1754- Archives of the Seminary.
[iv] The journal of Mssr. de Villiers has been published largely in the Summary of facts, known as the Memoir of the Duke de Choiseul, in 1756,

Coulon de Villiers

It was reported that Mssr. de Contrecoeur was to send the detachment of 500 Frenchmen and a few Indians the following day to go and drive out the English and avenge the death of Jumonville. The Chevalier le Mercier had been appointed to command this little troop. He was an excellent officer, "but," writes Mssr. de Villiers, "As I was senior to this officer, that I commanded the Nations, and that my brother had been assassinated, Mssr. de Contrecoeur honored me with this command, and Mssr. le Mercier swore to me, though deprived of the command, that he would be delighted to conduct the campaign under my orders."[i]

Mssr. Duquesne, informed of this change, wrote to Mssr. de Contrecoeur on July 19: "I should have been equally tranquil if the Chevalier le Mercier had commanded this troop, but it could not be refused to Sieur de Villiers, who is an officer of distinction and to whom the Indian has much confidence."[ii]

The details of this expedition are known. They will be found, moreover, in Mssr. de Villiers's journal and in most of the Histories of Canada. We take the liberty of referring the reader to it [see appendix H].

Let us note only that the expedition was fortunate. On July 3, the detachment was before the fort of Necessity. It was necessary to fight in broad daylight and uncovered but that did not prevent the Canadians from showing much ardor. The English defended themselves, but after a battle which lasted ten hours, they consented, according to their proposal, to capitulate to avoid the assault.

On the same evening, the articles of capitulation were signed by James Mackay,[126] Ge. Washington and Coulon-Villier.

Then the French commander returned his troops in good order to Fort Duquesne, where he arrived on July 7 at four o'clock.

This brilliant victory had a great resonance throughout the colony.

On July 25, Duquesne wrote to Mssr. de Contrecoeur:

---

etc. It was reprinted in its entirety by the Louisiana Historical Society in 1905, according to a copy made by ourselves on a copy preserved in the Seminary of Quebec. We list it in the appendix [H].

[i] Journal of de Villiers.
[ii] Archives of the Seminary.

Louis, le Grand Villiers

> Nothing could be more desirable, sir, than the pretty affair which has just taken place at the top of the river Malengueulée,127 since it reconciles bravery, prudence, and humanity. In my opinion, this is the most beautiful thing that has happened in Canada, because it is rare that in this country we have seen fighting in front of Banners and that it is usually only by surprise that the enemy is attacked.... Everything happened according to my desires, the lesson is good and I expect it will be encrusted in the memory of the English and the Indians.[i]

On the 30th of the same month, Bigot,128 after congratulating Contrecoeur for his handling of the affair of Fort Necessity, added: "....and the Sieur de Villiers has executed on his part the orders which you gave him."[ii]

Towards the end of July, Mssr. de Villiers returned to Montreal, bringing to Mssr. Duquesne the letters of Mssr. de Contrecoeur. The governor wrote to the latter on August 14, 1754: "I was very glad to embrace this officer who has just served the state and his country so well."[iii]

The governor was not content merely to congratulate de Villiers, but he recommended him to the minister. On October 10, 1754, after having asked for the Cross of Saint-Louis of Messrs. Contrecoeur and Péan, he added:

> I have reason to hope, my lord, you will not refuse to procure the same decoration to Sieur de Villiers after the brilliant action which he has just completed on the Ohio River, that every soldier will have difficulty in believing in a country where only wars of ambush are known, and you will have seen in his journal the wisdom and prudence with which this brave officer conducted himself despite his resentment at the assassina-

---

[i] Archives of the Seminary.
[ii] Ibid.
[iii] Ibid.

tion of his brother. [*For if he had not been able to restrain the Indians and the Canadians, not an Englishman would have escaped their fury.*][i]

Duquesne's praise and recommendation had no effect at that time, and de Villiers was decorated only three years later.

However, Mssr. de Villiers had not arrived in good health (at least that is what Mssr. Duquesne wrote in a letter to Contrecoeur), and he does not appear to have moved away from Montreal during the winter.

Soon it was learned that the English were to make a general attack on Canada in the spring. The forts Duquesne, St. Frédéric, and Niagara seemed particularly threatened.

Mssr. de Villiers was sent to the latter post to cover the fort and prevent the incursions of the English. He remained there five months.[ii] He had to leave at the end of June, because on the 23rd Mssr. Duquesne wrote to Mssr. Laperriere,[129] then at Niagara; "I need not recommend to you to have for the Sieur de Villiers all the attention he deserves, and you will find on the part of this captain all the return you may desire."[iii]

De Villiers had a detachment of 200 men to form an observation camp;[iv] it was sparse, but when the danger seemed more threatening, he pulled the necessary help from the surrounding posts. On August 21, Mssr. Benoît[130] wrote to Mssr. de Contrecoeur, at Fort Presque Isle, that "on the advice of Mssr. de Villiers, he sent to Niagara all the detachments of the Belle-Riviere."[v]

The arrival of these reinforcements and the news of the defeat of Braddock, discouraged Shirley[131] and he abandoned the idea of attacking Niagara for this year at least.

---

[i] General correspondence, vol. 99, p. 275. [*Pease & Jenison. eds., Illinois on the eve of the Seven Years' War, 904.*]

[ii] *Mémoires*, de Gaspé, 1895 edition, p. 136.

[iii] Archives of the Seminary.

[iv] Mssr. de Lignons to Mssr. de Contrecoeur, July 31, 1755. Archives of the Seminary.

[v] Archives of the Seminary.

Louis, le Grand Villiers

The retreat of the English commander and his fifteen hundred men restored tranquility to Niagara, and Mssr. de Villiers was recalled to Montreal. "You will leave," wrote Mssr. de Vaudreuil[132] to Laperriere, "from the 15th to the 20th of November, with Mssr. de Villiers, to return to Montreal together."[i]

During the winter of 1755 – '56, Mssr. de Vaudreuil prepared to dislodge the English from Chouaguen. This campaign was reserved for Montcalm,[133] who arrived at Quebec in May 1756. It was crowned with success, and Mssr. de Villiers distinguished himself there. It was he who, after having fortified himself at Niaoure [*Sackets Harbor, N.Y.*], commanded the observation camp, harassed the enemy, and prevented them from communicating with the upper country.[ii] At the siege of Chouaguen, he commanded the right column, and was charged with preventing the English from leaving the fort.

Finally, on August 14, Montcalm was master of the three forts, and on the evening of the same day, at eight o'clock, Mssr. de Villiers left to carry to Mssr. de Vaudreuil the five flags the English had left in the square.[iii]

It may be thought that he was well received by the governor!

Mssr. de Vaudreuil, who had already recommended him to the Court the previous year, wrote on November 8, 1756, proposing him for the Cross of Saint-Louis: "I must add to the observations I had the honor to make you Last year in favor of this officer, the successes he had had as he commanded the observation camp I had set up within reach of Chouaguen to intercept the enemy's aid. The expedition of the three forts after which he rejoined the army at Carillon and remained there during the campaign."[iv]

---

[i] Letter of Oct. 19, 1755.—Archives of the Seminary.

[ii] *Journal de Montcalm.*

[iii] Journal of Mssr. de Léry. In his book, *La jeunesse de Bougainville*, Mssr. de Kerallain, so well informed, writes (p.46) that Bougainville's dispatch to Montreal brought the glorious news. Bougainville said in his diary that he arrived in Montreal on August 26 at 10:30 o'clock and dispatched the day before the Fort de la Présentation. Had not Monsieur de Villiers already accepted the surrender?

[iv] Archives of the Marine.—Copy in Seminary.

Montcalm, who had arrived in Canada and was unkind to certain Canadian officers who took part in this campaign, found that Mssr. de Villiers was a good officer.[i]

We shall soon see that Montcalm will recognize all his merit.

When the campaign was over, Mssr. de Villiers returned from Carillon to Montreal, where he spent the winter in garrison.

It is known that at the time of the surrender of Fort Necessity, the French commander had been handed over, as hostages, two English officers: Jacob Van Braam[134] and Robert Stobo.[135] The latter took advantage of his stay at Fort Duquesne, where he had been left almost entirely free to play the part of a spy. He even drafted the plan of the fort and sent it to the enemy. The letter accompanying this plan was found in the papers of Braddock after the battle of Monongahela.

Indignant, Mssr. de Vaudreuil sent the two hostages before a council of war. The trial opened in October 1756, in Montreal, where Van Braam and Stobo had been held for a long time.

Called to testify, Mssr. de Villiers appeared November 3, 1756, and declared his names, etc., as follows: "Louis Coulon Esquire, Sieur de Villiers, captain of infantry, aged 47, resident stationed in Montreal, Rue St-Paul, Notre-Dame Parish."[ii]

He was questioned about a conversation he had heard during the winter of 1755, in Montreal, at Mssr. de St-Luc's,[136] a conversation in which Stobo confessed to having written the letter in question.

During the trial, Mssr. de Villiers and Stobo declared that they knew each other well.

The council of war condemned the traitor to have his head cut off, which was not carried out.

The year 1757 was particularly remarkable for the capture of Fort William Henry. In this campaign, de Villiers, at the head of 300 volunteers and some Indians, distinguished himself continuously.

As early as June 24, Montcalm, writing to Vaudreuil to inform him of the success of two French detachments and that of Mssr. Rigaud de Vaudreuil,[137] saying: "Mssr. de Villiers, of whom I cannot

---

[i] *Montcalm à Lévis*, August 17, 1756—Collect. Lévis.
[ii] Archives of the Marine 1756.—Copy at Seminary

praise too much, this officer marched yesterday, with that zeal for which you know him, but unsuccessfully, to cut off a retreat from a small party of Indian enemies.... This officer, whose reputation is well made, does not need any action to increase it, but he will profit well from all those that fortune will present to him in the war."[i]

This, indeed, was a fine praise, and yet it was only at the beginning of the campaign, which ended in the capture of [*Fort*] William Henry, and during which de Villiers did not hesitate.

So much intelligence, activity, and bravery deserved a reward. She arrived in the autumn of 1757. In the month of May preceding, Moras[138] had written to Montcalm that de Villiers had been appointed Knight of Saint-Louis.[ii]

Mazas[iii] puts this appointment on May 1st. It included: "de Sermonville,[139] de la Corne la Colombière,[140] de Villiers, Le Gardeur de Repentigny,[141] and Chevalier le Mercier, captains in the troops of Canada."

On September 9, Montcalm wrote to Bourlamaque[142] that Mssr. de Vaudreuil had just received a letter of advice from the graces of the colony.[iv] In the list he provided, Montcalm appointed Mssr. de Villiers.

The brave captain did not long enjoy his new decoration.

In October, being in Quebec, he fell ill and on the 26th, Montcalm wrote to the Chevalier de Lévis.[143] "I'm worried about de Villiers. I believe he has smallpox. If you know in Montreal, do not say anything."[v]

De Villiers, in fact, had smallpox, and died on November 2, 1757. On the same day, Montcalm imparted this sad news to Lévis: "I am, my dear sir," he said, "inconsolable at the loss of poor Villiers. Do not write to his widow, but speak to her and tell how much I regret the death of her husband, and that, independent of all that

---

[i] *Doc. Rel. à la Nouvelle-France,* IV, p. 111.
[ii] Cf. *Lettres de la Cour de Versailles,* p. 67.—Coll. Lévis.
[iii] *Histoire de l'Ordre de St-Louis,* vol. II, p. 172.
[iv] Montcalm to Bourlamaque—Letters of Bourlamaque, p. 193.
[v] Montcalm to Lévis.—Letters, Coll. Lévis, p. 72.

she deserves herself, I shall always be glad to show her on every occasion the singular esteem I had for Villiers."[i]

On the 6th of the same month Montcalm wrote in his diary: "The Sieur de Villiers, one of the best officers of the colony, and best known for his actions, died of the smallpox on the 3rd, which is universally regretted."[ii]

Mssr. de Vaudreuil also appreciated this excellent officer. On November 2, he announced to the minister the death of Mssr. de Villiers: "I have the honor to inform you that Mssr. de Villiers, captain, etc.... has just died on the moment of the smallpox. It is a pity, my lord, that such an excellent officer died of this malady, after having exposed himself to the greatest dangers, the services he has constantly rendered, especially since the war, and the expedition to Fort George. It deserves my regrets; it is a great loss that we endure."[iii]

Mssr. de Villiers had died on November 2. He was buried the next day in the church cathedral of Quebec.

Here is the record of burial: "On November 3 of the year one thousand seven hundred and fifty-seven was buried in the parish church, Mssr. Colon, Squire Sieur de Villiers, captain of a marine company, Knight of Saint-Louis, who died the day before at the age of forty-eight, and there were present Messrs. Parent and Grave, and many others of any status (signed) J. F. Recher,[144] parish priest."[iv]

The name of baptism is not found in this record. Msgr. Tanguay believed that this was Antoine. We have shown that he was mistaken. And, as in 1757 there remained only two brothers of the Villiers family, Louis and François, and the latter died only in 1794. It follows that the one of which we have just given the record of burial can be none other than Louis.

Mssr. de Villiers had married in Montreal, on December 29, 1753, Marie-Amable Prud'homme,[v] with whom he had a daughter,

---

[i] Letter of Montcalm to Lévis, p. 72.
[ii] p. 316.
[iii] Archives of the Marine, 1757—Copy at Seminary
[iv] Archives of Notre Dame of Quebec.
[v] Archives of Notre Dame of Montreal.

Louise, baptized on June 3, and buried on September 6, 1755. He is not known to have other children.[i]

As with most of the Canadian officers, Mssr. de Villiers was more brave than rich, and his widow retained more or less resources. Mssr. de Vaudreuil knew this, and in the letter, he addressed to the minister to announce the death of Mssr. de Villiers, he said: "He leaves a widow not very fortunate, for whom I cannot dispense with interest. More than anything else, my lord, to beg you to be willing to procure her a pension from the king in consideration of the important services of her late husband."[ii]

This request was heard because in 1760 Madame de Villiers received a pension of 150 livres.[iii]

After a widowhood of nearly three years, Madame de Villiers married in Montreal on September 15, 1760, Michel Mougon de Jarimeau, siegneur de la Garde, captain in the Barry regiment.[iv] The author of the *Dictionnaire généalogique* does not mention any children born from this marriage. [*Tanguay, and by inference, Gosselin, is mistaken on the name of the second husband of Louis Coulon de Villiers's widow. Fauteux in his work, "Quelques officiers de Montcalm," recorded:*

> *AVICE (Michel-Marie-Charles), chevalier de Montgon de Surimeau*
>
> *Was captain in Berry upon the arrival of this regiment in Canada, in 1757. Recommended twice for the cross of St. Louis, at the end of 1759 and at the end of 1760, he was knighted March 5, 1761. Here are his records of service according to the regulations of Aquitaine, the regiment where he was paid with the other officers of Berry, after his return to France:*
>
> *"Montgon Surimaux (Charles, Chevalier de); born May 25, 1725, in Niort, Poitou; lieutenant on October 31, 1745; Captain November 12, 1746; reformed captain en second in 1749; substitute captain on April*

---

[i] Tanguay, III, p. 168.
[ii] Archives of the Marine.—loc. cit.
[iii] Moreau St-Méry Collection—Copy at Seminary.
[iv] Tanguay, III, p. 168.

12, 1756; abandoned in 1764. Comes from Berry incorporated. A note of 1763 adds: Good captain."

He was the son of Charles-Amateur Avice, siegneur de Montgon et Mothe-Claveau, in Poitou, lieutenant-colonel of cavalry, and Blanche-Colombe de Razilly. On September 15, 1760, he married in Montreal lady Amable Prudhomme, 23 years old, widow of Louis Coulon de Villiers, captain, and daughter of Louis Prudhomme and Louise Marin.

According to Beauchet-Filleau, Charles Avice, chevalier de Montgon de Surimeau, was appointed lieutenant of Marshals at Niort in 1773, and died March 12, 1780. In 1789, his widow survived, because it appears on the State of Pensions, since 1758, a pension of 554 livres, in consideration of the services of her first husband, Captain Louis Coulon de Villiers.

Mssr. de Surimeau had from his marriage with Amable Prudhomme six children:

1. Colombe, born December 30, 1761, married May 27, 1781, Philippe Jau, knight, Sgr de Chantigné;

2. Marie-Pétronille-Rose, married to N... Viault de Breuillac;

3. Gabriel-Amateur-Louis, born October 15, 1764;

4. Louise-Françoise-Catherine, born on September 28, 1766, and buried on October 12, 1786;

5. Marie-Amable, born on July 17, 1768, and died on March 18, 1787;

6. Charles-Antoine-Jean Avice de la Carte, born in Cherveux, March 30, 1771, and died May 14, 1836. During the emigration he was standard-bearer of the army of Condé and knight of Saint-Louis. Married in 1801 Marie Maixende de Chesne de Vauvert, including 5 children.

The name of the officer of Berry has often been distorted, but it is still Tanguay who went the furthest by calling him Michel Mougon de Jarimeau (Dictionnaire, 6, 125). Although he was commonly called Mssr. de Surimeau, his patronymic name was Avice.[145]]

Louis, le Grand Villiers

We have now to add some explanations and clarifications on a point that we preferred to not discuss in this place so as not to interrupt the flow of our narrative, that is to say, is Louis de Villiers actually the avenger of Jumonville?

For us, we do not doubt it, despite tradition, or rather, with the tradition that it is François.

Indeed, this tradition will be true if applied to what happened in 1756 when the Chevalier de Villiers, from the Illinois with the intention of avenging his brother Jumonville, attacked and took Fort Granville. It would be like a second vengeance, and we could explain how it could be confused with the first in 1754.

Besides, this tradition can be contrasted with another no less respectable and closer to events. We want to talk about that of the family of Gaspé allied to Coulon de Villiers.

Ignace Aubert de Gaspé, who had married Marie-Anne, sister of the Mssr. de Villiers, was part of the expedition ordered by his brother-in-law de Villiers against Fort Necessity.[i]

He ought therefore to know, and Madame de Gaspé, likewise, who was the commander of the expedition, and often spoke in the family, and of Jumonville and his avenger. Ignace Aubert de Gaspé and Marie-Anne Coulon de Villiers were the grandfather and grandmother of the author of the *Ancienne Canadiens*, and the latter, in the notes he has added to his work, writes "My great uncle Coulon de Villiers died of the small-pox when he was over sixty years of age [sic: 47], incessantly reiterating: 'I, to die in a bed like a woman! What a terrible fate for a man who has so often faced death on the battlefield! I had always hoped to shed the last drop of my blood in fighting for my country!'"[ii]

And let no one say, because Mssr. de Gaspé does not give the Christian name, that these words may be applied to all the Coulons; For there was only one who died of the smallpox after 1754, and it is Louis; we have proved it.

One more word. Bossu,[146] a contemporary of whom we have already quoted, wrote about le Chevelier's expedition in 1756: "We

---

[i] Archives of the Seminary—Papers of Gaspé.
[ii] *Anciens Canadiens,* Edition, 1877, p. 215. [*The English translation is taken from* Canadians of Old *translated by Pennée, 323.*]

must not confuse Mssr. de Villiers, surnamed le Grand Villiers, who was to avenge the death of Jumonville, immediately after his assassination in 1753 (sic), with the Chevalier de Villiers, who commanded this detachment."[i]

This sentence is without comment. To these proofs we add another, if not certain at least probable, drawn from the signatures of the two brothers. We know of only one from François; It is of 1762 and is in the registers of Saint-Louis of New Orleans.

Mssr. Cruzat has kindly sent us a photograph of it, which we reproduce here.

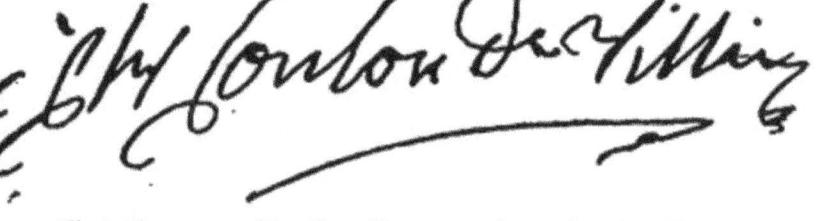

Ill. 6. Signature of Le Chevalier François Coulon de Villiers.

---

[i] Bossu, *Nouveaux voyages*, etc., Paris, 1768, p. 212.

As for the signatures of Louis, they are varied, but they all resemble each other. We give three. The first is that of his marriage certificate, in which there can be no doubt that it is his.[i]

Ill. 7. Signature of Louis Coulon de Villiers.

The second signature was taken from the works of Winsor[ii] and Abbe Daniel;[iii] it is not said that it is the signature of Louis, but it does not resemble that of any of his brothers.

Ill. 8. Signature of Le Grand Villiers.

The third is extracted from a facsimile of the capitulation, preserved at the Seminary of Quebec.[iv]

---

[i] Listed on the Register of N.-D. from Montreal.
[ii] *Narrative and critical History of America.*
[iii] *Histoire des grandes familles.*
[iv] This faxsimile is by P.-L Morin.

Coulon de Villiers

These last three signatures of de Villiers seem to us very much in the same hand; More or less large or more or less heavy, according to the pen, ink or paper, perhaps, they remain nevertheless similar and it would be difficult to attribute the signature of the capitulation to the Chevalier de Villiers if one judged by what we know of him.

It will be noted that at the capitulation Louis signed "Coulon-Villier" and not "Coulon de Villiers" and still less "Coulon et Villiers" as Ferland stated.[i]

These proofs, so as not to be without reply, may have some value, and we give them to be more complete.

[*The other signatures of the capitulation given here are, of course, that of James Mackay, captain of the British independent company from South Carolina, and George Washington, provincial colonel of the Virginia Colony.*]

Ill. 9. Signatures from the capitulation of Fort Necessity.

---

[i] *Cours d'histoire*, II, p. 509. Ferland notes on the preceding page that several copies of this capitulation were made and signed by Mackay, Washington, and Villiers. We wonder whether the signature given by Winsor and Father Daniel was not taken from one of these copies.

VI. François Coulon de Villiers,
known as le Chevalier

François de Villiers was, of all the sons of Nicolas-Antoine, the one who furnished the longest career. What we know of his statement of service proves that he did not lack from the other Coulons anything for bravery or activity. Although he has been confused with some of his brothers, and particularly with Louis, it is easy enough to distinguish him from others, at least as far as his military career is concerned, because, in official documents, he is almost always nicknamed le Chevalier.[147] What we lack is precise information about his private life and we should not be surprised. An officer of Louisiana, and, therefore, almost always absent from Canada, François de Villiers left here few traces. It is from Louisiana that we have come up with the details we are going to give of the alliances and the death of le Chevalier, and it is there also that we must go and seek all that will be missing from these notes.

The place and date of birth of le Chevalier de Villiers cannot be clearly ascertained. In the record of his third marriage, in 1762, he was said to be a native of Montreal and his record of burial in 1794 listed him as 91 years old, which would place his birth at 1703.[i]

Are these indications correct? We do not think so. The registers of Montreal are complete for this period. We have had them carefully examined and the record of baptism is not there.

The record of burial shows that François, at his death, was 91 years old, but we know that Nicolas-Antoine de Villiers, the father, did not marry until the end of 1705 or the beginning of 1706, and presumably, we cannot put the birth of François in 1703. Moreover, between the years 1706 and 1712 the other children: Marie and Madeleine, Nicolas-Antoine, and Louis follow each other closely.

Msgr. Tanguay does not speak of François in his *Dictionnaire généalogique*. For us, here is what we think.

François de Villiers, like his brothers and sisters, was born in Verchères, and in the marriage certificate he is said to be a native of Montreal, which can be understood as the region of Montreal. As for the date of his birth, we place it between the years 1712 and 1715.

---

[i] Registry of Saint-Louis, New Orleans

Coulon de Villiers

The records of Contrecoeur are totally missing for the years 1712, 1713, and 1714.[i] It follows that we could not find the baptism certificate.

What convinces us even more is that tradition in the family of François places his birth in 1712, and that Mssr. Villiers du Terrage, in the *Derniers jours de la Louisiane française*, places his birth to the year 1715.

To distinguish himself from his brothers, no doubt, François was called le Chevalier de Villiers. And it may be well to remark, *Chevalier* does not necessarily signify the Cross of Saint-Louis. One could be a knight long before being decorated. Such was the case for the latter.[ii] [*As shown in the previous chapter, while François was "always or almost always" referred to as le Chevalier, his brother Louis was also at times recorded with that moniker.*]

François de Villiers was at St. Joseph's River with his father and his brothers. He took part in the battle against the Sauk, September 16, 1733.

Three days afterwards, he accompanied his brother Nicolas-Antoine, who had pursued his enemies. During the combat which took place when they were joined, le Chevalier was wounded in the arm with a shot. At least this is what Beauharnois [148] and Hocquart[149] say in their letter of November 11, 1733, in which they recount the last blow and indicate the number of the dead and the wounded: "On the side of the Sieur de Villiers, his brother, cadet *à l'aiguillette*, was wounded with a gunshot in his arm,"[iii] In other letters, the governor says that Villiers, a cadet *à l'aiguillette*, was wounded in the affair against the Foxes in the action where his father was killed. We rather stick to the one we have just quoted.

---

[i] Letter from the Abbe Ducharmo to the late Abbe Rhéaume, 9 Dec. 1901.—Archives of the Seminary.

[ii] "The eldest son of a baron, the third son of a count, the fifth son of a marquis were called Knights without belonging to any order of Knighthood."—*Bescherelle*, quoted by Mssr. B. Sulte, who adds that they have imitated all this in New France.—*Bulletin des Recherches Historiques*, VIII, p. 36.

[iii] General correspondence, vol. 60, p. 134.

Documents subsequent to these letters tell us that this is le Chevalier.

Nicolas-Antoine de Villiers, who had remained commander of the fort by the death of his father, sent the news to the governor by his brother and Douville *fils*. "The Srs. de Villiers, wounded, and Douville *fils*, arrived tonight from Montreal," wrote Beauharnois on November 11th.[i]

[*Gosselin is mistaken, likely due to the reference to le Chevalier, in concluding that François was the Villiers brother wounded in the arm during the fight with the Sauk and Meskwaki. Surgeon Major Joseph Benoist recorded in June 1734, "I...certify that Monsieur Louis Coulon de Villiers, a cadet in the aforesaid troops, has been wounded by a shot in his left arm." As we have already mentioned, Louis writes of his being wounded in the La Baye affair in his 1754 letter to the Minster of Marine. As a final confirmation, we turn to François himself, who in his 1777 petition to the King of Spain, stated: "In the chase, another brother of mine named Villiers was wounded."[150]*]

On the same day [*November 11, 1733*], the governor wrote to the minister, suggesting certain promotions, and after recommending to him Nicolas-Antoine for an appointment, he added: "If you advance, Monsignor, de Villiers the eldest, it will create a vacancy that his brother who has just been wounded will fulfill very well."[ii] This vacancy of an ensign that was requested of him was perhaps granted shortly afterwards, but then he was only ensign *en second*. [*Again, Gosselin mistakenly concluded that François, not Louis, was wounded in 1733. It was the wounded Louis who was promoted from cadet to ensign* en second *following that fight. François received his promotion three years later.[151]*] In a list of promotions, on November 4, 1740, Beauharnois designated several young officers for the rank of ensign *en pied*, and among them was "de Villiers wounded in the affair of the Foxes, now at the Chickasaw."[iii] [*Again, this reference is to Louis, not François.*]

---

[i] General correspondence, vol. 60, p. 134. The governor is then at Quebec.

[ii] General correspondence, vol. 59, p. 37.

[iii] General correspondence, vol. 74, p. 89.

Coulon de Villiers

Indeed, le Chevalier had taken part in the expedition against the Chickasaw. The different accounts of this affair, which can be found in volume 44 of the Moreau St-Mery collection, indicate the names of Mssr. de Villiers and of le Chevalier de Villiers.[i] We also know that Jumonville was there.[ii]

In the same year (1740) Bienville,[152] Governor of Louisiana, wrote about a Coulon: "He is wise, intelligent, and has very strong feelings for the service of the colony."[iii] The name of le Chevalier is not found in this note, it is true, but we believe that it applies to him, since he seems to have taken part in the government of Louisiana.[iv]

We see by a list of officers who served in the different posts in 1743 that Chevalier de Villiers commanded at St. Joseph's.[v] He would have replaced his brother Nicolas-Antoine who returned to Quebec City around that time. [*It likely was Louis who commanded at St. Joseph's, as François made no mention of it in his 1777 petition to the King of Spain but indicates instead that he was assigned to the Illinois district.*]

An order from the governor to Mssr. DeMuy,[153] July 9, 1746, informs us that he was to command in the upper country, under his orders "the Sieur Chevalier de Villiers, at the head of the Pottawatomi, Winnebago, Illinois, who descend with him."[vi] [*Again, this was most likely Louis, not François.*]

In 1748, the Chevalier de Villiers was still only an ensign *en pied*. That year, he was proposed for the rank of lieutenant: "Cher. de Villiers, a good officer with much service, has found himself in actions and was wounded in that where his father and one of his brothers were killed." And further on, in the chapter on pensions, one adds: "Cher de Villiers, an ensign *en pied*, wounded in action where his father and one of his brothers were killed."[vii] [*Convinced that it was François who was wounded with his father, Gosselin*

---

[i] Report of Richard, 1899, p. 32.
[ii] *Etats de services.*—Archives of the Seminary.
[iii] Villiers du Terrage—*Derniers années de la Louisiane*, etc., p. 87.
[iv] Louisiana and the country of the Illinois had been handed over to the king by the French East India company in 1731.—Cf. Ferland, II, p. 466.
[v] General correspondence, vol. 79, p. 158.
[vi] Archives of the Seminary.
[vii] General correspondence, vol. 91, p. 164.

François, le Chevalier de Villiers

continues to confuse him with his brother Louis. It was Louis who was wounded with his father, and it was Louis who was promoted to lieutenant in 1748. François wrote in 1777, "In 1746, I was promoted to lieutenant, spent eight years in this rank at various garrisons and detachments in the Illinois District."[154]]

These reiterated recommendations prove, if not the goodwill of the minister, at least the excellent memoir of the Governor of Canada.

The inventory of Nicolas-Antoine's property, in 1752, shows us the Chevalier François lieutenant in Mississippi. He was made captain the following year. A memorandum dated April 1, 1753, at Versailles, announces that Mssr. de Montigny[155] will replace the vacant lieutenancy by the advancement of the Sieur Chevalier de Villiers, made captain.[i] [*It was Louis who was promoted to Captain in 1753. François was promoted the following year.*]

Varin[156] wrote the same thing to Contrecoeur[157] on September 15.[ii]

The documents tell us nothing about le Chevalier de Villiers during the years 1754 and 1755. It is not impossible that he was present at the capture of Fort Necessity but not as commander. He had, however, to make several trips from Louisiana to the forts of the Belle-Riviere: "he has made all the campaigns of the Belle-Riviere since my arrival in the colony," wrote Vaudreuil[158] in 1758.[iii]

[*François provided the definitive answer that it was not he, but rather, his brother, Louis, who avenged the death of Jumonville by vanquishing Washington and Mackay[159] at Fort Necessity. In his 1777 petition to the King of Spain, François Coulon de Villiers wrote:*

> *At the start of the [Seven Years' War], Jumonville, another of my brothers, was assassinated by the English while he was informing them of his commandant's orders.... Shortly thereafter my other brother, [Villiers,] went there with a detachment of five hundred men to*

---

[i] Archives of the Seminary.
[ii] Ibid.
[iii] Archives of the colonies—Louisiana, General corresp.—Vaudreuil arrived in Canada in July 1755.

> take vengeance for [Jumonville's] death. He attacked and seized Fort Necessity, defended by a garrison of seven hundred men and twelve cannons. He killed more than three hundred of them and obliged the remainder to surrender and sign a document in which they admitted killing Jumonville treacherously.[160]]

Bossu tells us[i] that in the spring of 1756 le Chevalier de Villiers obtained permission from the commander of the fort at Chartres to raise a party of French and Indians to avenge Jumonville, his brother, assassinated by the English before the war.

De Villiers was charged at the same time to conduct a convoy of provisions for Mssr. Dumas,[161] commander at Fort Duquesne. He left Fort de Chartres on April 1, 1756,[ii] and on August 8, Vaudreuil wrote to the minister:

> The provisions which Mssr. Dumas had requested of the Illinois had arrived.... Mssr. le Chevalier de Villiers, who commanded the escort of these provisions went up to Fort Duquesne with a boat of 18 thousand.... Mssr. de Villiers brought with him a chief and four Illinois warriors. He made them smoke with the Shawnees; the peace will be solid. The Shawnees appear disposed to send one of their chiefs with Mssr. de Villiers to complete the cohesion.
>
> These Illinois return home, very angry to have made a journey of about 20 days with Mssr. de Villiers without having found the opportunity to strike.[iii]

When Mssr. de Vaudreuil wrote these lines, he did not know that the Illinois were going to find an opportunity of signalizing themselves at the capture of Fort Granville.

---

[i] *Nouveaux voyages*, vol. I, pp. 211-212.

[ii] A letter from Kerlérec to the minister, dated December 23, 1757, places this expedition in the preceding spring, consequently in 1757. This is an error: it took place in 1756, as all the documents prove.

[iii] Archives of the Marine.—(Copy at Seminary)

François, le Chevalier de Villiers

There are several accounts of this expedition,[i] but the most complete is that of Kerlérec[162] to the minister. It is dated December 23, 1757, and begins thus:

> I have the honor to inform you that the Chevalier de Villiers, an infantry captain in the service of this colony, detached to the Illinois post, and whom I had ordered to convey the supplies of food which Mssr. MaKarty[163] sent last spring to Mssr. Dumas, the commanding officer of Fort Duquesne, carried out this mission with as much prudence and distinction as possible.
>
> Scarcely had this officer handed over to Mssr. Dumas, in very good order, the provisions with which he was charged, that he wished to go into the English camp (the season opposing his visit to the Illinois). Guided first by the desire to contribute to the glory of the King's arms, he was also delighted to take advantage of all the opportunities that presented themselves to avenge the death of Sieur Jumonville, his brother, assassinated by the English.[ii]

Dumas acquiesced to the wishes of de Villiers and permitted him to go towards Fort Cumberland to prevent the English from communicating from one fort to the other.

Embarking with a detachment of 60 men, both French and Indians, de Villiers had already traversed 60 leagues of country when the want of provisions and illness compelled him to retrace his steps and to return to Fort Duquesne, whence he had left twenty-five days earlier.

Once recovered, he again asked permission to go against the English, which was granted him. Kerlérec continued:

> The Chevalier de Villiers then set out on July 13 with 22 Frenchmen to go to the village of Attiquer [*Kittanning*] (a distance of 15 leagues from Fort Duquesne) where he raised a party of 32 Indians of the Wolves

---

[i] Cf. Bossu, loco cit; *Journal du Montcalm*, p. 111. Doc. rel. To New France, 1756, etc.
[ii] Cf. *Dernières années de la Louisiane française*, p. 87.

Coulon de Villiers

> [*Munsee*], Shawnees, and Illinois, who formed a detachment of 55 men, with whom he left the village on the 17th of the same month, with the intention of going to the Englishman George Croghan's [164] fort [*Fort Shirley*], but his guide having mistaken his way, he found himself on the 30th at noon in sight of Fort [*Granville*]. They discovered three men whom he wanted to encircle, but having been seen, they fled into the fort despite a few shots.[165]

The fort was well guarded, and de Villiers saw only one means of seizing it: to set it on fire. After the fort had been invested by a part of his people, he employed the rest of his men in transporting dry wood near a bastion and setting it on fire, which the enemy could not extinguish. The breach was opened, and le Chevalier proposed at dawn to raid with bayonets fixed at the end of their guns, at which time the garrison, which had lost its commander, two officers, and six soldiers, opened the gates of the fort, and surrendered with discretion. This garrison still contained 30 soldiers. There were also 3 women and 7 children. Thanks to their pathetic harangues, "de Villiers succeeded in saving them all from the fury of the Indians, who wanted to burn some of them."

[*François described his capture of Fort Granville:* "After a month, I left again to seize Fort Granville, defended by four bastions, a 200-man garrison, and artillery. On the eve of my arrival, 150 soldiers [in the fort] deserted, and only fifty remained to endure twenty-four hours of combat. Finally, I succeeded in setting fire to the fort, killing the commandant and fifteen men, capturing the remaining thirty-five, and spiking the cannons."[166]]

De Villiers finished burning the fort, spiking the cannon, seized the powder and flour that were there, and returned to Fort Duquesne with his prisoners. He arrived there on August 12.

Kerlérec, to whom we have borrowed all these details, concludes his letter thus:

> I think it my duty to represent to you that it is of the essential interest of the service that this officer should receive some marks of satisfaction from the King. To procure him the Cross of Saint-Louis, and this favor

will have a noticeable effect upon the soldiers entrusted to my orders. I dare even tell you that it is especially necessary in the dependence of the Illinois, where the service cannot be more difficult, that it is well that these gentlemen learn by trial that if the work is great, the reward of the monarch is always proportionate.

For their part Vaudreuil and Montcalm[167] wrote to France, and the latter said to Mssr. de la Bourdonnaye:[168] "The Chevalier de Villiers, lieutenant, brother of Mssr. de Jumonville, assassinated by the English, and Mssr. de Villiers, a captain who this year led a very brilliant campaign on Lake Ontario, this Chevalier, I say, came, with 55 men, to burn Fort Granville in Pennsylvania."[i]

In his turn, the Chevalier de Villiers had avenged his brother Jumonville. This second blow made by a Villiers against the English, to come two years after the first, was nevertheless regarded, and with reason, as a vengeance. Thus, it is easy to understand how little by little the dates were confounded and that we ended up seeing only one fact, one vengeance, that of 1754.

Kerlérec's excellent recommendation did not have the expected effect: the Cross of Saint-Louis, which the Chevalier so well deserved, was not to come until two years later, but he continued to serve with zeal.

A note appended to a letter from Mssr. de Vaudreuil, September 28, 1757, informs us of the Chevalier's titles on this date: "Mssr. François, Chevalier, Squire Sieur de Villiers, lieutenant of an infantry company detached from the Louisiana, acting as a staff officer at Fort de Chartres, has the honor to represent you...."[ii]

In the spring of 1758, he was again instructed to conduct a convoy of provisions to the Belle-Riviere.[iii]

On April 18, of the same year, Vaudreuil wrote to the minister:

---

[i] O'Callaghan, *Doc. de New-York*, X, p. 490.

[ii] Ministry of the Colonies—Louisiana. General correspondence 1755-1757.—This note, and the letter of Montcalm to the Bourdonnaye, (1756) agree to give de Villiers the rank of lieutenant; He had been a captain since 1753 [*sic: 1754, see page 145, or 1757, see page 170*].

[iii] *Journal de Montcalm*, p. 366, June 13, 1756—Coll. Lévis.

Coulon de Villiers

> Mssr. le Chevalier de Villiers, whom Mssr. de Macarty, commander in the Illinois, had accordingly ordered me to march on Virginia at the head of an Indian party. Might have surprised an English fort whose gate was open without the excessive force of his Indians, who made it out by running after three Englishmen, killed one of them, took the other, and the third retired to the fort; a woman went there with a spear. This party killed more than 500 animals.... The Chevalier de Villiers found more than thirty leagues of country, whose dwellings were abandoned on the river called the English River, 40 leagues above Sonnioto. This party took only four days on the river going across the mountains to the fort in question, and on returning it took many horses from the English, which they took to the Illinois.[i]

In the autumn of the same year de Villiers was still at Fort Duquesne. He took part in the brilliant victory that Aubry,[169] an officer of Louisiana, won over Major Grant[170] at the gate of the fort.[ii] He was one of the officers who most distinguished himself.

On November 20, Mssr. de Vaudreuil addressed to the minister the praise of Mssrs. Aubry and de Villiers. He wrote of the latter: "The second [*officer*] has served very well since a young age and has been in the campaigns of the Belle-Riviere since my arrival in the country and has always distinguished himself by his discoveries....and was particularly distinguished in the latter case by supporting Mssr. Aubry's detachment."[iii]

For his part, Mssr. de Kerlérec wrote on December 20, 1758: "The Sieur de Villiers, of whom I have just spoken, is the same, my lord, for whom I have asked for the Cross of Saint-Louis by my dispatch No. 132 of January 28, 1757. I have described the action of this officer, who took a fort from the English in 1756."[iv]

---

[i] General correspondence, vol. 103, p. 41.
[ii] Cf. Casgrain, *Montcalm et Lévis*, II, pp. 549 and following.
[iii] Archives of the colonies—Louisiana.
[iv] Ibid. As we see, Mssr. de Kerlérec here gives the true date of the capture of Fort Granville.

François, le Chevalier de Villiers

The long service of the Chevalier de Villiers, all those fine successes which had earned him so many good recommendations, ought to have touched the minister. This was not the case at the time, and de Villiers was only decorated the following year.

That year, 1759, the English made enormous preparations to attack Canada from all sides at once.

Fort Niagara, which Pouchot[171] had raised in 1756, was the most important of the posts in this region, and consequently one of the most exposed to attack by the enemy. Measures were therefore taken to put it in a state of defense.

At the call of the governor, the people of the West sent relief. They came from all directions, and Aubry, who had for his part the Chevalier de Villiers, brought six or seven hundred men from the banks of the Mississippi. He repaired to the fort at Presque Isle, and placed himself under the orders of Mssr. de Ligneris [sic: Lignery[172]], commandant of Fort Machault.

On July 6, General Prideaux[173] appeared before Niagara. Pouchot at once sent for the relief of the fort at Presque Isle and the surrounding posts.

On July 9, Prideaux ordered Pouchot to give him the fort; It was refused, as was expected, and the siege began. On the 23rd, Mssrs. De Ligneris and Aubry arrived with the requested assistance. Regrettably, Johnson,[174] who had replaced Prideaux, who had been killed shortly before, was informed of the arrival of the French detachment. He placed part of his army on the road through which Mssr. de Ligneris and his people were to pass while the Indians were spreading through the woods. Hidden by an abatis, the English could strike almost without danger. So, we can guess what happened. The little French troop taken unexpectedly, obliged to fight openly, against an enemy superior in number, was routed or cut to pieces. "The end of the battle," says Casgrain, from whom we have borrowed all these details, "is nothing but a massacre, the horrors of which have remained the secret of the solitudes of Niagara."[i]

Most of the officers were killed; The others, almost all wounded, were taken prisoners; among them was the Chevalier de Villiers.

---

[i] Cf. Casgrain, *Montcalm et Lévis*, II, pp. 167 and following.

Coulon de Villiers

Pouchot, understanding that it would be madness to resist any longer, resigned himself to lay down arms, and the capitulation was signed on July 25.

According to the articles of the capitulation, the garrison of Niagara and the prisoners were to be transported to New York. In the *Mémoires de Pouchot*, we read that before he signed the surrender, the English general proposed to stipulate that the garrison should be conducted to France. "He had not," he said, "at first thought of doing so, on the contrary he had decided to designate the most suitable place where the prisoners could be exchanged, which was done."[i]

According to these last words, there was, therefore, an exchange of prisoners in New York, and Mssr. de Villiers was able to return to Louisiana; Mssr. Villiers du Terrage informs us that the Chevalier passed into France with Aubry.[ii] The latter, according to the same author, would have arrived there only on February 24, 1761.[iii] If this date is correct, Mssr. de Villiers did not remain in France for a long time, at most one Year, since he was in Louisiana in June 1762.

[*François detailed his capture at the end of the French and Indian war in his petition to the King of Spain:*

> *In 1759, we again went out with another detachment to reinforce Canada, and, in passing, the settlement of Niagara, which the English had besieged. I was wounded in this action and taken prisoner by the Indians, who disrobed me from head to foot. They took me to their encampment, pouring blows and insults of all kinds on me. When, due to weariness or because of my wounds and ailments, I fell to the ground, they rained kicks and blows from their firearms upon me. Their only relief was to tell me that they intended to burn me on arrival [at their village]. Indeed, they would have done so had not the English had the humanity to rescue me from their hands and take me to*

---

[i] *Mémoires de Pouchot*, vol. 1, p. 201.
[ii] *Dernières années de la Louisiane française*, p. 201.
[iii] Ibid., p. 267.

François, le Chevalier de Villiers

New York. There I remained a prisoner for eighteen months, until the first of 1761. I was exchanged and finally went to France, where upon arrival I received the Cross of Saint-Louis as a reward.[175]]

Shortly after the capture of Niagara, but before news of it was published in Paris, François de Villiers was appointed Knight of Saint-Louis. Mazas[i] fixed the date of this appointment on September 7, 1759. However, a letter from the King, dated Versailles, August 1, 1759, addressed to Mssr. de Kerlérec, governor of Louisiana, gave orders and instructions to the latter to receive several officers from Louisiana, among whom was the Chevalier de Villiers.[ii] In any case, it was not too early. [*According to Fauteux: "He had been made Knight of Saint-Louis on September 7, 1759, but having, that same year, been made prisoner near Fort Niagara with Captain Aubry, he did not return to France until 1761, wherefore on March 27, new orders to receive him were sent to Count de la Serre." See appendix N, page 170.*]

Mssr. de Villiers, who had been stationed at Louisiana for a long time, continued to live there after the war had ceased. We know nothing of his history from 1762. [*See appendix L for François Coulon de Villiers's entire petition to the King of Spain wherein he details his career in Louisiana up to 1777.*]

He died in St. Louis, New Orleans, on May 22, 1794, and was buried the next day in the cemetery of this parish. The burial record of which we have the copy in Spanish with the French translation, reads as follows: "On the twenty-third of May of the year one thousand seven hundred and ninety-four I, the Vicar of the parish of St. Louis of New Orleans, buried the body of Messier François Coulon de Villiers, a native of Canada, a knight of the Royal Order of St Louis, married to Dame Marie de Livauduis. The night the deceased passed he was the age of ninety-one, with the sacraments of Penance, Viatic and Extreme Unction, which I administered to him with

---

[i] *Histoire de l'Ordre Royal*, etc., vol. II, p. 170.
[ii] Archives of the colonies 1747-1762.—Series P, vol. 3, p. 124. (Toledo Mssr. Cruzat furnished to him by Mssr. de Puntalba.)

the solemnity corresponding to these said offices. Present record this said month and year. (Signed) Fr. Louis de Quintallina."[i]

The original clearly says 91 years old, "noventa y un anos," however, we still believe that he should have written it 81 instead.

The *Annals* of the Ursulines of Quebec report that on the tomb of Mssr. de Villiers, who died in Louisiana, the following words were written: "Rejection of a noble race.... It is in the midst of misfortunes that he showed his goodly heart."[ii]

This epitaph, to which reference is made here, is not that of the Chevalier, as might be supposed, but that of Charles-Philippe Jumonville Coulon de Villiers, son of François and Delle de Livaudais his wife in third nuptials. Here is this epitaph in its entirety:[iii]

Rejection of an illustrious race
Unceasing to the blows of the fate opposing his goodly heart
In the narrow path of honor
From his confessions, always he followed the path.

Good blood cannot lie. It is not surprising that Charles Coulon de Villiers was the worthy son of Chevalier François, who was one of the most distinguished officers of his time in both Canada and Louisiana.

If, as we think, the Chevalier de Villiers was not the avenger of Jumonville at Fort Necessity in 1754, we can always say with truth that he was the second avenger of the victory he won in 1756 at Fort Granville.

François de Villiers had married three times. He had married first, [*in*] 1740, Elizabeth de St-Ange de Bellerive, sister of the last French commander in Illinois, with whom he had four children. [*Elizabeth was the daughter of Robert Groston de Saint-Ange, who cooperated with Nicholas-Antoine Coulon de Villiers, the father, in the 1730 siege of the Meskawki when François was a cadet. That Saint-Ange served most of his career in Louisiana and the Illinois country, may explain why François spent most of his career in that*

---

[i] Mssr. J.-W. Cruzat has provided us with both.
[ii] Vol. III, p. 41.
[iii] We owe this reference to Mssr. J.-W. Cruzat.

region, rather than in Canada with his brothers. Elizabeth died at Fort de Chartres on March 6, 1755.[176]] His wife from his second marriage was Madeleine Marin, daughter of Paul Marin,[177] captain at Fort Le Boeuf; she left him a son.

On June 28, 1762, François de Villiers wedded in his third marriage Geneviève [*Énault*] de Livaudais, who died in New Orleans in 1803: she left a son whose epitaph we have given above.

There are still descendants of the Chevalier de Villiers in Louisiana, and probably in Florida and Havana.

Marc, born of his marriage with Madeleine Marin, remained faithful to Spain at the cession of 1803, immigrated to Pensacola, Florida, with his family, then with his sons passed to Havana where he died around 1840.

One of the latter's daughters, Marie-Suzanne-Alice married Jose-Ignace Cruzat on September 30, 1814, and was the grandmother of Mssr. J.-W. Cruzat of New Orleans, to whom we owe so much for the preparation of this work.

We give in the appendix the genealogy of the Chevalier de Villiers as supplied to us by Mssr. Cruzat himself: he understands only the sons and grandsons of François. Since our work is not one of genealogy, we shall be forgiven for not having pushed our research further.

To conclude these notes on the brothers Coulon de Villiers we summarize.

First, all the sons of Nicolas-Antoine Coulon de Villiers and Angélique de Verchères, were born in Canada and not in France.

Second, it is certain that Nicolas-Antoine, the eldest of the Coulons, was the vanquisher of Noble[178] at Les Mines, but not of Washington at Fort Necessity.

It seems to us very probable if not certain that the avenger of Jumonville in 1754 was Louis le Grand Villiers and that François was likely the second avenger in 1756. [*We now know with certainty that Louis was the brother who vanquished Washington and sacked Fort Necessity based on his 1754 letter (appendix I) in which he details his campaign against Washington and also states that he was formerly the commandant of Fort Miamis, based on the July 13, 1750, contract in which he gives his full name as the* commandant at Fort Miamis, and based on François's 1777 petition (appendix L) in which he states that it was his brother who "attacked and seized Fort Necessity."]

Thirdly, one cannot truthfully say that of the seven brothers who composed this family, six were killed on the battlefield.[i] Let us note instead:

CHARLES-FRANÇOIS, born June 14, 1721, and died five months later, did not die on the battlefield.

PIERRE, if it is the same as Lespiney de Villiers, died from illness at Beaubassin in 1747 [*albeit during an active campaign in Acadia during King George's War*].

NICOLAS-ANTOINE, clearly died from his wounds, but he was not killed in combat.

LOUIS, taken by the smallpox in 1757, did not die in armed combat, either.

Finally, the CHEVALIER FRANÇOIS, who died at the age of 91 (likely 81 years), also had to die in his bed.

That leaves only JUMONVILLE who was killed, and we know one other [*DAMONVILLE*] who was killed in 1733 while fighting with his father against the Sauk.

Besides, it was not necessary to die in combat in order to bring credit to the homeland. Nicholas-Antoine, Louis, and François Coulon de Villiers proved it superabundantly. [*While it cannot be said that all were killed in battle, it can be said that all were killed, wounded, or died of disease in the service of their king.*] If death did not lay them down on the battlefield, it was not that they had fled the opportunities nor lacked courage: their hour had not come.

Four members of this family, the father, two sons, and a son-in-law, had lost their lives in the exercise of their duty. Two others had been seriously wounded. It was already enough to prove that the Coulons were not stingy with their blood when it came to the defense of the country.

---

[i] Cf. Bossu, *Nouveaux voyages*, I, p. 213; Sargent: *Braddock's Expedition*, p. 56.

VII. THE DAMSELS DE VILLIERS

We would reproach ourselves with finishing this work without adding a word about the damsels de Villiers. We have already named them, but here we want to state what their alliances were and make known those of their children whose names have come down to us.

The two elders, MARIE and MADELEINE, were at the Ursulines of Quebec in 1720 and 1721.

I. On August 7, 1720, MARIE married Alexandre Dagneau-Douville[179] in Montreal.[i]

MARIE-LOUISE, born on February 16, 1734, was married on April 23, 1759 to Pierre-Philippe d'Aubrespy de Lafarelle,[180] a knight, an officer of the Bearn regiment. Msgr. Tanguay does not indicate any other children from this marriage. According to the same author, Madame Douville died before 1740, because that year, on September 13, Mssr. Douville had a girl born from his marriage with Marie Courtemanche.

Curiously enough, another child of Mssr. Douville, MARGUERITE, who entered the Hôpital-Général on May 23, 1772, at 26½ years of age, was also listed as a daughter of Marie Coulon de Villiers. And yet she was born after 1740. Tanguay ascribed her baptism on November 12, 1744, and listed her mother Marie Courtemanche. She took the religious name of Marguerite Pierre de St-Amable, made her profession on November 25, 1773, and died on December 23, 1782.[ii]

[*The Douvilles also had two sons. In 1754, Louis Coulon de Villiers wrote to the Minister of Marine regarding his victory over Washington at Fort Necessity, in which he mentions a nephew, "I also Beg My Lord to have Consideration for my nephew Dagneau-Douville, who Is a Cadet, and who did His duty well in this latest campaign, in which he caught a musketball in the foot."[181] Cadets generally entered service by the age of fifteen, and this age would put his birth at 1739 or earlier.*

Yves Drolet in his work, Genealogical Tables of the Quebec Noblesse from the 17th to the 19th Century, *lists four children of Marie*

---

[i] *Dictionnaire généalogique*, III, p. 218.

[ii] Cf. *Msgr de St- Vallier et l'Hôpital- Général*, p. 722.

Coulon de Villiers and Alexandre Dagneau-Douville: LOUISE-ANGELIQUE, born May 12, 1731, at Montreal, and died February 27, 1808, at Montreal; MARIE-LOUISE, previously mentioned, died at Aspiran, France; ALEXANDRE-RENÉ,[182] born July 22, 1736, at Fort Frontenac, Quebec, married May 28, 1764, Madeleine-Félicité Ricord at Guadeloupe, and died there in 1789; and JOSEPH, born between 1737 and 1739 and killed in the Ohio valley April 7, 1756.[183] Of this last son, Hunter, writes "On March 23[, 1756,] Captain Dumas,[184] commanding at Fort Duquesne, ordered Ensign Dagneau-Douville, with a party of fifty Indians, to scout beyond Fort Cumberland and if possible to destroy English magazines on Conococheague. On April 7, while Douville was attacking a settlers' fort on Cacapon River, some twenty-five miles east of Fort Cumberland, he was surprised and killed by a Virginia detachment."[185] This may have been the same cadet who served under Louis Coulon de Villiers and was wounded in the battle at Fort Necessity.]

II. MADELEINE Coulon de Villiers, twin sister of the former, married three times. She first married at the end of 1727 or at the beginning of 1728,[i] François Duplessis-Faber, who was killed in 1733 with his father-in-law.

From this marriage was born GENEVIEVE baptized in Montreal on November [5, 1728,] and buried in the same place on April 22, 1729.[ii]

Four years after the death of her first husband, December 30, 1737, Madeleine de Villiers remarried in Montreal, to Claude Marin.[iii] [186] Both were at St. Joseph's River in Illinois in 1742 and 1745. Mssr. Marin signed: Laperriere-Marin, and his wife: Villiers de la perrière, or Mme. de Villiers la perrière.[iv]

According to the author of the *Dictionnaire généalogique*, a daughter, MARIE, born of this marriage would have been buried at Ste-Foy, on April 13, 1748. It seems to us that Monseigneur Tanguay

---

[i] Tanguay says 1727; the marriage contract passed in Montreal before Adhémar is June 11, 1728; the husband is appointed to the record: François Lefebvre Duplessis-Faber.—Note from Mssr. Ph. Gagnon.
[ii] Tanguay, III, p. 545.
[iii] Ibid, V, p. 514.
[iv] Registry St. Joseph of Illinois.

used here a bit of supposition. Indeed, the act of burial upon which he leans does not bear the Christian name of the father, nor the name of the mother, nor even that of the child.[i] How, after reading this act, could the author of the *Dictionnaire* conclude that this child was called *Marie* and that she was the daughter of *Claude* Marin and *Madeleine* de Villiers? This, we cannot answer.

Was not this child wet nursed at Ste-Foy rather Marie-Charlotte, baptized on August 11, 1746, and daughter of Joseph Marin and Charlotte De Fleury (de la Gorgendiere) whose names join in the registers of Ste-Foy at that time? We present the case without solving it.

Finally, Madeleine de Villiers, who had become a widow a second time, joined in a third marriage with Joseph Damours Sieur des Plaines,[187] on July 29, 1754, at Quebec. We do not know of any children from these last two marriages.

III. MARIE-ANNE de Villiers was born in 1722. She entered the Ursulines of Quebec on October 12, 1733, and retired on May 29, 1735.[ii]

On June 30, 1745, she married Ignace-Aubert de Gaspé[188] in Quebec City. The eight children from this marriage were: MARIE-ANNE-ANGÉLIQUE; PIERRE-IGNACE; GENEVIEVE; IGNACE; MARIE-ANNE-JOSEPH; PIERRE-IGNACE; LOUIS-IGNACE; and MARIE-CATHERIN.[iii]

Father Daniel does not name the last two.[iv]

Madame de Gaspé died at St. Jean-Port-Joli, where she was buried on March 18, 1789.

Philippe Aubert de Gaspé, the author of Les *Anciens Canadiens*, was her grandson.

---

[i] Registry of Ste-Foy. Here is the record in all its bareness: "On April 13, 1748, I buried in the Cemetery of Notre Dame de Foy a little daughter of Mssr. Marin, who was wet nursed by Antoine Samson, aged about two years. (Signed) Leprévost, priest."

[ii] Note from the Reverend Mother Mdm. of the Assumption.

[iii] Tanguay, II, p. 63.

[iv] *Histoire des grandes familles*, p. 363.

IV. Madeleine-Angélique de Villiers, born January 20, 1726, was, we believe, the last of the family. On October 23, 1749, she married Charles-Thomas de Gannes Falaise at Three Rivers.[i]

Tanguay introduces us to five daughters born of this marriage; They all died before 1759.[ii] They were: Marguerite-Anne; Marguerite-Angélique; Charlotte; Gabrielle and Marie-Antoinette. This list is not complete since in 1767, on February 16, the *Gazette de Québec* published the following notice: "Demoiselle Angélique Villiers wife of Mssr. Charles de Gannes Sqr. Chevalier de la Falaise, informs the public that for her advantage and that of her children, she renounced by public deed to the community of her and her present husband in France and the intention to remain so, etc."[iii]

Madame de Gannes Falaise then lived at Maskinongé.

In 1773, she had her inventory registered at Three Rivers; She said she was a widow from her first marriage with Charles Falaise.[iv]

V. Marguerite de Villiers, married, one knows not when or where, Pierre de Gannes Falaise, brother of the previous one. A daughter, Marie-Anne, born of this marriage, was buried at Pointe-du-Lac on September 27, 1750.[v]

---

[i] Registry of Three Rivers.—Note of Rev. P. Odoric, O. F. M.
[ii] *Dictionnaire*, etc, III, p. 275.
[iii] Note due to the kindness of Mssr. Pierre-Georges Roy.
[iv] Registry Closing of inventories. - Notes by B. P. Odoric, O. F. M.
[v] Tanguay, III, p. 275.

[*On the following pages is the map,* Partie Occidentale de la Nouvelle France ou du Canada, *or "Occidental part of New France or Canada: by Mssr. Jacques-Nicholas Bellin, Royal Engineer and Marine to serve the Intelligence of Business and State present in America, communicated to the Public by the Heritiers de Homan, in the year 1755." It depicts the Pays d'en Haut or upper country, the region upriver from Montreal, and known today as the Great Lakes region.*[189]]

Ill. 10. Occidental part of New France or Canada

Map: Great Lakes Region (French colonial map)

LAC ALIMIPEGON

On ne connoît point le Cours de toutes ces Rivières.

LAC SUPERIEUR

- Isle Royale
- Isle Maurepas
- I. Pontchartrain
- I. Philippeaux
- I. S. Anne
- Cap Hoquart
- Baye de Michipicoton
- Anse aux Sables
- Minabawien
- Havre Beauharnois
- Pointe de Kirueournan
- La Grande Isle
- Les SAUTEURS
- Michillimakinac aux Bois Blanc
- Fort et Mission abandonnés
- Anse au Tonerre

LAC MICHIGAN

- Baye des Noquets
- I. du Castor
- Baye de Saguinam

PAYS DES RENARDS

- Lac aux Outaouacs
- Lac des Vieux deserts
- Mines de Cuivre
- Mine de Plomb
- Village de Malomines
- Baye des Puans
- LES SAKIS
- Mission de S. François Xavier

PAYS DES MASCOUTENS

- Portage des Chenes
- Fort de Chicagou
- Village de Miamis
- Village de Poutouatamis
- Sources Portage du Theakiki
- R. S. Joseph
- Sources la Riviere Ouabache

PAYS DES ILINOIS

- Village d'Ilinois
- Le Rocher
- Lac Timitroui
- Fort des Miamis
- Les Forts à fleurs Chateaux ruinés
- Kaskasquias et Tamarouas
- Le Missouri R.
- Mine de Plomb

PAYS DES MIAMIS

- Lac

Rivers: R. aux Groseilles, R. Cachée, R. des Quicapoux, R. Pagnitane, R. Quiouconon, R. Noire, R. aux Ailes, R. au Canot, R. Quiscousing, R. à la Mine, R. des Macopins, R. aux Sable, R. Blanche, R. Moulon, R. au Raisin, R. à la Barbue, R. Marameg, R. Noire

Fleuve Mississipi

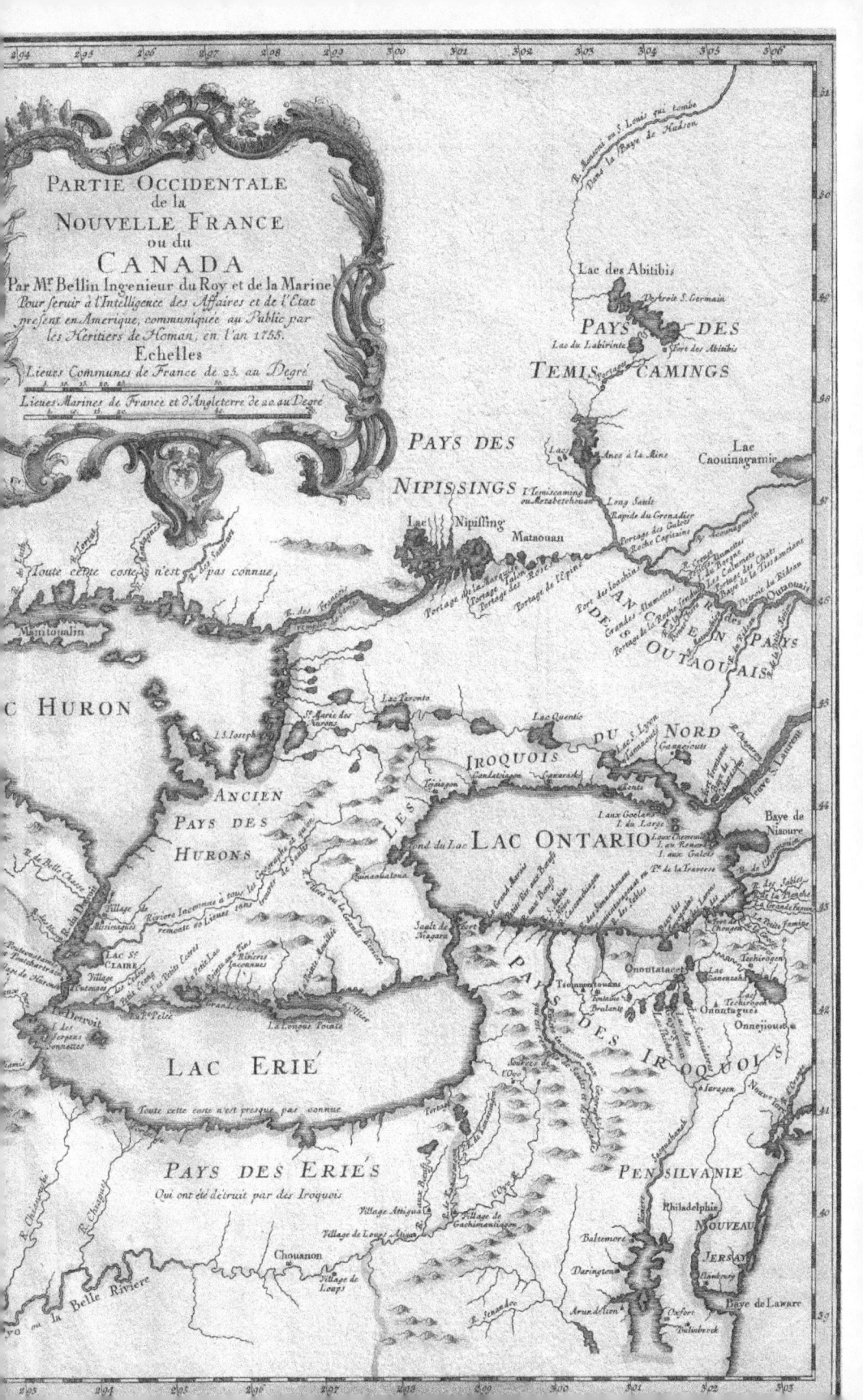

PARTIE OCCIDENTALE
de la
NOUVELLE FRANCE
ou du
CANADA
Par M.r Bellin Ingenieur du Roy et de la Marine
Pour servir à l'Intelligence des Affaires et de l'Etat
present en Amerique, communiquée au Public par
les Heritiers de Homan, en l'an 1755.
Echelles
Lieues Communes de France de 25. au Degré.

Lieues Marines de France et d'Angleterre de 20. au Degré.

Appendices

A. 1730 De Villiers Report of Destruction of the Fox

[*Following is the September 23, 1730, letter of Nicolas-Antoine Coulon de Villiers to Beauharnois detailing his siege and destruction of the Meskwaki two weeks earlier. The following English translation of the letter is taken from* Wisconsin Historical Collections, *edited by Reuben Gold Thwaites.*[190] *This appendix was not included in Gosselin's original publication.*]

Monsieur—I Had the honor of sending you a report on my first journey to le rocher,[191] with the nations to prevent the renards from passing over to The Iroquois.

The first step I hasten to take on my arrival here, is to dispatch to you a canoe, in which I send my son,[i] in order that he may have the honor of informing you of the blow inflicted by me, at the head of the French and savages, upon the renards, who were going to join The Iroquois and who were stopped by The poutouatamis, mascoutins, quikapoux, And The jllinois of le rocher.

On the 6th of August two mascoutins came to us here, who had been Sent expressly by their chiefs, to inform me that the renards had struck The poutouatamis, quikapoux, mascoutins, jllinois, And the Latter, in revenge, had pursued them and found them marching in a body with Their women and children in the direction of the jroquois; and had come to blows with them. Our people then numbered only About Two hundred men, as one Hundred had been allowed to depart on the previous day. The attack began at Ten o'clock in the morning. They defeated the renards and put them to flight, But the latter rallied and gained renewed vigor; they fought until nightfall. In this affair Our people had Six men killed, and three wounded. One of our Bravest war-chiefs, named Okeia, was among

---

[i] This was, doubtless, Louis Coulon de Villiers, who afterwards attacked Washington at Fort Necessity. For a biographical sketch, see *Wis. Hist. Colls.*, v, pp. 118, 119.—Ed. [*As we have seen, this was not Louis, but, rather, the eldest son, Nicolas-Antoine.*]

1730 De Villiers Report

the dead, and Pindigaché, another chief, was Wounded. The renards had seven men killed And thirty wounded. During The night, The poutouatamis posted themselves on a hill in the prairie and dug holes in the earth by way of a fort. On their side, The renards with their families took possession of a small grove of trees and fortified themselves. On The following day, they parleyed with one another to gain time and to obtain assistance. During these parleys, the Pouatouamis sent Papissa, with a young man to the oüyâtanons to ask aid of the tribes and the French at that post. The mascoutins sent to ask me to join the poutouatamis and to likewise come to their assistance.

The jllinois in the same manner, sent messages to the caokias. As soon as I heard the news I notified the Sieur Denoyelles,[192] and sent two Savages to Detroit, but they did not reach there in time. I started from my post on the 10th of August, with the French Who were then in a condition to March, and with all the savages here, including Poutouatamis, Myamis, and Saquis and proceeded to the place where the renards were. On the way I took with me The quikapoux and maskoutins, making about 300 men in all. Monsieur de St. Ange[193] was already there with 100 Frenchmen and 400 savages, including Kaôquias, missouris, and Peôrias, and The 200 of our savages who had already fought with them. The Ouyatanons and péanguichias also arrived on the same day as I did, so that in a short time we numbered About 1400 men. I was about to forget one particular circumstance, Monsieur, While Papissa was among the ouyatanons, the renards also sent two men there with a Collar [*viz.: belt of wampum*] and calumets [*viz.: peace pipes*] to ask their aid against the Poutouatamis, maskoutins, and quikapoux, against whom they had just fought, and who were watching them; at the same time they asked them to leave the road open to enable them to go in peace with their families to the jroquois. The ouyatanons replied that they would assist them; that they would remain where they were and fortify themselves and that they would soon see them.

The renards' fort was in a small Grove of trees, on the bank of a little river running through a vast prairie, more than four leagues in circumference, without a tree, except Two groves about 60 arpents from one another. Monsieur de St. Ange had camped with His savages on the left bank of the river and had built redoubts to prevent their obtaining Water, but they had excavated underground passages leading to the River. I camped, with my savages and the Frenchmen who had joined me, on the right of their fort, where I erected two others, with a Cavalier in each to beat them back into their own And prevent them from descending into the ditches they had outside. I had a trench opened to approach them more closely, without risk to anybody and had an attempt made to set fire to their fort. This trench made them uneasy, and caused them to move about more than usual. As soon as they saw that the earth was being excavated, a shower of gun-shots fell in good fashion.

The ouyatanons who apparently were unwilling to completely break Their promise to them, asked me to allow them to call a man who was their ally; saying that thereby they might get some Illinois women whom they held in captivity. I allowed them to do so, on condition that I should see no other meat Come out of that village than my own. This they promised, but, on the contrary, that man came out, with four Slaves and a Collar, which he presented to me on behalf of the renard. I would not listen to him. I said that it was Illinois flesh that I asked for, and that I would have no other. He returned and in several trips brought me what I wanted. The Saquis took advantage of this delay, and approached the fort in spite of the French, who were on guard there. They got out a number of children and gave food to the renards, so that I was obliged to open fire on the fort, to compel them to retire.

Our tribes were very anxious to spare the renards' lives, and proposed an act of treachery to me. Their design was that I should promise Them their lives, that I should make them come out And that they would fall on them. It was in nowise their intention to do so; their only object was to secure captives. I opposed this, seeing that it could only result in sparing the lives of those wretches, who would undoubtedly Continue on their way to The jroquois. Every day they found fresh subjects on which to speak to me. They came back twice with their children and with collars, to move me. But although they had been pale, I made them turn as if painted red, by telling them that all their words were in vain And that they were not to come back again. They addressed themselves to Monsieur de St.

1730 De Villiers Report

Ange, who listened to them no more than I did. Nevertheless, we fired some shots at them as they re-entered their fort. They suffered much from hunger because, for four days previous to Their flight, they lived only on *apichimonts*.[i] Monsieur de Noyelles arrived with the nations of His post, which gave us a reinforcement of a hundred men; these would have been very Useful to us, had the Savages been willing to mount guard night and day, but as soon as the least bad weather set in, they would not come out of their cabins and we were not enough Frenchmen to man the entire contravallation.

The Renards held out for twenty-three days. On the 8th of September, we had the finest weather in the world until an hour from sunset, when a Terrible storm of wind and rain arose which lasted until the night, which was very dark and Foggy, so that, in spite of all I could say to our Savages, I was unable to make them guard all The outlets. The Renards took advantage of this to come out of their fort and flee. We perceived this at first from the crying of the children which we heard, and we learned it from a Sauteux woman who came into the trench to surrender. I at once prepared to pursue them at day-break. We followed them with Our Savages and routed them, and more than 200 warriors were killed. No other chief Escaped except Licaouais, of whom, however, we have no information. The others were made prisoners and placed in The hands of the Kaôquias, who will assuredly not spare their lives. Those who escaped from us threw away all they had, even to their powder-horns in order that they might escape; but few remain. The prisoners told us that they had fought against The Scioux in the spring and very likely this is true. I Found their village very small, although I do not refer to that in which they were shut up, But to two Of their Camps which I saw in the prairies where they had lived during The summer. Our Quicapoux and mascoutins did wonders on the expedition, and all did equally well, vying with one another. Had it not been for The desertion of 300 Kaôkias who had only just abandoned Monsieur de St. Ange, and for the absence of 100 men from my camp who had gone Hunting to supply us with food, not a single Renard would have escaped. I can assure you, Monsieur, that we

---

[i] Note on original manuscript: "these are Their coverings made of Skins."

made The renards fast, but that we fasted almost as much as They. My son, who has just come out of The action, will give you whatever details I may have omitted. I take the liberty, Monsieur, of begging your protection for Him. I have had no more urgent desire, than to Send Him to you that he may have The honor of bringing you this News.

All our nations are preparing to go in the spring to pay you their homage, and, at the same time, to tell you of their dead, Especially Louis Lamech; they are Oüyénamégousy, Pindigaché, oüataouaségo and Ouéfigué, who kept the Renards in sight all summer Without abandoning them, with the quikapoux and mascoutins.

The sieur de Villiers, the younger, adds[i] that the nations returned home well pleased with the compliments they had received from Monsieur His father, each one in particular and all in general, so that it was impossible to say who had done best on that occasion, all having displayed uncommon ardor and courage.

That in order to thank Monsieur The commandant and the officers, all the chiefs of the nations, at the head of their troops, had sworn and protested that if ever any Nation were rash enough to attack the French, they would shed the last drop of their blood to avenge them; that they come to give them a tangible proof of their friendship and attachment for Them, after destroying their enemies; That this memory would never be Effaced from their hearts And that they would Carefully impress it upon Their descendants.

---

[i] What follows is an addendum to the letter of De Villiers, set down from the oral account of his son, the messenger.—Ed.

B. 1733 Beauharnois-Hocquart Letter of Captain de Villiers's Death

[*Following is the November 11, 1733, letter of Beauharnois and Hocquart to the French Minister that Gosselin referenced on page 24 of his* Notes sur la Famille Coulon de Villiers, *and page 23 of this translation. The following English translation of the letter is taken from* Wisconsin Historical Collections, *edited by Reuben Gold Thwaites.*[194] *This appendix was not included in Gosselin's original publication.*]

Monseigneur—Monsieur De Beauharnois had the honor by his letter of the first of July last to inform you of the orders that he had given to the Sieur De Villiers whom he had sent back as Commandant at la Baye, and of the manner in which he was to act regarding the Renards [*viz.: Foxes or Meskwaki*]. The result has not fulfilled our expectations.

The Sieur De Villiers, the younger, an Ensign in the Troops, who has succeeded to the Command of that Post through the death of his Father, has sent one of his brothers and The Sieur Douville[i] with Letters giving us the particulars of what happened in the month of September last at the Post of La Baye.

Monsieur De Villiers, the Commandant of that Post arrived there on the 16th of the said month of September alone in his Canoe. He had left at a distance of half a League from there The Sieur De Repentigny,[ii] a Lieutenant, who was Commandant at Michilimackinac, together with 200 Savages; Outawacs, folles avoines, and sau-

---

[i] The ensign was probably Louis Coulon de Villiers, called "le grand Villiers;" [*Thwaites is mistaken. The ensign was Nicolas-Antoine, the eldest son and namesake of Captain Coulon de Villiers, and the brother that he sent to Beauharnois was the wounded Louis;*] for his biography, see Wis. Hist. Colls., v, p. 119. Alexandre Dagneau, Sieur Douville, was married to Marie Coulon de Villiers in 1730.—Ed.

[ii] Probably the elder son of Pierre de Gardeur de Repentigny, who accompanied Duluth (see *Wis. Hist. Colls.*, xvi, pp. 119, 123); and elder brother of the Repentigny who later commanded at Mackinac.—Ed. [*Jean-Baptiste-René Legardeur de Repentigny, see 178-n.19*]

teux, and about 60 French. The Sieur De Villiers had given Him orders to be ready to march as soon as he heard The signal of 3 gun-shots and he had also detached his son, The Ensign, with 10 Frenchmen and 50 Savages to the petit Cacalin,[i] a passage by which the Renards might escape.

When Monsieur De Villiers arrived at the French fort, he at once sent for The Saki Chiefs to inform Them of Their father's Intentions. The chiefs came to Him and he explained to Them that their father had granted the remnant of the Renards who were with Them, their lives; But on the condition that they should submit to his orders and go to Montreal. After a Council which lasted some time, as the Sakis Chiefs gave no positive answer, Monsieur De Villiers sent 4 of them back to Their fort[ii] to tell their tribe that if within a certain time they did not send the Renards to him, he would go and get Them Himself. When the specified time had elapsed without the Renards appearing, and when Monsieur de Villiers, whom the sieur De Repentigny had joined, saw that The Sakis were not coming back, he resolved to go to their Fort in person accompanied by two of his Children, by the Sieur Douville, the younger, his son-in-law, and by 7 or 8 French to ask Them to Deliver up The Renards to Him. He had just given orders to the Sieur De Repentigny to guard The approaches to the Sakis' fort with The remainder of the French lest the Renards should escape. When Monsieur De Villiers arrived at the Door of the fort he asked the Sakis for the Renards. He found there some armed Sakis who told him to withdraw, And when he tried to enter a Savage approached Him with uplifted Tomahawk and at The same moment three gun-shots were fired, one of which killed one of the Sieur De Villiers' sons at his side. The Father and the French discharged their pieces and this was followed by other volleys from the Sakis by which Monsieur de Villiers was killed, and three French were wounded.

---

[i] Now called Little Kaukauna, in Brown County, Wis., about ten miles above the present city of Green Bay, on Fox River.—Ed.

[ii] This appears to have been situated on the lake shore, opposite the French fort, on the east side of Fox River, near the present city of Green Bay.—Ed.

Monsieur De Repentigny who guarded The aproaches [sic] on the side of the woods, ran up and was killed a moment afterward in a sortie that the Sakis made against Him. The Sieur Duplessis, a Cadet in the Troops, and six other French met the same fate. 200 of our Savages who had remained in the French fort went to the Assistance of the others and when the Sakis saw them coming they withdrew into Their fort. 3 of them were killed.[i]

Three days after this action The Sakis evacuated Their fort during The night and The Ensign, Sieur De Villiers, who had returned from le petit Cacalin, assembled all the French and Savages—Outawacs, folles avoines and Sauteux—and pursued The Sakis and overtook them about 4 o'clock in the evening 8 Leagues from the post.[ii] He attacked them and fought Them until night. 20 Sakis and 6 Renards were killed in this last fight; 9 were mortally wounded besides others who were wounded and whose number is not known. On the side of sieur De Villiers, his brother, a Cadet *à l'aiguillette*, received a gun-shot wound in the arm; The Sieurs Daillebout, the des Musseaux brothers,[iii] and 8 other French were also wounded while two others were killed.

The Outawacs lost 9 men, the grand Chief of The nation being among the number; The folles avoines 6; The sauteux 2 and 4 wounded in all.

Monsieur De Beauharnois will at once give the necessary orders to attack The Sakis and The remainder of the Renards to

---

[i] For the tradition preserved among the Indians and French of this event see "Grignon's Recollections," *Wis. Hist. Colls.*, iii, pp. 204-206. The name there given as "De Velie," is doubtless De Villiers. [*"Grignon's Recollections" is provided in appendix D.*] Another form of the tradition, is given in *Wis. Hist. Colls.*, viii, pp. 207, 208. Dr. Draper dated this 1730, because of his knowledge of De Villiers's attack of that year, and not of this embroilment in 1733. The Sieur Duplessis was a son of the former commandant at La Baye, and son-in-law of De Villiers.—Ed.

[ii] This is about the distance of Little Butte des Morts, near the present city of Appleton, and thus would coincide with tradition.—Ed.

[iii] The Sieurs Daillebout, and the brothers Des Musseaux were all relatives, descendants of Charles D'Aillebout, a prominent judge at Montreal during the 17th century, and Catherine le Gardeur. Thus they were also relatives of De Repentigny.—Ed.

avenge The blood of the French that has been shed, and he will concert with Monsieur hocquart regarding The expense that will have to be incurred. He has The honor to submit to you by a private Letter the Names of the officers who are to replace those who have been killed. We unite with him in asking you for their promotion which they deserve, and a pension for Madame De Villiers, to provide for her subsistence and that of her numerous family, Since she is a widow with 10 children. The Sieur De Villiers who was Wounded and the Sieur Douville, the younger, arrived this evening from Montreal. Fortunately The Vessel *Le Saint Joseph* of L'Isle Royale which sailed this morning, had been compelled to put back in consequence of a leak. It will sail tomorrow at daybreak And we have barely time to write you this Letter.

We remain with very profound respect, Monseigneur, Your very humble And very obedient servants.

BEAUHARNOIS
HOCQUART

QUEBEC, November 11th, 1733.

C. 1734 Beauharnois Letter of Captain de Villiers's Death

[*Following is a subsequent letter dated October 5, 1734, from Beauharnois to the French Minister, in which he justifies his connection with what the French ministry considered a fiasco at La Baye. In so doing, he shamelessly places all blame for the affair on Captain Nicolas-Antoine Coulon de Villiers despite orders from Beauharnois directing de Villiers, "If that Wretched Remnant will not obey, to kill them without thinking of making a single Prisoner, so as not to leave one of the race alive in the upper Country If possible."195 Beauharnois provides additional details of the incident in which Captain de Villiers was killed along with his son, Damonville, and his son-in-law, Duplessis-Faber. The following English translation of the letter is taken from* Wisconsin Historical Collections, *edited by Reuben Gold Thwaites.196 This appendix was not included in Gosselin's original publication.*]

Monseigneur—You do me the honor of informing me by your letter of the 20th of April last that his Majesty causes an explanation to be given me, by his despatch to Monsieur Hocquart and myself jointly of his intentions Regarding what concerns each nation. I have seen what His Majesty is pleased to point out to me on this Subject, and I venture to assure him that this matter has always received my chief attention since I have Been in this Colony. You will Observe, Monseigneur, by our reply to the King's memorial, the measures that I continue to take to restore tranquillity [*sic*] in the upper Country.

It would have been difficult for me to forestall the events that gave rise to the troubles there in connection with the Sakis and Renards, and after having had the honor of informing you by our joint letter of the 11th of November last of what had caused the unfortunate affair of la Baye, I would add that it should be attributed less to the remnant of the Renard nation, than to the slight precautions observed by the Sieur de Villiers on that occasion. What I had had the honor of telling you, Monseigneur, in the preceding years, respecting the condition to which the Renards were reduced, was authentic; and there was no reason to think that so small a number as those that remained and implored mercy on all sides, could cause any trouble in the upper Country, especially after the assurance I had received, as I had the honor of informing you, that the Remainder of that Nation, after trying in vain to effect an alliance with all the other nations, who had refused them, saw no other way of saving their lives than by coming and throwing themselves on their Father's mercy. Nevertheless, although this information came to me from all sides, and, moreover, appearances gave me no reason to suspect anything else, still, the inconstancy of the savages and the little reliance that can be placed in their promises led me to think of the measures that should be taken to prevent the consequences that might result from that affair, in the event of the Renards succeeding in corrupting some nations, and in finding a refuge among them.

To that end I had ordered the Sieur de Villiers by special instructions to take every proper precaution, through the nations that are faithful to us, to bring in the remainder of the Renards, or to destroy them if he could not succeed in doing so. I had expressly recommended to him before attempting anything, to make sure of the Sakis (as being Those who seemed to me the most to be suspected) for the success of the undertaking, And with that object I had given him a large collar [*viz.: belt of wampum*], accompanied by presents and two medals for the two most noted chiefs of that Nation,—a Course that seemed all the more suitable since those savages had Until then manifested naught but Hostility toward the renards and had also refused their alliance. The precautions that I took were calculated to strengthen the resolution they had taken, and to estrange them more and more from the Renards. If those measures, Monseigneur, had been Followed as I had arranged them, I can assert that Matters would not have reached such an extremity. As far as I was concerned, they were the Best measures that I could take, and They seemed to me all the more safe since I entrusted their execution to an officer who had always displayed great prudence in his actions. Monsieur de Villiers's conduct on that occasion gave a different aspect to the affair. That officer, who was ordered to act with the most gentle means, and to send word to the friendly nations to deliver up the Renards to him or to destroy them utterly, began by talking of war at Michilimackinac; and without heeding the commands that had been given him, he marched straight to la Baye with thirty French and a hundred folles avoines Savages, whom he gathered on the way; and he ordered the Sieur de Repentigny to follow him with thirty French whom he also had with him and a hundred Outaüacs. On approaching the post of la Baye, the Sieur de Villiers left the Sieur de Repentigny with his party half a league from the fort of the Sakis with orders to proceed there on hearing the signal of three gun-shots; and after embarking in his canoe to continue his route, he despatched his eldest son with ten Frenchmen and fifty savages to the petit Cacalin, a place by which the Renards might escape from the Sakis' fort, and he kept with Him only sixteen men, whom he divided into two parties to blockade the fort. To say nothing of the fact that all these manœuvres were contrary to the orders that he had received to adopt only the gentlest measures to secure the Subjugation of the Renards, and that for the Carrying out of his design, he had with Him but those sixteen men (for the savages of his party had asked him to allow them time to hold a feast), he acted in this affair with still less prudence and circumspection since—in addition to the fact that there was no question of coming into conflict with the Sakis or with any other nation to secure the Renards—the Very objection of the Sakis at the outset to deliver up the remainder of that nation, and their request to Him not to use violence to get them because it was not yet time, should have induced him to have had some consideration for the Sakis, and to have attempted to win them by means of the presents that I had entrusted to him, especially as his forces were not yet assembled. The Sieur de Villiers, not heeding all these considerations and guided solely by rash Bravery and courage, brought on the misfortune that happened, which it was impossible for me to foresee owing to the measure that I had taken. He tried to enter the Sakis fort, He being the tenth, to force and tear down the barrier, in the hope that such boldness would overawe them. Some Chiefs told him to withdraw; that their Young men had no longer any sense and that if he persisted he would be a dead man. Nothing stopped that Officer. A gun-shot Was fired by a Sakis or by a Renard, and killed the son of the Sieur de Villiers who was at his side. The Father fired his gun at the first who presented himself, and this Was followed by a volley from the warriors of the Village and he was killed. I would have had the honor, Monseigneur, of giving you these particulars last year in our joint letter on the subject of this affair, had I been informed of them. But the news only reached me last Summer, and I was all the more surprised at it, since the orders I had given to the Sieur de Villiers were very different from the manner in which would, in truth, have done honor to the French, had he (although Without orders) employed his forces more judiciously.

You will observe, Monseigneur, in the reply to the King's memorial the measures that I have taken to prevent the Consequences of this affair and to put an end to the same, if possible by conciliatory means as far as the Sakis are concerned. I have occasioned as little expense as possible to His Majesty, and he will not be able to hear of the Success of our efforts before next year.

I remain with very profound respect, Monseigneur, Your very humble and very obedient servant.

BEAUHARNOIS

QUEBEC, October 5th, 1734.

D. Grignon Reminiscence of Captain de Villiers' Death

[*The following is Captain Augustin Grignon's recollection providing an alternate version of the September 16, 1733, La Baye affair between Captain Nicolas-Antoine Coulon de Villiers and the Sauk and Meskwaki, in which the elder de Villiers was killed along with his son Damonville and son-in-law Duplessis-Faber. The recollection was recorded by Lyman C. Draper in the summer of 1857 when Grignon was seventy-seven years old. Grignon refers to de Villiers as Captain De Velie. This account is from* Wisconsin Historical Collections, *edited by Reuben Gold Thwaites.*[197] *This appendix was not included in Gosselin's original publication.*]

As the details of the war which eventuated in the expulsion of the Sauks and Foxes from the Fox River Valley in 1746 [sic], are of much interest, I shall give them as fully as I have learned them from the lips of my grandfather, CHARLES DE LANGLADE,[198] who took an active part in some of the occurrences narrated, and from other ancient settlers and Indians.

The Outagamies or Foxes were at this time located at the Little Butte de Morts, on the western bank of Fox river, and some thirty-seven miles above Green Bay. Here they made it a point, whenever a trader's boat approached, to place a torch upon the bank, as a signal for the traders to come ashore, and pay the customary tribute which they exacted from all. To refuse this tribute, was sure to incur the displeasure of the Foxes, and robbery would be the mildest punishment inflicted. This haughty, imperious conduct of the Foxes, was a source of no little annoyance to the traders, who made their complaints to the Commandants of the Western posts, and in due time these grievances reached the ears of the Governor of Canada.

Captain DE VELIE was at this time Commandant of the small garrison at Green Bay. He was relieved by the arrival of a new officer whose name I have forgotten, and the new Commandant brought with him demands for the Sauks of the village opposite the fort, who had hitherto demeaned themselves well, to deliver up the few Foxes living among them, in consequence of intermarriages or otherwise. All were readily given up, except a Fox boy, who had been adopted by a Sauk woman. DE VELIE and his successor were dining together, and becoming somewhat influenced by wine, some sharp words passed between them relative to the tardiness of the Sauks in surrendering the Fox boy; when DE VELIE arose, and taking his gun and a negro servant, crossed the river to the Sauk village, which was surrounded with palisades or pickets. He found the Sauks in council, and was met by the Sauk chief, of whom he demanded the immediate surrender of the remaining Indian. The chief said he and his principal men had just been in council about the matter, and though the adopted mother of the youth was loth to part with him, yet they hoped to prevail upon her peaceably to do so. The chief proceeded to visit the old woman, who still remained obstinate, and DE VELIE renewing his demands and immediate compliance, again would the chief renew his efforts; and thus three times did he go to the sturdy old woman, and endeavor to prevail upon her to give up the boy, and returning each time without success, but assuring DE VELIE that if he would be a little patient, he was certain the old squaw would yet comply with his demands, as she seemed to be relenting. But in his warm blood, the Frenchman was in no mood to exercise patience, when he at length drew up his gun and shot the chief dead. Some of the young Sauks were for taking instant revenge, but the older and wiser men present begged them to be cool, and refrain from inflicting injury on their French Father, as they had provoked him to commit the act. By this time DE VELIE, whose anger was yet unappeased, had got his gun re-loaded by his servant, and wantonly shot down another chief, and then a third one; when a young Sauk, only twelve years of age, named MA-KAU-TA-PE-NA-SE, or *The Black Bird*, shot the enraged Frenchman dead.

The garrison was too weak to attempt the chastisement of the Sauks, but upon the arrival of a reinforcement, joined by the French settlers, CHARLES DE LANGLADE among them, the Sauks were attacked at their village, when a severe battle occurred, in which several were killed on both sides, and the Sauks finally driven away. In this Sauk battle, two of my father's uncles were among the slain on the part of the French. The Sauks now retired to the Wisconsin river and located themselves at Sauk Prairie, where they still resided, and had a fine village, with comfortable houses, and apparently doing something in mining lead, when CARVER visited the country in 1766, but which appeared to have been several years deserted when I first saw the place, in 1795, as there were then only a few remains of fire-places and posts to be seen. The brave young Sauk, BLACK BIRD, became a distinguished chief among his people, and Mssr. LAURENT FILY, an old trader, told me many years since, that he knew BLACK BIRD well at the Sauk village at the mouth of Rock river, and that he lived to a good old age—and FILY added, that he was the same person who in his youth had so fearlessly shot DE VELIE.

E. French Account of the Battle of Les Mines

[*Following is the French Government's report regarding the February 1747 Battle of Les Mines, also called Minas or Grand-Pré, including the articles of capitulation signed by Nicolas-Antoine Coulon de Villiers. It was translated by Edmund B. O'Callaghan and originally published in the 1855 New England Historical and Genealogical Register.* [199] *This appendix was not included in Gosselin's original publication.*]

Mr. de Ramezay[200] being unable to march in consequence of a severe bruise he received on the knee in his journey to Minas,[i] the Canadian detachment, consisting of about 300 men, including French and Indians, set out on snow shoes from Beaubassin[ii] on the 23d January (1747) for Minas, under the command of Captain [*Nicolas-Antoine*] Coulon [*de Villiers*], for the purpose of driving off the English who had come to settle there. It arrived at Pegiguet[iii] on the 10th of February. Capt. Coulon having reconnoitred the enemy's position, divided his force into 10 subdivisions so as to make a simultaneous attack on as many houses in which the enemy was quartered to the number of 500, instead of 250 as had been already reported. After marching all night, he found himself, on the morning of the 11th, in a position to commence the attack, which he did. The enemy had sentinels at each house and kept good watch. Mr. de Coulon received, shortly after the first shock, a musket ball in his left arm, which obliged him to retire from loss of blood. The then houses that were attached were all carried, with the exception of only one which had cannon, and

---

[i] In that part of the Township of Horton which borders on the basin was situated the French village of Minas. No traces of it are now to be seen except the cellars of the houses, a few aged orchards, and groups of willows, the never failing appendages of an Acadian settlement.—*Haliburtons Nova Scotia*, II. 115.

[ii] Beaubassin was situate on the river La Planche, at the head of the Bay of Fundy, and is now called Lawrence.

[iii] Now Windsor, on Avon River. Haliburton says the Indian name signifies, the junction of two rivers.—*Ibid.*, II. 100.

French Account of the Battle of Les Mines

which had been abandoned by the Micmacs, four of their men having been put *hors de combat* by the first fire. The command having develoved on Captain Chevalier de La Corne,[201] he attacked and carried the house occupied by Colonel Noble[i] [202] and his brother, and Mr. How[203] member of the Council at Port Royal. He remained in the house and prevented the approach of the enemy, whom he obliged to take refuge in a stone house in which they had some cannon. The firing had been unceasing from the commencement of the attack in the morning, until three o'clock in the afternoon, when it terminated. In this space of time, the enemy have had 130 men, including six officers,[ii] killed on the spot, 34 wounded and 53 taken prisoners. On our side, we have lost 6 men, viz.: 3 Canadians, a farmer belonging to Port Toulouse, and two Micmacs; had 14 wounded, including Capt. de Coulon and Cadet Lusignan.[204] Captain How being dangerously wounded, requested Capt. de La Corne to send for an English Surgeon to staunch his wound, the French Surgeon being, at the time, engaged in attendance of Mr. de Coulon. This occasioned the sending of hostages on our part, and a suspension of hostilities until the English Surgeon was sent back. It was then that two English officers came out of the house and advanced with a French flag towards the house where Mr. La Corne lay, who sent out to receive them. They proposed to him a cessation of hostilities until 9 o'clock the following morning. He granted their request, but perceiving, at a very early hour the next day, that they were leaving their houses and collecting the cattle, he sent to notify them that if they did not return to their houses at once, the armistice should terminate. Mr. [*Goldthwait*],[205] the English commandant,[iii] came to see Mr. de La Corne in company with another officer, and after having excused himself, commanded all his men to go in again

---

[i] Colonel Arthur Noble. For some account of him, see *Williamson's Hist. of Maine*, II. 250.

[ii] Col. Noble, Lieutenants Lechemere, Jones, and Pickering and Ensign Noble.—*Haliburton*. The name of the sixth does not appear.

[iii] Haliburton, in his account of this battle, says, that "after Col. Noble's death the English formed themselves into a body under Capt. Morris, the grandfather of the present Surveyor General of Nova Scotia."—*Hist. of Nova Scotia*, II. 132. This conflicts with this authentic report, which shows, that Benjamin Goldthwait was the Commanding Officer.

to their houses; asked to capitulate, and submitted his terms in writing: Mr. de La Corne after consulting with his officers, agreed to a portion of these terms, and told Mr. [*Goldthwait*] to make haste with his decisions, as a prompt renewal of the attack had been determined on. The Capitulation was thereupon signed, and is as follows:—

CAPITUALTION GRANTED BY HIS MOST CHRISTIAN MAJESTY'S TROOPS TO THOSE OF HIS BRITANNIC MAJESTY AT GRAND PRÉ

1. A detachment of his Most Christian Majesty's troops will form themselves into two lines in front of the stone house occupied by his Britannic Majesty's troops, who will take their departure for Annapolis Royal within twice twenty-four hours, with the honors of war. Six days' provisions, haversack, one pound of powder and one pound of ball.

2. The English prisoners in the hands of the French will remain prisoners of war.

3. The shipping seized by the troops of his Most Christian Majesty cannot be restored to his Britannic Majesty's troops.

4. As there was no pillage except by the Indians their booty cannot be restored.

5. The sick and wounded belonging to the English actually in his Britannic Majesty's hands, will be conveyed to the River *Aux Canards*, where they shall be lodged by order of the French Commandant, and supported at his Britannic Majesty's expense until they be in a condition to be removed to Annapolis Royal, and the French Commandant shall furnish them with Letters of Protection, and they shall be at liberty to retain one of their Surgeons until they be restored to health.

6. His Britannic Majesty's troops actually at Grand Pré will not be at liberty to bear arms at the head of the Bay of Fundy, that is to say, at Minas, Cobequitte and Beaubassin, for the term of six months from the date hereof.

On the acceptance and signing of these terms on the one side and on the other, his Britannic Majesty's troops will bring with them a flag, and march to-day from their guardhouse, of which his Most Chritian Majesty's troops will take possession, as well as of

French Account of the Battle of Les Mines

Grand Pré and of all the munitions of war, provisions and artillery which his Britannic Majesty's troops now have.

Done at Grand Pré, the 12th of February, 1747.
(signed) COULON DE VILLIER, Commander of the French Party.
BENJAMIN GOLDTHWAIT, Commander of the English, who hath signed with thirteen others.

In consequence of the above, the King of England's troops marched out, and the French took possession of Grand Pré, and of all the stores provisions and artillery, consisting of two 4 pounders and three swivels.

⚜

Ill. 11. Battle of Grand-Pré, by Charles W. Jefferys.[206]

F. Contrecoeur's Summons Borne by Jumonville
[*This appendix was labeled "I" in Gosselin's original publication.*]

Summons borne by Mssr. de Jumonville, an officer of the troops of the most Christian King, to the commander of the English troops, if he finds them on the lands of the King's royal domain.

Sir,
It has already come to my attention by way of the Indians, that you have come armed and with forces on the lands of the King, my master, although I am unable to believe it; but not neglecting anything to be informed of it, I detach Mssr. de Jumonville to see for himself, and in case he finds you there, to summon you by the King, and by virtue of the orders of my general, for you to withdraw peacefully with your troops; without which, Monsieur, you oblige me to compel you to do so by all the means which I consider most effective for the honor of the King's arms.

The sale of the lands of the Belle-Riviere by the Indians to you is so weak a title that I cannot refrain, Sir, from repelling force by force. I warn you, that if after this summons, which will be the last I give you, should there be an act of hostility that it will be up to you to answer it, since our intention is to maintain the union which exists between two Princes as friends.

Whatever may be your plans, Sir, I flatter myself that you will have for Mssr. de Jumonville all the consideration that this officer deserves, and that you send him back to me immediately to inform me of your intentions.

I'm waiting with respect, Sir, Your most humble and very obedient servant,

Contrecour

Made at the camp of Fort Duquesne for copy
The 23rd May 1754.

Summons Borne by Jumonville

On the reverse of the copy which we have before us, Mssr. de Contrecoeur wrote in his best hand: "This last summons to the English, if Mssr. de Jumonville finds them in his exploration, of May 23, 1754." Afterwards, but with another ink, he added: "He found them, and they killed him when read."[i]

[Here it may be fitting to list the casualties from Jumonville's detachment, originally listed by Vaudreuil and provided by Mssr. Edmond Mallet:

Among those killed were Joseph Coulon, Sieur de Jumonville, a native of Saint-Ours, Montreal, aged 36; Deroussel, of Quebec; Caron, of Quebec; Charles Blois, of Pointe Claire; Gerome, of La Prairie; L'Enfant, of Montreal; Paris, of Mille-Iles; Languedoc, of Boucherville; Martin, of Boucherville, and La Batterie, drummer.

The prisoners were: the ensign Drouillon, the cadet Boucherville, the cadet Dusablé, the cadet Louis-Paul, de Sorel [sic: Vaudreuil did not indicate that Louis-Paul was a cadet]; Baptiste Berger, of Varennes; Augustin Bonvouloir, of Longueil; Joachim Parent, of Soulanges; Nicolas Milles, of La Chine; Ducharme, of La Chine; Joseph Brown, of Montreal; Albert Ouimet, of Mille-Iles; Joseph Duchâtelet, of l'Assomption; Joseph Larabel, of Longue Pointe; Girardin, of l'Ile Jésus; Lavigne, of Varennes; Morisseau, of Repentigny; Trouin, of Repentigny; Collet, of Charlesbourg; Homnier, of Montreal, and Laforce.[207]*]*

---

[i] Archives of the Seminary of Quebec.

Ill. 12. *Assissinat de Jumonville au fort de la Nécessite.*

[Assassination of Jumonville at Fort Necessity *by illustrator Jules Claye appeared in* La Régence et Louis XV *by Alexandre Dumas published in 1857 more than a century after the incident that sparked the Seven Years' War. Depicted is a British soldier shooting Ensign Coulon de Jumonville in the head while he reads his peaceful summons. A French soldier holds aloft a white flag, a Mingo warrior passively looks on, Colonel Washington restrains the musket of another soldier, and a large and well-constructed Fort Necessity looms in the background.*

This romanticized artistic rendition follows closely the accompanying narrative of Dumas. "But at a short distance from the fort, suddenly a fusillade broke out, and Mssr. de Jumonville perceived that he was completely surrounded. Then he advanced alone between those who attacked him and his little troop, to whom he ordered to stop, made a sign with his hand, and, acknowledged as a parliamentarian, began to read his letter."[208] *Dumas's narrative and Claye's illustration are indicative of a 19th century French perspective of the event. Both stray from the historical record and differ significantly from the English version.*[209]]

G. Captain Contrecoeur's Order to Jumonville

[*Following is the order that Captain de Contrecoeur provided to Ensign Jumonville dated May 23, 1754. This English translation of Contrecoeur's order to Jumonville is from the 1757 publication:* A Memorial, Containing a Summary view of Facts, with their Authorities, in answer to the Observations sent by the English Ministry to the Courts of Europe.[210] *George Washington viewed this order as evidence of French duplicity with espionage being the primary purpose of Jumonville's detachment. This appendix was not included in Gosselin's original publication.*]

Be it known, that the Captain of a company belonging to the Detachment of Marines, Commander in Chief at the Ohio, Fort Du Quesne, the Peninsula [*Presque Isle*] and River Beef [*Le Boeuf*], hath given Orders to Mssr. de Jumonville, an Ensign of the Troops, to depart immediately with one Officer, three Cadets, one Voluntier [*sic*], one English Interpreter, and twenty eight Men, to go up as far as the High-Lands, and to make what Discovery he can; he shall keep along the River Monaungahela [*sic*], in Pettiaguas [*viz.: dugout canoes*] as far as the Hangard [*viz.: storehouse*]; after which he shall march along, until he finds the road which leads to that said to have been cleared by the English. As the Indians give out that the English are in their march to attack us (which we cannot believe, since we are at Peace) should Mssr. de Jumonville, contrary to our Expectation, hear of any Attempt intended to be made by the English, on the Lands belonging to the French King, he shall immediately go to them, and deliver them the Summons we have given him.

We further charge him, to dispatch a speedy Messenger to us, before the Summons be read, to acquaint us of all the Discoveries he hath made; of the Day he intends to read them the Summons; and also, to bring us an Answer from them, with all possible Diligence, after it is read.

If Mssr. de Jumonville should hear that the English intend to go on the other Side of the Great-Mountain (The Apalachian [*sic*]

Coulon de Villiers

Mountains), he shall not pass the High-Lands, for we would not disturb them in the least, being desirous to keep up that Union which exists between the two Crowns.

We charge Mssr. de Jumonville to stand upon his Guard against every Attempt, either from the English or Indians. If he should meet any Indians, he shall tell them he is travelling about to see what is transacting on the King's Territories, and to take Notice of every road, and shall shew them Friendship. Done at the Camp at Fort Du Quesne, the 23d of May 1754.

Signed, C<small>ONTRECOEUR</small>.

H. 1754 Journal of Louis Coulon de Villiers
[*This appendix was labeled "II" in Gosselin's original publication.*]

The copy of Mssr. de Villiers's journal, which we give here, differs somewhat, if not in substance, at least in form, from that which was published by the Historical Society of Louisiana, and which we had furnished ourselves.

It is a copy made for Mssr. de Contrecoeur, who wrote in his hand on the reverse: "Copy of the journal of Mssr. de Villiers, of July 3, 1754."

It included only the journal proper, and Mssr. de Contrecoeur had neither the words spoken to the Indians, nor the result of the conference of officers, nor the order given to Mssr. de Villiers, nor the articles of the capitulation. As these documents may bear interest, we have thought it necessary to put them in their place in the course of the journal; [*they are delineated by block quotes*]. We borrow them from the copy already published, except the articles of the capitulation which we transcribe from a facsimile made by P.-L. Morin and preserved in the archives of the Séminaire de Québec. [*Phrases inside {braces} are from the handwritten copy of de Villiers's journal from Augustin de Boschenry de Drucour, knight of the Royal and Military Order of Saint-Louis, Colonial Governor of Île-Royale in New France, dated September 6, 1754, part of the Moreau St-Mery collection in the Library and Archives Canada, but which were not in the version presented by Gosselin.*[211]]

Journal of the campaign of Mssr. De Villiers, from his arrival at Fort Duquesne until his return to the fort.

I arrived June 26, at Fort Duquesne about eight o'clock in the morning, with the different nations, of which the Mssr. le General had given me to command.

I learned upon arriving that Mssr. de Contrecoeur[212] had made a Detachment of five hundred French and eleven Indians[213] from the various Nations from the Belle-Riviere, that he had entrusted the command to Mssr. le Chevalier Mercier,[214] and who was to depart the next day.

As I was senior to this officer, that I commanded the Nations, and that my brother had been assassinated, Mssr. de Contrecoeur honored me with this command, and Mssr. le Mercier swore to me, though deprived of the command, that he would be delighted to conduct the campaign under my orders.

I assembled the Indian habitants to make them accept the hatchet, which Mssr. de Contrecoeur presented to them, with a belt to each Nation, pronouncing them this speech with seven strings in his hand.

> By Seven strings of wampum.
>
> My Children I invite you all by these strings to listen to my word, which is that of your father Onontio;[215] I unclog your ears to hear well and unclog your throat so that my words will fall to your heart and you feel the same pain that I feel.
>
> By seven Strings of Wampum.
>
> My children, your father Onontio informs me that he has sent you here only to work for good affairs, we have also come with this view. But he orders me at the same time that if someone insults me, to crush him, and that he does not doubt by your attachment to his will that you follow our example and help us to avenge him. You are not ignorant of the murder committed against me. I will speak to you all with an open heart because I have nothing hidden for the real children of Onontio.
>
> {By a Belt to each Nation.}
>
> I tell you my children that I came here only to work for good affairs; that I have found the Englishman, and that I have summoned him to retire according to the orders of your father; that I have furnished them with their wants to go in peace to their homes. I learned from your brothers that they came to strike your father; I sent an officer to parley with them and work to maintain peace. They assassinated him. My children, my heart aches, and I send the French tomorrow to avenge me. You have arrived my children when I have already delivered the shoes, the powder, and the [*musket*]

balls. And I invite you, the other people, Sioux of the Lakes, Huron, Abenaki, Iroquois of Fort de La Presentation, Nipissing, Algonquian, and Ottawa, by this belt to come and accept the hatchet to accompany your Father and help him crush the English who have violated all the strongest Laws by assassinating bearers of words. Next to this hatchet, two barrels of wine to make you a feast, having no beef here.

It is Mssr. de Villiers whom I place at your head to guide you and serve you as a father. He is going to avenge the death of his brother. Those who love him will follow his example. I invite you to do whatever he commands you.

By four strings of Wampum, you other wolves,[216] if you are the true children of Onontio, I invite you, by these strings, to follow the example of your brothers.

One of the Iroquois chiefs replied that their father Onontio had sent them only to work for good affairs, as they did not wish to disturb the earth, and that their father had assured them that they would only observe, and to maintain Peace.

The Warriors nevertheless carried away the hatchet, the Belts, and the two Barrels of wine, which had been provided to let them feast.

Two hours later the council was recalled, and all the Nations accepted the hatchet, the song of war was sung, and the Chiefs demanded the following day to make their shoes, and things were arranged to perfection.

The 27th. We continued to work on the preparations for the campaign, Mssr. de Contrecoeur called on Mssrs. le Mercier, de Longueuil,[217] and me to deliberate on what should be done in the campaign, considering the place, the strength of the enemy, the assassination he had committed against us, and the peace which we had intended to maintain between the two crowns. Here is the result of this conference:

> Result—that it was proper to march with the greatest number of Indians and Frenchmen as possible, to go and meet the English to avenge ourselves and to

chastise them for having violated the most sacred laws of the Civilized Nations.

That the action they have done deserves to have no regard for lasting Peace.

That as the King's intention was to maintain the peace between the two crowns, as soon as the blow has been made and they have been driven from the lands of the King's Domain—the commanding officer will send one of the prisoners to the English commandant of the nearest place, to inform him that our intention was to support the summons we have given them to withdraw from the lands of the King's Domain, and avenge the assassination they have done to us.

That now they must feel the price of the unworthiness of their action.

That the King's intentions, which tend only to peace, will always be seconded. It will be up to the commander only to withdraw peacefully from the King's lands, and as soon as the answer conforms to the rights of His Most Christian Majesty, we will prevent our troops from continuing their incursions and regard the English as our friends.

That as to the prisoners who have been taken in the strike, as soon as they have returned those whom they have seized, we will send back to them those who are in the hands of the French.

That our Indian habitants, indignant at such an unheard-of and surprising action, they declared by going to avenge their Father, that they no longer wished to return the prisoners who will be in their hands; but let us not doubt that the General would implore them—as he already did all he could—to recover the prisoners, without flattering himself that he could succeed. If the English settlers withdrew from our lands, that we would go as far as their homes so as to destroy them and treat them as enemies until the full satisfaction and change of conduct of that nation.

Done at Camp of Fort Duquesne June 27, 1754.
(Signed) DE CONTRECOEUR, DE VILLIERS,
LE MERCIER, and LONGUEUIL.

The Chiefs then came to announce to Mssr. de Contrecoeur that the warriors were going to follow me, and that they who had come to work for good affairs would remain with him.

The 28th. Mssr. de Contrecoeur handed me my order to leave, conceived in these terms:

> We Captains of a Company of the Marine detachment, Commandant in Chief of the party of the Belle-Riviere, of the forts Duquesne, Presque Isle, and River Le Boeuf. The Sieur de Villiers, Captain of Infantry, is ordered to depart immediately with the detachment of French and Indians, whom we entrust to him to meet the English Army. He is ordered to attack them if he sees a day to do so and destroy them if he can to chastise them for the assassination of our messenger, which they did to us by violating the rights of civilized nations.
>
> If the said Sieur de Villiers can no longer find the English, and they are withdrawn, he will follow them as much as he deems it necessary for the honor of the King's Arms. And if they should be cut off and he does not have day to fight them, he will ravage their cattle and will try to fall on their convoys to defeat them whole.
>
> Despite their impetuous action, recommend to the said Sieur de Villiers to avoid all cruelty as much as he can.
>
> If he can beat them to avenge us for their bad conduct, he will detach one of the prisoners to announce to the English Commandant that if he wishes to withdraw from the lands of the King and send back our prisoners, we will prevent our troops from regarding them as our enemies in the future.

He will not let them know that our Indians, indignant at their action, have declared that they will not return the prisoners in their hands; but that we do not doubt that the General will do for them as he has done in the past.

As we rely entirely on the prudence of Mssr. de Villiers in all the cases which we cannot foresee, we will approve of all that he will do in consultation with himself in these cases with the captain only. Made at the Camp of Fort Duquesne on June 28, 1754.

Signed CONTRECOEUR.

As soon as my orders were received, we distributed and loaded the provisions, and we left the fort about ten o'clock in the morning.

At that time, I ordered to have Indian scouts[218] on land to avoid any surprise, and I joined a few cadets who relieved each other as well as the Indians during the rest of the journey. I was to camp seven or eight arpents[219] above the first fork of the riviere mal engueulée, although I did not intend to take this route.

I assembled the Indians and asked them for their opinion. They deferred the route to the Chief Sonontouan[220] of the Belle-Riviere, as he was better acquainted with the locale. It was decided, though the road was longer, that it was fitting to take it, the river being poorly navigable. Seeing that if the Englishman had continued his march he might have gained the storehouse,[221] and also, the other arm of the river might be liable to run out of water.

The Indians made me aware that the Mississauga[222] band was missing, that it might have been a blow, which would hurt them greatly, but I reassured them on that point.

The 29th. The Mass was celebrated in the camp, after which we proceeded with the usual precautions. I saw the Mississauga, who were coming to join me, and who brought us letters from Mssr. de Contrecoeur. We had no events that day and made good progress.

The 30th. We proceeded to the storehouse, which was made of stacked logs, well crenelated [*viz.: outfitted with loopholes for firing muskets*], and about thirty feet long by twenty-two feet wide. As it was late and I did not want to do anything without consulting with the Indians, I camped at twice the range of a musket.

I summoned the Chiefs in the evening, and I deliberated with them on the precautions to be taken for the safety of our pirogues [*viz: dugout canoes*], the provisions which we left in reserve, and the people who were to guard them. I made them consider the advantages of the storehouse, from which twenty men could make a strong resistance; they all agreed. It was then proposed to arrange for the scouts, in order to obviate the jealousy which arises among the Nations when there is an appearance of partiality, and it was concluded that there would be but a very small number near the camp, that the others would return to meet us as soon as they had knowledge of something, that on the contrary, those who would discover the camp, would do so during the night, and would come so that we might strike at daybreak.

The 1st of July we were able to store our pirogues safely, we arranged our effects and all that we could do without in the storehouse. I left there a good sergeant with twenty men and a few sick Indians. We distributed ammunition and began marching about eleven o'clock. We found the road so difficult that by the first post the chaplain was no longer in a condition to continue the journey. He gave us the general absolution and returned to the storehouse. We saw some tracks which made us suspect that we were discovered.

About three o'clock in the afternoon, having no news from our scouts, I sent back others who met our first men and were about to shoot, but fortunately, they ceased to take the exchange. They returned to us and announced to us that they had been on the road which the English had made, that they had seen no one there, and that it appeared that they had not been there for three days. We no longer doubted that the English were informed of our advances. We continued our journey, however, to a dwelling, which was situated advantageously from discovery on all sides, and arranged the troops in such a manner as to defend themselves, and we passed the night anticipating the return of our scouts.

The 2nd. At daybreak, we set out on our march without the scouts having arrived. After having walked for some time, I resolved not to continue until I had positive news, and I sent scouts to the road. Meanwhile, Indians who had remained in the storehouse came back and had captured a prisoner, who claimed he was a deserter. I questioned him and threatened him to be hanged if he imposed on me. I learned that the English had quit their post to rejoin their fort, and that they had brought back their cannon. Our last scouts arrived and told me that the former had seen the tracks of ten or twelve men and that they no longer doubted it was theirs [*the English*]. I continued on my way and arrived at the sight of an abandoned house where some of our people saw what appeared to be the deserted camp of the English, and we went there. This place consisted of three houses surrounded by a few posts and fences, the protection of which was commanded by the neighboring heights. I sent scouts and made a search of everything. There were several caches of tools and other ancillaries that I had removed. As it was late, I encamped the detachment, which had been harassed by bad roads while the weather was rainy, and there we were alerted occasionally by Indians pursuing a few animals.

I again questioned the Englishman, alternately intimidating him then giving him the hope of reward. I informed the Indians of all that he said to me, and the resolution that I would not expose them rashly. We had rain all night.[i]

---

[i] [*The information that the English prisoner gave de Villiers on July 2, was pivotal in convincing that officer to rapidly move on the English forces and attack at the soonest opportunity, which he did the following day. De Villiers did not record in detail what information the prisoner provided him, but it likely was similar to information that Mssr. de Contrecoeur obtained from another English deserter captured a few days earlier. De Contrecoeur may have had the deserter escorted to de Villiers to ensure that officer could interrogate him personally. Lieutenant Léry recorded the following in his journal on July 7, 1754:*

> *Sunday at noon a messenger arrived from Belle-Rivière. Mssr. de Contrecoeur wrote that Mssr. de Villiers had left Fort Duquesne the 28th of June with 700 Frenchmen and savages to attack the 400 English who were marching on Belle-Rivière. He enclosed the deposition of an English deserter.*
>
> *Denis Kaninguen, deserted from the English camp yesterday morning, arrived at Fort Duquesne today, June 30th.*

1754 Journal of Le Grand Villiers

The 3rd. At daybreak, I prepared for departure and invited the Indians to furnish scouts. The weather was rainy, but I foresaw the necessity of preventing the enemy in the labors which he might make. I even flattered myself that he was less watchful in such foul weather.

The Nipissing and Algonquin did not want to pass, I told them that they could stay. I set out with the other Nations, which shamed

---

He reports that the English army is composed of 430 men, including 30 Indians.

That they learned that 300 French and 400 Indians left the French camp, which made them decide to retrace their steps to their fort in a meadow the length of a rifle shot, that the English have no food, having only sixteen cows and ten oxen left, some of which they eat every day, without bread. Every other day ten to twelve sacks of flour reach them.

The government of Philadelphia did not want to furnish men to make war on the French, and South Carolina furnished only ten soldiers, Virginia gave three hundred men. He reports that Mssr. de Jumonville was killed by an English detachment which surprised him. The officer had advanced to communicate his orders to the English commander, in spite of the musket-fire on the French. Mssr. de Jumonville was wounded, and had fallen. Thanihison, an Indian, came to him and said, "You are not dead yet, my father," and struck him several blows with his hatchet, which killed him.

Mssr. Drouillon, ensign en second of Mssr. de Jumonville, with all the rest of the detachment of thirty men, was seized. Mssrs. de Boucherville and Du Sable, cadets, and Laforce, storekeeper, are among the prisoners. There were ten or twelve Canadians killed, and the prisoners were sent to the city of Virginia.

The English had only very little food.

He reports that if the French do not go into English territory, the English will no longer want to come to the French.

On leaving the English camp, the said Denis Kaninguen was pursued by a horseman whose thigh he broke with a rifle shot. He took this man's horse, and came at full speed to the French camp.

Léry, Journal of Chaussegros de Léry, 27-28.]

the first to the point of joining me, except for two, before my departure.

Two of my first scouts came to join me and told me they captured three prisoners who came from the Shawnee and that they had put them in the storehouse, which was confirmed to me by a letter that they handed to me from the sergeant whom I had left there.

We marched all day in the rain and sent out scouts one after another. I stopped at the place where my brother had been assassinated and saw a few corpses there.[223]

{When I was three quarters of a league [*about two and a half miles*] from the English fort I ordered to march in columns with each officer in his Division to be able to dispose of it according to the necessity.} I dispatched scouts to go to the camp, twenty others to support them, and I advanced in orderly formation when they came to announce that we were discovered, that the English were in battle array to attack us. As I was told they were close at the very least, I put the troops in battle formation suitable for woodland combat. It was not long before I noticed that the scouts had misdirected me, and I ordered the troops to advance on the side from which we might be attacked. As we had no knowledge of the locale, we presented the flank to the fort, whence they began firing cannon upon us. I perceived almost at the same time the English in battle formation on the right who came toward us. The Indians and we let out a yell and advanced to them, but they did not give us time to make our discharge, as they retired to their entrenchments, which held their strength, so we endeavored to invest the fort. It was conveniently situated in a meadow, the woods of which were in range of a musket, and we approached them as much as possible, so as not to expose the subjects of his Majesty in vain. The fire on both sides was very lively, and I went to the place that seemed to me the most suited to wiping them out with a sortie. We succeeded in extinguishing the fire of their cannon with our musketry. It is true that the fervor and zeal of our Canadians and soldiers worried me because I could see that we would soon be without ammunition. Mssr. le Mercier proposed to me to work to make fascines[224] to secure our posts and to tighten the English in their fort during the night and totally prevent them from slipping out. I ordered Mssr. de Bailleul[225] to go and gather as many people as possible to assist the quarter which could be attacked by a general sortie, and during this time we captured caches of food, ammunition, and merchandise that encouraged the Indians and militia.

The fire of the enemy was rekindled at six o'clock in the evening with more vigor than ever and lasted till eight o'clock. As we had been soaked by the rain all day, the detachment was very tired, and the Indians announced their intent to depart the next day, and being told there were drums beating in the distance and cannon fire, I proposed to Mssr. le Mercier to offer the English to parley. {He was of the same opinion,} and we shouted that if they wished to parley with us we would cease fire. They accepted the proposition. A Captain in the attack came to see where I was. I detached Mssr. le Mercier to receive him, and returned to the meadow, where we told them, that, not being at war, we wished to avoid the cruelties on the part of the Indians to which they would expose themselves if they obstinately persisted their resistance. That night we would deprive them of all hope of escape, that we now consented to give them pardon, having come only to avenge the assassination of my brother made by violating the most sacred Laws, and compelling them to free themselves from the lands of the King's Domain, and we agreed with them to grant them capitulation, of which the copy is here attached:

> Capitulation accorded by the commandant of His Majesty's most Christian troops to that of the English troops now in the fort of Necessity which was built on the grounds of the King's Domain, this 3rd of July at 8 o'clock in the evening.
>
> **Know ye.**
>
> As our intentions have never been to disturb the peace and good harmony which prevailed between the two Princes, but only to avenge the assassination that was made upon one of our officers bearing a summons and on his escort, as also to prevent any settlement on the grounds of the Domain of the King my master.

To these considerations, we want to grant pardon to all the Englishmen who are in the said fort on the following terms.

Article 1st.

We grant the English Commander to retire with all his garrison to return peacefully to his country and promise to prevent him from being insulted by our Frenchmen, and to restrain as much as we can in our power all the Indians who stand with us.

2nd.

He will be allowed to go out and take away all that belongs to them except the artillery and munitions of war which we reserve for ourselves.

3rd.

That we grant them the honors of war, that they will go out drums beating with one piece of small canon, willing to prove to them that we treat them like friends.

4th.

That as soon as the articles are signed by both parties, they will lower their English flag.

5th.

That tomorrow at daybreak a French detachment will go to make the garrison pass and take possession of the fort.

6th.

That, as the English have no horses or oxen, they will be free to put their effects in caches to come and fetch them when they have obtained horses, and will be able to leave guards there in such numbers as they wish on the conditions that they will give their word of honor to no longer work at any settlement in this place nor below the rise of the land during the year from that day.

7th.

That, as the English have in their power an officer, two cadets, and, generally, the prisoners whom they had made in the assassination of Sieur de Jumonville, and promised to send them with safeguards to Fort Duquesne, situated on the Belle-Riviere, and that for the sake of this article and this treaty, Mssrs. Jacob Vanebrane [*sic: Van Braam*][226] and Robert Scobo [*sic: Stobo*],[227] both Captains, will be held hostage until the arrival of our Canadians and Frenchmen above mentioned. We are obliged on our side to give escort to bring back safely the two officers who promise us our French within two and a half months thereafter.

Made in duplicate on the posts of our barriers, the day, year and hour of that above.

          JAMES MACKAY[228]
          G^E WASHINGTON
          COULON-VILLIER

 We envisioned that nothing could be more advantageous to the Nation than this capitulation, as it is so unnatural in time of peace to make prisoners who in wartime would have been harmful in that they would have consumed our provisions. {Also, they agreed to sign that they had committed assassination by the devilish strike on my brother.} We had hostages for the safety of the French who were in their power, we made them leave the country as it belongs to the most Christian King, we obliged them to leave their cannons which consisted of nine pieces, we had destroyed all their horses and cattle, and we made them sign that the pardon we gave them was only to prove to them how much we wanted to treat them as friends.

 Could we expect such considerable advantages from the view of the enemy, almost as numerous as ourselves, who had been waiting for us for several days, who had seen us from within the midst of their fort in which they had nine cannon, and were attacked only on sight by the Indians' musketry who are inhabitants unaccustomed to this military discipline. Therefore, I owe the success of this undertaking only to their valor, to the firmness of the officers, and to the example of the cadets who formed this party.

 That very evening, the articles of the capitulation were signed, and the two hostages for whom I had asked were at the camp.

 The 4th. At the break of day, I sent a detachment to take possession of the fort. The garrison filed out, and the number of their dead and wounded left me to pity them despite the resentment which I had for the manner in which they had destroyed my brother.

Our Indians, who had adhered to my will, professed to pillage; I opposed it. But the English, still frightened, fled from their pavilion and left their banners and one of their flags. I demolished the fort, and Mssr. le Mercier caused their cannon to be broken, as well as that which was granted to them by the capitulation, the English having been unable to carry it away.

I hastened to depart after having broken the barrels of spirits to avoid the obvious disorder that would inevitably ensue. One of my Indians took ten Englishmen whom he brought to me, and whom I sent back by another, who reported to me that coming behind the English to their assistance were 200 men with a Great Chief.

I had two Frenchmen killed in this attack and [*the Indian slave of Mssr. Pean*[229]], seventeen wounded, including two Indians, not counting numbers of wounds so slight that they did not need the help of the surgeon. I made about two leagues this day and had our principal infirm carried by our detachments on litters.

The 5th. I arrived about nine o'clock at the abandoned English camp. I broke the fortification and burned the houses, after which I continued my route, having detached Mssr. de la Chauvignerie[230] to burn those in the surrounding area. I was encamped three leagues beyond.

The 6th. I left early in the morning and arrived at the storehouse. About ten o'clock we made arrangements for the pirogues, fed the detachment, recovered the reserve provisions, and found some caches, after which I burned the storehouse.

I embarked and marched until six o'clock in the evening, where I was obliged to camp by a very heavy rain which lasted all night.

The 7th. I continued my route, after having detached Mssr. de la Chauvignerie to inform Mssr. de Contrecoeur of the success of our campaign. As I went, I burned the settlements that I found, and at four o'clock I handed the detachment to Mssr. de Contrecoeur.

{Signed COULON DE VILLIERS ※}

Ill. 13. Washington Surrenders, by Felix O. C. Darley (1822-1888).

Illustration of Colonel George Washington signing the articles of capitulation at Fort Necessity.

I. Villiers Seeks the Cross of Saint-Louis

[*After his victory over the English at Fort Necessity, Louis Coulon de Villiers returned to Montreal at the end of July. In September of that year, he wrote to the Minister of Marine requesting that the King honor him with the Cross of Saint-Louis, the honorific of knighthood that was bestowed on his older brother Nicolas-Antoine in 1748 following that Villiers's victory at Grand Pré. He also wrote seeking back pay owed him. Attached to Le Grand Villiers's letter was a copy of his journal and the surrender terms signed by Mackay, Washington, and Villiers. Following is an English translation of de Villiers's letter, as translated and edited by Joseph L. Peyser and published in his book,* Letters from New France.[231] *This appendix was not in Gosselin's original publication.*]

My Lord,

    I have the honor of Sending you Attached herewith, the journal, the Capitulation, and other items concerning the campaign I have just waged, relating to the Ohio River settlement. you will see thereby, My Lord, the Outcome of this Trip, and that it would have been enjoyable for me to go personally to report on my Mission to you; I Hope, My Lord, that it will please you, having done the best that I could, seeking only to merit the Position that I have the honor of occupying. You will see, My Lord, by means of the attached documents, The murder of my brother Jumonville by the English. I made them feel the effects of The affront that they inflicted upon us by the force of our weapons, having Violated the most Sacred Laws of civilized Nations.

    I Hope that My Lord will find my Performance acceptable and that he will be willing to grant me the honor of His patronage, having lost my whole family in the King's service. When my brother Coulon had completed the Acadian action, he was made a Knight of Saint-Louis and the major of Three Rivers. I Would be very Pleased with my duty If you would be willing, My Lord, to honor me similarly with the Cross of Saint-Louis and the majority of Detroit which I think might Be Vacant by the promotion of Monsr de Céloron.[232]

Villiers Seeks the Cross of Saint-Louis

In sum, My Lord, You are the master of my fate, I have no patronage and I Hope for everything, in your GRANDEUR.

In 1750 I had the honor of Being detached by Monsr the Marquis de la Jonquière[233] to go bring the miamis back to reason. I succeeded, and I believe I rendered a great service to this Colony, since they Were Slaughtering the French wherever they found them, and they even Killed two of my Soldiers under me about one thousand feet from my fort, and by dint of Negotiating with this Nation I had them come back to their senses. This was the key to the other Nations: the hurons, Pianguichias, and ouyatanons Came back As Soon as they saw the miamis Surrender. Monsr The marquis de la Jonquière had granted me one thousand Crowns per year in pay; indeed he paid me the first year, being Alive; Monsr de Longueuil[234] Commanded [next], and I received nothing; Then Monsr The marquis Duquesne[235] and when I asked for my pay upon my return, he told me that there was no money at all; however all the other officers of the other posts have definitely been paid. After Having Sacrificed myself to the service, losing two years of pay does not seem fair to me, having done my duty well, as I prove in the Attached Attestation by Mssr. de Céloron.

I do not mean by this to complain about my General [Duquesne], but to present precisely, My Lord, my reasons, And I Hope from Your reward for my services, and those of my whole family, all of whom perished in the war. It is I who Was shot in the arm during The attack of the Foxes. I also Beg My Lord to have Consideration for my nephew Dagneau-Douville,[236] who Is a Cadet, and who did His duty well in this latest campaign, in which he caught a musket-ball in the foot.

I have the honor of Being with very deep respect, My Lord,
Your very humble And very obedient Servant

COULON DE VILLIERS

At MONTREAL the 9th of 8bre 1754

J. The "Jumonville" of Thomas[i] and Washington

[*Due to the controversial manner of his death, Jumonville became the symbol with which the French monarchy rallied her allies in the first truly global conflict: The Seven Years' War. The slain ensign was memorialized in song and verse, perhaps most famously the Jumonville: Poëme by Mssr. Antoine Léonard Thomas in 1759. While widely cited, it is rarely quoted or even printed, much less translated into English. Following is an article published in Henry B. Dawson's July 1862 edition of* The Historical Magazine.[237] *This appendix was not in Gosselin's original publication.*]

> When the tidings of this affray crossed the Atlantic, the name of Washington was, for the first time, heard in the saloons of Paris.... The death of Jumonville became the subject for the loudest complaint; this martyr to the cause of feudalism and despotism was celebrated in heroic verse, and continents were invoked to weep for his fall.

Bancroft thus alludes to a poem on an event in Washington's early life, which few have seen; and which figures, we think, at least in a separate form, in few collections of American history. It may therefore be worth the space to give some analysis and appreciation of the Jumonville of [*Mssr.*] Thomas, Membre de l'Académie Française. It is curious as a contrast to the poetical passage of our great historian, like him exalting a chance collision into a struggle between liberty and despotism. Unfortunately for mankind, despotism was on all sides. The blood that flowed in all our border wars, flowed in wars evoked by ambition in courts, fanaticism in popular leaders here, the despotism of the prince, the minister, or the mob.

Few of our writers give the work of Thomas more than a passing notice, though few omit all mention of it. Winthrop Sargent, in

---

[i] *Jumoville : Poëme*, Par M. Thomas, P. E. L'U. D. P. Quod genus hoc hominum ? quæve hunc tam barbara morem Permittit patria. *Virg. Æneid.* 1759. 8vo, 59 pp.

The "Jumonville" of Thomas and Washington

his "Braddock's Expedition," gives some idea of the poem, and introduces an extract; but his is the longest reference which we have met.

Thomas, the author, was more esteemed for his panegyrics than his poems, and Jumonville did not win him immortality. It is scarcely mentioned in works on French literature; and its want of local accuracy in the description of American scenes and men, its tameness and lack of real poetic creation, justify beyond a doubt the fate that has befallen it.

Why waste time on it then? Simply because Washington is the incarnation of evil in the poem, the Satan of this Paradise Lost, though English readers will wonder to hear that the name of Washington does not once occur in the poem. Those better acquainted with the [*exigencies*] of French verse will comprehend the difficulty of making Washington flow in the line, and the advantage to be derived from the use of some general term.

In the preface to his poem, Thomas describes the affair in which Jumonville fell, with some exaggerations; he proceeds to state the "slight changes," poetical licenses, adopted by him. Pegasus disdains the harness. "A poem," says Thomas, "should not be a dry gazette." For the brother of the fallen Jumonville merely to force *le Commandant Anglais* to capitulate at Fort Necessity, was not enough to satisfy poetical [*vengeance*]. Our poet accordingly makes the fort carried by storm, most of the defenders slain by fire and sword, and the rest bound in chains on the smoking ruins of the ramparts. The poem, divided into four cantos, opens thus:

> Fair Peace has vanished: o'er our head anew,
> See in the stormy sky fresh tempests brew;
> The Thames hoarse murm'ring through the sedgy plain,
> Arms her vast fleets to crush thy glory, Seine!
> The Spree which erst nor name nor glory knew,
> But crept obscurely sands unnoticed through,
> Now fearful in its wide-spread watery waste
> Calls Victory to its banks in eager haste;
> Drags down its haughty tide each noblest crown,
> And muttering rolls o'er thrones she topples down—
> Wound fain in fetters hold the Danube bound,
> Roused by the storm to all of portent sore,

Coulon de Villiers

> See Tagus foaming on Iberia's shore,
> Quiver beneath his hand his golden urn,
> His kindling wrath in fury soon to burn.

Then follows a passage on the folly, misery, and cruelty of war, closing:

> Fierce Britons, rivals ever of fair France,
> Upon these graves your frenzy fills, but glance!
> You, whose bold reason in its pride extreme
> Itself a pure ray deems of essence the supreme;
> Ye men of thought, ye sages all presumed,
> By whom all mortals are to be illumed,
> 'Tis little to have forged the sword of war,
> To lavish for earth's woes your golden ore;
> Your impious hands have wrought on every side,
> Deeds' Time's dark veil will ne'er from memory hide.
> Assassins, pirates, perjured robbers too,
> How black a picture for the future's view!
> The Muse who holds the pen of immortality,
> And graves in solid bronze austerest verity,
> Saves from the shadowy mists of envious time,
> Alike distinguished worth and famous crime.
> Lo! I retrace a deed that must overwhelm
> With deep abiding shame your guilty realm.
> May I, Jumonville, here embalm thy fame,
> In verse undying hallowed to thy name,
> And limning to the world thy murderer's rage,
> Make all with horror read the blood-stained page.
> And you, whose valor and intrepid zeal
> Plunged in the brigand's heart the avenging steel,
> Permit my hand to bind the laurel now,
> As victory's prize upon each warlike brow.

This is followed by an invocation of his country and his king as his Apollos, and the action of the poem begins.

Louis had restored peace to Europe, and the soldier, returned to his plough, looked forward to a tranquil life, when the English, that people—

> Slave to a Cromwell, tyrant to its kings,

jealous of the commercial progress of France, smarting under the remembrance of the defeat of Fontenoy, again plunged Europe in war. The colonies of France are poetically and vaguely described, and the neighboring English colonies alluded to. The beginning of hostilities is then described; but our readers will remember that in the French view, the Ohio was then in Canada:

> Canadian peaceful fields at once invade
> The English hosts in warlike guise arrayed.
> The clarion's note, the sudden din of arms
> Proclaims of stormy war the dire alarms.
> Their flags displayed where'er their bands appear
> Summon red carnage to that hemisphere.

The Ohio, like the European rivers, then appears, roused from his grotto, and beholds with alarm the advancing hosts of England. These roll on, preceded by Discord, with Treason at their side. The erection of Fort Necessity—

> Invasion's naught; these murderous brigands,
> Perfidious robbers of our wasted lands,
> To screen their project from a vengeful storm
> In these wild woods a guilty shelter form,

is followed by an address to that impious citadel. Fame announces to the French that the English had crossed the frontier. Each Frenchman burns to rush to the field; but their chief withholds them and determines to send a prudent envoy to remonstrate. Jumonville and De Villiers, two brothers, are then introduced, their early life depicted, their coming to America, and their touching adieu to their mother. Jumonville is chosen as envoy, and embracing his brother departs, ending the first canto.

The second canto contains the great event of the poem, the fall of Jumonville; and that portion is here given almost entire:

> On speeds the Gaul, till now his kindling eye
> Britannia's guilty ramparts can descry.
> At once of countless guns the tempest dread
> Presages death that mutters o'er his head.
> Jumonville halts—he bids the English cease.
> He comes the bearer of the words of peace.

Coulon de Villiers

Aloft he holds the papers that he bears
The voiceless tokens of the trust he wears.
The firing stops, and in its darksome womb
The bronze enkindled holds the fiery doom.
They press around him, and more pleasing sounds
Succeed a moment to wild anger's bounds.
Thus when in ocean roused by furious storms
Calm gliding o'er its billows all reforms
And naught is heard but breakers' distant roar,
As muttering still they die upon the shore,
Such stormy waves the furious Britons seemed
When Gallia's envoy thus his task redeemed:
'Illustrious foes, who guide Britannia's car,
In peace her yeoman brave, her heroes in wild war,
To whom with us God gave this western shade,
I come not now in warlike guise arrayed,
To dip in generous blood my cruel hand
Or settle new disputes by murderous brand.
A herald, sheltered by law's ægis here,
I claim fair France's rights by treaties clear.
Each rising State its certain limits knew,
And nature's self the lines eternal drew.
These rocks on rocks that rise toward the sky,
Our fathers held a barrier bold and high;
And treaties yielding to great nature's laws,
Confirmed her work with unison applause.
Yet boldly you these ramparts known have passed,
Ohio sees your standard o'er her cast.
Must we by warlike passions cause to cease
In streams of blood the world's profoundest peace?
Our endless strife revolts the human breast,
Two worlds in tears bewail this murderous zest.
This right, this fearful right to slaughter men,
Too long has made this earth a tiger's den.
Our recent war struck fear to every breast
From South to North, from East to distant West.
Let us forbear the struggle to renew
And bleeding wounds to open here anew.
The movements in this wilderness begun,

> May all convulse that live beneath the Sun.
> Equal by nature, equal too in toils,
> Live on in friendship undisturbed by broils;
> Respecting each the oath that binds our soul,
> Let virtue be our guide, and no State craft control.
> That each in peace eternal's happy rest
> May...' at these words his kindling zeal addressed,
> Pierced by a murderous ball but aimed too well,
> Prone at his assassin's feet Jumonville fell.
> His death-weighed eyelid thrice to heaven he raised,
> And thrice to upper light his eyeball glazed;
> The tender memory of his lovely France
> Can e'en in death that noble soul entrance.
> He dies; and trampled 'neath inhuman feet,
> His mangled limbs all vile dishonor meet.

Such is the description of the fall of Jumonville, followed by an indignant burst against the violation of all law. He then describes the fall of the other French, and the escape of a wounded Indian, who reaches the French fort, and dies while attempting to tell what happened; able only to utter the name of Jumonville, as he sees Devilliers, the brother of that officer. The second canto ends with Devilliers' preparations to proceed to the spot to ascertain the real state of facts.

The third canto opens with the march, and the first night amid the gloom, Jumonville's spirit appears, and, when addressed by his brother, calls for vengeance. In the morning the march is resumed; and, prepared by the apparition, Devilliers finds on the battle-field the mangled remains of his brother, and is filled with grief and desolation. His lament over his brother, is not without merit. Sorrow soon gives place to thoughts of avenging the crime:

> At once he cries: "What, shall we weeping stand?
> Frenchmen and warriors, we, with armed hand?
> We weep! and he, the felon, cause of all our woe,
> Mocks the sad tears his crimes have called to flow.
> We weep! and have we naught but tears to shed?
> Brother! forgive this tribute to the dead;
> Such idle pity must rouse thy disdain;
> Thy spirit craves the blood of Saxons slain.

Coulon de Villiers

> On, my brave friends, heroic scourge of crime,
> To offer on the walls a hecatomb sublime!
> Jumonville guides you; and his shade in wrath,
> Of each death-speeding blow will guide the path."
> He spoke, and towards the walls in crime disgraced
> Pressed his good war-steed's generous flanks in haste;
> Twice galloped round it, and with searching ken
> Measured with eager glance that caitiff den.
> So, in the deserts of dark Afric's land,
> The lion's mate, before whom none will stand,
> Robbed in her absence of her precious birth,
> Follows the hunter's footprints in the earth;
> In fury foaming, thirsting for his life,
> Flies to his den, though fitted for the strife,
> And bristling crouches for a bold advance,
> While lightnings flash from each avenging glance.

The fourth canto opens with Fort Necessity invested, and depicts at length the siege, the fierce cannonade on both sides, the breach, the assault, and the final overthrow of Washington and his troops, fighting to the last. The fort is taken; and then, "by the aid of saltpeter hurled through the air, the walls as they fall make those deserts tremble. Olympus resounds: a frightful dust with its thick veil obscures the light." And the canto ends with a reproachful address to the English, about the best portion of the poem, in which he alludes to Braddock's defeat, the ravages of the Indians, the conquest of Minorca, the defeat of Byng, and the ravages in English Africa and India, as so many more blows of heaven's vengeance.

> The avenging gods whose justice hath no end,
> Thus to their doom the boldly impious send.
> Scourge of the world! ambitious race and line,
> Dread mortal arm, and dread the wrath divine.

The reader will thus have at least some idea of the plan, style, and spirit of this historical poem; the subject of which is an act of Washington's, and which treats not only Jumonville's death, in which he was the main actor, but of his surrender at Fort Necessity, and that battle of Monongahela in which he displayed his greatest qualities.

K. Portrait of Le Chevalier de Villiers

[*This appendix was labeled "III" in Gosselin's original publication. The illustration provided was a slightly different version and was positioned at the beginning of chapter VI.*]

Ill. 14. Le Chevalier de Villiers.[238]

This portrait and the notes which follow are graciously provided by Mssr. J.-W. Cruzat.

The original of this painting was first owned by Marc Coulon de Villiers, son of François, and then passed to his son-in-law, Arnould Guillendard, who lived in Pensacola. During the Civil War the portrait disappeared. Fortunately, the Louisiana branch of the de Villiers had made a copy of it today in the possession of Mssr. Geo. Villeré of Louisiana. It is from this copy that we have drawn all those which have appeared for some twenty years either in the United States or in Canada.

L. 1777 Petition to the King of Spain

[*Following is Le Chevalier François Coulon de Villiers's petition to the King of Spain. It was attached to a memorial written by Governor Bernardo de Gàlvez to José de Gàlvez dated March 21, 1777. This autobiographical letter provides in le Chevalier de Villiers's own words his recollections of his military service and some of the events of his brothers. It is central in eliminating the confusion that historians have continued to make between the events from the various careers of the Coulon de Villiers brothers. It is interesting to note that the primary reason for the petition is that very confusion caused by the shared name, De Villiers, of two unrelated officers: François and a younger officer named Balthazar de Villiers, who was, according to the petition, mistakenly promoted in the Spanish King's service to a position that was intended for François. This English translation of the petition was published in* Louisiana History: The Journal of the Historical Association *by Gilbert C. Din.*[239] *It is reprinted here with express permission from the publisher and Dr. Din. Bracketed words that are not italicized reflect Dr. Din's comments. This appendix was not in Gosselin's original publication and has aided greatly in shedding new light on his now century old research.*]

Cover Letter of Governor Bernardo de Gálvez to José de Gálvez

I pass to Your Excellency the following memorial of Don Francisco Coulon de Villiers, who petitions from His Majesty's charity the rank of captain with assignment to this city [New Orleans] and the salary that persons of this class enjoy. I consider him deserving of this favor, not only because of the merit he has earned in the service of France, according to what he explains in the accompanying declaration, but because my predecessor, Don Antonio de Ulloa, found him in the province when he arrived and had proposed him for captain in the battalion he intended to create. [He, however,] was not included for the reasons he states in his memorial.[240]

D*E*V*ILLIERS'S* P*ETITION TO THE* S*PANISH* K*ING*

Don Francisco Coulon DeVilliers, present *alcalde [ordinario]*[241] of this city of New Orleans in the province of Louisiana, Knight of the Royal and Military Order of Saint-Louis, and infantry captain, which I have been with the troops assigned by His Most Christian Majesty [referring to the King of France] in this same colony, to the royal feet of Your Majesty with the greatest submission, state: that in recognition of the merits of my services that are included in the accompanying memoir, the first Spanish governor of this province, Don Antonio de Ulloa, had proposed me to Your Majesty as a captain in the battalion that he tried to form for garrison duty at this capital and its dependent posts. He assigned me, meanwhile, to command the district of Natchitoches, which borders the Presidio of Los Adaes in the Province of Texas. There I remained until His Excellency, Count O'Reilly,[242] took possession in the name of Your Majesty. I was unable to go [to New Orleans] immediately upon [O'Reilly's] arrival because of low waters in the Red River. During this time, he created the present Battalion of Louisiana. To it, by error or because of the similarity in surnames, he appointed Don Balthazar de Villiers, who had been a lieutenant in the French army, as company captain, which Your Majesty had deigned to confer on me. Despite the many representations I made upon my arrival here, he [O'Reilly] merely replied that it was not now time to act because he had already sent to Your Majesty the names of the officers for the corps. But upon his arrival in Spain, he would mend his error, a promise that to date has not been kept. In recognition of this:

At the royal feet of Your Majesty, I humbly seek that you deign to concede to me in compensation the rank of retired army captain with the salary assigned to that office in the same manner that all retired captains who are attached to the headquarters staff of this city enjoy. By this grace and those I hope to receive from Your Majesty's royal benignity, I shall live eternally grateful.

Coulon de Villiers

ATTACHMENT TO THE PETTION

Declaration of the services of Don Fran^co Coulon DeVilliers, Knight of the Royal and Military Order of Saint-Louis, retired captain of French infantry and present alcalde of the city of New Orleans, capital of the Province of Louisiana.

In the year 1720, in Montreal I entered as a cadet in the service of His Most Christian Majesty. In 1730 I made my first campaign with my father, who had an order to march against the Fox Indians. In this expedition, we killed 800 men.[243]

In 1733 I returned with my father against the same Indians who had taken refuge in the Sac's fort. In this action, my father was killed when he advanced to set fire to the fort's gate. My brother Damonville and my brother-in-law Duplessis experienced the same fate there. My other brother, Coulon, then took command and, for three days, we continued fighting, until the Indians abandoned the fort and fled. So we chased them from two in the afternoon until dawn the next day, when we were forced to abandon the pursuit so as not to fall into an ambush. In the chase, another brother of mine named Villiers was wounded.

In the year 1736, I was appointed sublieutenant in Louisiana. In 1740, under the command of Chevalier St. Laurent, I participated in a campaign against the Chickasaw Indians, in which we fought them for two days within sight of their fort. We killed many people and finally forced them to sue for peace and cease their incursions for some time.

In 1746, I was promoted to lieutenant [and] spent eight years in this rank at various garrisons and detachments in the Illinois District. During this time, my brother Coulon spent a winter on the snow in Acadia at the head of three hundred men. He attacked six hundred Englishmen entrenched at the same place, killing three hundred twenty of them and taking many more prisoner.[244] In the battle, he was gravely wounded and died from his injury after a short time. My other brother, Lepinay, also died in the same fight.[245]

On another occasion against the Iroquois, the Indians captured my uncle named Duverger Daubusson.[246] They burned him while spread-eagled for five consecutive days, after which he expired from the torment.

1777 Petition of François Coulon de Villiers

At the start of the [Seven Years' War], Jumonville, another of my brothers, was assassinated by the English while he was informing them of his commandant's orders. The commandant had commissioned [Jumonville] to ask the English commander to withdraw from French territory, where [the English] had tried to form a settlement in the name of His Britannic Majesty. Shortly thereafter my other brother [*viz: Louis Coulon de Villiers*], went there with a detachment of five hundred men to take vengeance for [Jumonville's] death. He attacked and seized Fort Necessity, defended by a garrison of seven hundred[247] men and twelve cannons.[248] He killed more than three hundred[249] of them and obliged the remainder to surrender and sign a document in which they admitted killing Jumonville treacherously.

In 1754, I received a patent as captain. Two years later, I was sent with a detachment to reinforce Fort Duquesne at more than five hundred leagues upriver. A month after my arrival, the commandant assigned me to a party of fifty men, half of them French and the rest Indians, to attack Fort Cumberland, sixty leagues farther to the north. Before that fort, I fell ill, and I was forced to entrust command to a subaltern officer and retire to Fort Duquesne.

After a month, I left again to seize Fort Granville, defended by four bastions, a 200-man garrison, and artillery. On the eve of my arrival, 150 soldiers [in the fort] deserted, and only fifty remained to endure twenty-four hours of combat. Finally, I succeeded in setting fire to the fort, killing the commandant and fifteen men, capturing the remaining thirty-five, and spiking the cannons.

In 1757, I again left Illinois with two hundred Indians to travel four hundred and fifty leagues to the Virginia territory to attack an English fort. During the siege, I made several raids and took many prisoners. But I was unable to force the fort's surrender due to the bad will of the Indian allies caused by poor weather and my lack of food and munitions.

In 1758, under orders from Chevalier Aubry,[250] I went out again from Illinois with a detachment to reinforce Fort Duquesne. Major Crane [*sic: Grant*] was marching against it at the head of 900 troops, whom we shattered, killing the larger part of them and taking the rest prisoner.[251] A few days later, we marched against Royal

Fort Annon,[252] whose garrison came out to fight us. The combat lasted six hours. We killed many people and forced the others to shut themselves up again in the fort. But we were unable to seize it because of our lack of artillery to combat their cannons. After those two operations ended, we returned to Illinois.

In 1759, we again went out with another detachment to reinforce Canada, and, in passing, the settlement of Niagara, which the English had besieged. I was wounded in this action and taken prisoner by the Indians, who disrobed me from head to foot. They took me to their encampment, pouring blows and insults of all kinds on me. When, due to weariness or because of my wounds and ailments, I fell to the ground, they rained kicks and blows from their firearms upon me. Their only relief was to tell me that they intended to burn me on arrival [at their village]. Indeed, they would have done so had not the English had the humanity to rescue me from their hands and take me to New York. There I remained a prisoner for eighteen months, until the first of 1761. I was exchanged and finally went to France, where upon arrival I received the Cross of Saint-Louis as a reward. Soon I was sent to New Orleans to take charge of my company and continue my merits. I remained in service until the general discharge of 1763, when His Most Christian Majesty found it convenient to reduce this colony to the status of economic outpost, retaining in it only four companies of troops for the maintenance of law and order.

That small number of troops was insufficient for the indispensable garrisons necessary in the city and at its dependent posts. Mssr. D'Abbadie,[253] then the colony's director-general and commandant, decided to create two more companies. He conferred one of them on me, and I continued my service until some months after the arrival of the Spanish governor, Don Antonio de Ulloa. He, in light of favorable recommendations given to him regarding my conduct and seniority of forty-six years of service, of the various actions and campaigns in which I had participated and the unfortunate events in which I lost the greater part of my family, gave me command of the Natchitoches post, bordering the presidio of Los Adaes. That was until the court dispatched my patent as captain, which, he told me, he had solicited from His Catholic Majesty in the regiment

1777 Petition of François Coulon de Villiers

that was being formed to garrison this colony. I remained serving at the Natchitoches post to the satisfaction of the governor until several months after His Excellency, Count O'Reilly, took possession. He did not find me in the city because I could not get to it in time due to low and unnavigable waters in the Red River. He, possibly induced into error by the similarity of names, gave Don Baltazar de Villiers, a retired French army lieutenant and, consequently, my junior by at least twenty years of service, the company authorized to me in the Louisiana Battalion. This fatal error resulted in my losing, after forty-six years of service, the honor of entering His Catholic Majesty's service and reaping the rewards that I would have earned. Count O'Reilly pledged me his word that he would indemnify me upon his return to Madrid. It is a promise that no doubt has escaped his memory since until now it has not had an effect. Since that time, I twice have been named to the post of alcalde, an employment I hold in the current year to [the public's] general approval and applause.

Summary of the services and merits of the interested party in the preceding statement.

Forty-nine-and-a-half years of service without interruption, having begun in the year 1720 and continuing to the end of 1769.

Twenty campaigns and detachments in which I received several wounds and many times commanded as head of the expeditions.

My father dead with four of my brothers, a brother-in-law, and an uncle; two other brothers wounded and crippled; all without counting several of my nephews who also perished in [royal] service. For all of which, I hope that Your Majesty, in consideration of my zeal and that of my entire family, will concede me a reward appropriate to my seignority and services.

New Orleans, March 18, 1777.

F. CHER DEVILLIERS.

M. Genealogy of Chevalier de Villiers

[This appendix was labeled "IV" in Gosselin's original publication.]

First marriage.—François Coulon de Villiers married Elizabeth Groston de St-Ange [*born circa 1719.*[254] *She was the daughter of Robert Groston de St-Ange and Elizabeth Chorel de Saint Romain.*[255] *Ekberg and Person describe this wedding that occurred in 1740:*

> *This marriage, which linked two of the great military families of French North America, was arguably the most important marriage ever celebrated in the colonial Illinois Country, as the elaborate prenuptial contract abundantly reveals. The marriage was celebrated at Fort de Chartres, where Joseph Gagnon was priest. But one priest was not adequate for this grand occasion, so Father Rene Tartarin was brought up from Kaskaskia to participate. Tartarin and Captain Jean-Baptiste Benoist de St. Clair were witnesses in the marriage contract on the groom's behalf, and on the bride's side were Gagnon, Elisabeth Chorel (the bride's mother), and "Monsieur Louis de St. Ange Bellerive, officer commandant on the Wabash."*[256]].

Children:

1. *Isabelle*, born in 1740, married François de Volsay, captain of the Illinois. [*Ekberg and Person identify this daughter as Elisabeth and give the name of her husband as François de Volsey.*[257] *Cleary states that this was a failed marriage: "Elizabeth Coulon de Villiers sought the government's protection from her husband, Pierre Francoise de Volsey, a man she characterized as immoral, cruel, and greedy."*[258]]

2. *Joachime*, born in 1746, married François[-*Louis*] Picoté de Belestre, captain.

3. *Joseph*, born in 1747, died without children.

4. [*François-*]*Louis*, born in 1751 [*possibly 1746*], married Marie [*Genevieve de*] Fontenelle, in the Attakapas, Louisiana. [*He died May 18, 1818, at St Louisianandry Parish, Louisiana.*[259]] There are currently male and female lineage in Louisiana.

Second marriage - François Coulon de Villiers' wife from his second marriage was Madeleine Marin, daughter of Paul,[260] captain etc.

Child:

Jean-Marc Coulon de Villiers who married August 1, 1784, Josephine Catherine Griffon d'Anneville, who died in Havana.

Children:

    a. *Marie-Victoire*, born October 19, 1785, married Jean Innerarity.

    b. *Jean-François*, born August 9, 1786.

    c. *Marie-Joseph-Hugues*, married Arnould Guillemard.

    d. *Charlès-Marie-Hucher*, born February 20, 1795.

    e. *Marie-Suzanne*, born October 28, 1792; married September 30, 1814 to Jos.-Ignace Cruzat, who died November 18, 1860.

    f. *Marie-Jean*, born March 30, 1796.

    g. *Firmin*, born September 26, 1797.

    h. *Louis*, born August 17, 1799.

    i. *Manuel*, born August 19, 1801.

    j. *Felix*, born March 15, 1804.

Jean-Francois, Charles-Marie-Hucher, Marie-Jean, Louis, Felix, emigrated with the father to Havana.

Marie-Joseph Hugues died without children.

Manuel went to Spain where he married.

Marie-Victoire left descendants at Pensacola and Louisiana.

Marie-Suzanne (Madame Cruzat) and Firmin still have descendants in Louisiana; the descendants of Firmin which is in the female line nevertheless bears the name of de Villiers.

Third marriage. - François Coulon de Villiers married third, June 28, 1762, [Marie] Geneviève [Énault] de Livaudais [born 1736, died April 16, 1807[261]].

Child: *Charles-Philippe*, who married two times: first to Delia d'Acosta, of which he had:

Coulon de Villiers

    a. *[Francois]-Coulon Jumonville.*[262]

    b. *Claire-Jumonville de Villiers* who married Pierre Huchet de Kerniou.

    c. *[Marie-Ursula-]Amable* who married R. Ducros.

There are still descendants of Claire and Amable in Louisiana. Chs-Philippe married second Marie Frse Aimée Enoul Beaumont de Livaudais.

From this marriage six children were born:

    a. *Gustave*, married Stéphanie Guérin.

    b. *Louis*, Chevalier Jumonville, married: 1st Délie Buisson, 2nd Délie Commagère.

    c. *Alexander*, married Delia Vela.

    d. *Aimee*, married 1st Canon, 2nd Dupuy.

    e. *Celestine*, married Fleitas.

    f. *Odile*, married to Mssr. Guerin.

All have left posterity in Louisiana. The children of Louis and Alexander bear the name of Jumonville.

N. THE KNIGHTS OF SAINT-LOUIS IN CANADA

[*Aegidius Fauteux, in his 1940 work,* Les Chevaliers de Saint-Louis en Canada, *meticulously presented the history of the officers in Canada who were members of this renowned order. He presented the biographies of 318 knights who had served in New France. Fauteux admits that his list is far from complete, particularly concerning those officers who served in Canada only during the French and Indian War and then went on to serve in other French colonies after the capitulation. Nonetheless, his work is instrumental in presenting the historical significance of this prestigious award and the context in which it was sought after, bestowed, and respected. To provide context as to why membership in the Royal and Military order of the Knights of Saint-Louis was so coveted by the officers in Canada, we present here an abridged translation of Fauteux's work. This appendix was not in Gosselin's original publication.*]

In the parish registers and notarial deeds of a century or more ago, when it was the practice to display all the titles of the various persons appearing, there is one distinction which seems to dominate all the others, that of Knight of Saint-Louis. His proud possessors never forgot to take advantage of it, and the mention was always made of it in these words: "In the presence of Sieur X... Knight of the Royal and Military Order of Saint-Louis." Even when the proprietors had disappeared, honor remained and, in some way, reflected upon their sons, who did not fail to proclaim themselves, on many occasions, descended from knights.

We can scarcely blame this pride and even this ostentation, when we know of what consideration the dignity of Knight of Saint-Louis indeed surrounded men in this time, and in Canada perhaps even more than in France. From this profound consideration they have remained—although they themselves are long gone—a very significant trace in the subconscious memory of our people. I want to speak of the uniquely Canadian saying by which the brave gossips of our country are used to translating their opinion of people of more or less doubtful morality: "Oh! that one is not from the Cross of Saint-Louis."

It is fortunate that this phrase is sufficiently self-evident, for most of those who employ it are ignorant of the noble and great institution of which it remains the last vestige in popular memory. And among the others who can still relate it to its true origin, how many are there to whom it brings much more than a vague memory and quite imprecise?

The great chivalrous order founded by Louis XIV, however, has occupied too much place in our Canadian history that we do not learn to know it a little better, all as we are. I want to try to repair some of the forgetfulness in which they unfairly fell by tracing at least in great strokes this magnificent story.

It was by an edict of April 5, 1693, that the Royal and Military Order of Saint-Louis was created. It was already fifty years into the Sun King's reign. This half-century had been filled by incessant wars, which had made wide gaps in the armies of the nation, and the nobility, beset by all sorts of discontent, was on the point of confessing fatigue. France, however, needed brave warriors more than ever, for she had seen, the year before, rise against her at the same time the German Empire, Spain, England, Holland, and Sweden; in other words, the league of Augsburg. It was then that the Marshal of Luxembourg first proposed to institute honorary rewards capable of awakening, especially among the nobility, a warlike ardor which threatened to die out. At first sight Louis XIV understood the wisdom of the council. His genius made him read to the depths of the soul of France; he was dealing with the sons of the Gauls, lovers of glory, and, like Napoleon after him, he knew that with the lure of honor alone he could lead them to the ends of the earth. Already, no doubt, orders of chivalry existed in France. But the highest, the Order of the Holy Ghost, was reserved, like the Golden Fleece, for a small number of great people, and among all who, for whatever reason, played a role in the Canadian land, I can only find the Chevalier de Lévis who was part of it after becoming duke.

As for the two orders of St. Michael and St. Lazarus, they were already depreciated by dint of having been lavished too widely. The great king, moreover, wished to institute this time a purely military order, and, with marvelous wisdom, he insisted that this order

The Knights of Saint-Louis

should be a reward of value alone, and no longer, like the others, an appanage of birth.

Here is the edict that created the new order of chivalry. We shall see that by the nobility of language and by the elevation of thought, it is worthy in every respect of the great monarch from whom it emanates:

> Louis, by the grace of God, King of France and Navarre, to all, present and future, Greetings.
>
> The officers of our troops have signaled themselves by so many considerable acts of valor and courage, in the conquests of which it has pleased God to bless the justice of our arms, that the ordinary rewards are not sufficient for our affection, and to the recognition we have of their services, we have thought it necessary to seek new means to reward their zeal and fidelity.
>
> It is in this view that we have proposed to establish a new purely military order, to which, in addition to the external marks of honor which will be attached to it, we will assure, in favor of those who will be admitted to it, pensions that will increase as they become worthy of their conduct.
>
> We have resolved that we shall receive in this order only officers of our troops, and that virtue, merit, and services rendered with distinction in our armies will be the only titles to enter it.
>
> To these causes, in the opinion of our council, and of our certain science, full power, and royal authority, we have created, instituted, and erected, by the present, a military order under the name of Saint-Louis....

Louis XIV imposed from the beginning two essential conditions and *sine qua non* at the reception in the Order of Saint-Louis. First, it was necessary to be an officer in the land or sea troops; second, it was necessary to profess the Catholic, Apostolic, and Roman faith. And it was an admirable summary of the life of the Order's patron, Louis IX, who was both a great saint and a warrior. During the one hundred and thirty-odd years of its existence, the Order of

Saint-Louis underwent in its by-laws quite a number of modifications, for example as to the number of its dignitaries, as to the number of pensions to be distributed, as to the duration of the service, but never dared to touch the two fundamental statutes which his creator had established, and which required, together with the quality of an officer, the profession of Catholic faith.

The first condition was accepted without difficulty since it was a purely military order, but the second long raised the protests of the officers who belonged to the Reformed religion and who did not understand well that after having been aggrieved, they were not honored like the others. Marshal Saxe himself, despite his glorious victory at Fontenoy, was never made Knight of Saint-Louis because of his Protestant faith. It was not until 1759, after sixty-six years, that they finally surrendered to these claims, without however undermining the sacrosanct Ark of the Order of Saint-Louis, which remained inviolable and inviolate. A compromise was reached by instituting the Order of Military Merit, for the benefit of the officers of the Reformed religion.

Those proposed to be decorated had to produce a certificate of good life and morals and letters of catholicity. They were received only after this preliminary step. In principle, they were to be received by the king himself, who was the grand master of the Order, but, except in rare circumstances and when there was an exceptionally large promotion, the public and solemn meetings were reserved for the presentation of the insignia to the Grand Crosses and Commanders, and these being already knights, they did not constitute a receipt strictly speaking.

The Marquis de Valfons thus recounts, in his *Souvenirs*, a ceremony of investiture in which he attended:

> Three days before, all the Grand Crosses and Commanders, of which I was a part, had received a letter of invitation to go to Versailles and accompany the King to the chapel in the uniform dress of their rank.
>
> On the day of the festival, at half-past eleven in the morning, we were all in the first room of the chamber. The cabinet door opened, and the usher called seven commanders to whom the King, who had the red cord

on his coat, and the two plates, and the blue cord on his jacket, handed successively the Grand Cross that he took from the hands of Prince de Montbarrey, Minister of War.... Then they called those who were appointed to be Commanders; the King passed them the cord himself.... Then the usher took the general list of the Grand Crosses and Commanders of the Order and read successively the names by rank of seniority. Those who were present took their rank as they were appointed, outside the door of the King's chamber, beginning with the Grand Crosses....

We then crossed in a reversed column, two by two, the *Oeil-de-Boeuf*,[263] the large gallery, all the apartments, and descended by the small staircase, placing us on the right and left on benches in the order in which we arrived. The King, whom we preceded, placed himself on his *prie-Dieu*....[264] High Mass was said in song. A priest brought a louis[265] to the Duke of Chartres, as the first prince of the present blood. At the offering, he accompanied the King and gave him the golden louis.... Mass finished, we came out of the chapel as we had arrived, two by two, the youngest walking first. The Queen who had heard Mass in the tribune...placed herself in the salon of Hercules...with all her ladies in a semicircle.... She saw the commanders march past, who, observing the same order of march as the blue cords, crossed the apartments again, and carried the King back to his study, arranging themselves, as they arrived, on two hedges to let him pass. Everything ended there.

This meeting was held under Louis XVI in August 1779, sixteen years after Canada ceased to be a member of the Order, but I need not say that on such occasions they were no less ceremonious or less solemn at the time of Louis XV, and especially that of the Sun King, the most extravagant of monarchs.

To make known almost all that is necessary of the organization of the Order of Saint-Louis, it only remains to speak of the very decoration that its members wore. This decoration consisted essentially of a gold cross with eight spiked points, enameled with white, beveled with fleurs-de-lis of gold. In the center of the obverse, on an enameled field of guelles surrounded by a border of azure, also enamel with this inscription in gold letters: Ludov. Mag. Instit. 1693 (*Ludovicus Magnus Instituit 1693*),[266] there is depicted a Saint-Louis in armor of gold and covered with the royal mantle, holding in his right a laurel wreath and in his left the crown of thorns and the nails of the Passion. On the reverse side, also on a field guelles, a flamboyant unsheathed sword, the point passed through a laurel wreath, tied with a white sash, all encircled by a border of azure with these words in golden letters: Bell. Virtutis Praem (*Bellicae Virtutis Praemium*).[267]

Ill. 15. Grand Cross sash badge of the Order of Saint-Louis.[268]

The Knights of Saint-Louis

CHRONOLOGICAL LIST OF KNIGHTS OF SAINT-LOUIS OFFICERS OF CANADA

This list includes only the officers who were part of the Canadian troops, that is, infantry troops detached from the navy. It does not include any of the officers of the so-called land forces who came to Canada between 1755 and 1760 with the battalions of the Queen, Saar, Royal Roussillon, Guyenne, Languedoc, Béarn, and Berry, under the orders of Baron Dieskau, the Marquis de Montcalm, and the Chevalier de Lévis.[i] The list does include the officers of the Royal Corps of Artillery and the Corps of Engineers, who came from France at the same time, because they were really part of the troops of Canada, and in no way belong to the regular regiments mentioned above.

By officers of Canada I mean here the officers of Acadia and Ile Royale as well as those of New France. All, although serving under different governments, served in what is today Canada and can be said were all from Canada, and until the end, there was between them a close relationship, with New France providing a large number of her own to Acadia or Ile Royale and vice versa.

[*The following abridged list contains those individuals—forty-three in all—who appear in this work,* Coulon de Villiers: An Elite Military Family of New France. *The leading numbers correspond to Fauteux's original numbering, which was sorted chronologically according to when each officer was received as a Knight of the Royal and Military Order of Saint-Louis.*]

2 – *Louis-Hector, chevalier de* CALLIÈRES, son of Jacques de Callières and Madeleine Potier de Courcy, born in Normandy around 1646. Served for twenty years in the army and was captain in the regiment of Navarre when, on April 10, 1684, he received the provisions of governor of Montreal, instead of François-Marie Perrot. In 1699, he succeeded Mssr. de Frontenac as governor of New France. Died a bachelor in Quebec City on May 26, 1703. He was

---

[i] The author is preparing a special study on the French regiments of the Seven Years' War in Canada. [*Fauteux died within a year of publishing* Les Chevaliers de Saint-Louis en Canada, *and any subsequent work of his remained incomplete and unpublished.*]

made Knight of Saint-Louis on February 1, 1694, the first officer in Canada to receive this honor. As there was no other knight in the country who could be delegated to receive him, he was allowed to carry the cross while awaiting his reception. He was not received until 1698, at Quebec, at the same time as Mssrs. Frontenac and Crisafy, by Mssr. de Vaudreuil, who had been knighted in France on May 1st of the same year. (Mazas, I, 138).

5 – *Philippe de RIGAUD de Vaudreuil*, son of Jean-Louis de Rigaud de Vaudreuil and Marie de Chateauverdun, born in 1643 in Revel (Haute-Garonne). Officer in the King's Musketeers for 15 years, he was appointed in 1687 Commander of the marine troops in Canada. He was captain of ships on May 5, 1695, governor of Montreal on May 2, 1699, he became governor-general of New France on August 1, 1703. Died at Quebec on October 14, 1725. He married at Quebec on November 21, 1690, Louise-Elisabeth, daughter of Pierre de Joybert and Marie-Francoise Chartier de Lotbinière; she died in 1740 in Paris. Made Knight of Saint-Louis while he was in France on May 1, 1698, he was promoted commander with honors on June 18, 1712, then honorary Grand Cross on April 24, 1721.

9 – *Charles LEMOYNE, first baron of Longueuil*; eldest son of Charles LeMoyne and Catherine Primot, born in Montreal on December 10, 1656. After serving first in France as an officer for several years, he returned to serve in the troops of Canada where he was made lieutenant on March 17, 1687, reformed[269] captain on February 28, 1691, Guards of the Navy[270] on January 1, 1694, and captain at the same time. Appointed major of Montreal on May 27, 1706, he became lieutenant of the king[271] at the same place on May 5, 1710. Governor of Three Rivers May 7, 1720, he became governor of Montreal December 20, 1724. Had been made baron of Longueuil, on January 20, 1700. Died in Montreal on June 7, 1729. He had married first in Paris, by contract at the Chateau de Versailles May 7, 1681, Claude-Elisabeth, daughter of Armand Souart and Marie Jobart; she died in 1724. He married second at Longueuil, September 17, 1727, Marguerite, daughter of Charles Le Gardeur de

Tilly and Genevieve Juchereau; she died in 1742. Knight of Saint-Louis on July 3, 1703. (Mazas, II, 106).

12 – *Claude de RAMEZAY*, son of Timothée de Ramezay and Catherine Gribouillard, de Gesse, bishopric of Langres. Lieutenant in Canada on May 8, 1683, Captain on March 1, 1687, Governor of Three Rivers on July 1, 1690, Commander of the Troops on April 28, 1699, lieutenant of the king in Montreal on May 22, 1701, then Governor of the same city on May 15, 1704. Died in Montreal on August 1, 1724. On November 8, 1690, married Marie-Charlotte, daughter of Pierre Denys de la Ronde and Catherine Le Neuf. Knight of Saint-Louis on June 1, 1705, after Laffilard.

26 – *Jacques TESTARD de Montigny*, son of Jacques Testard de la Forêt and Marie Pournain, born in Montreal on February 23, 1663. Lieutenant reformed in Canada on March 17, 1687, lieutenant in Acadia in 1691, served in Canada in the same rank in 1700, captain in 1710, died in Montreal on July 10, 1737. Had married first in Quebec, September 24, 1698, Marguerite, daughter of Mathieu Damours des Chauffours and Marie Marsolet; she died in 1703, and second in Quebec, on February 28, 1718, Marie-Anne, daughter of Louis de Laporte de Louvigny and Marie Nolan; she died in 1763. Knight of Saint-Louis on June 12, 1712, according to Laffilard.

34 – *Jean-Baptiste LEMOYNE de Bienville*, son of Charles LeMoyne and Catherine Primot, born in Montreal on February 23, 1680. His brother François having been killed in 1691, he received the Bienville surname that it bore. Guards of the Navy in Brest in 1697, then in Rochefort in 1698. It was on March 11th of this last year that he was named ensign in Acadia. In 1702 he was second in command in Louisiana under his brother Iberville, and lieutenant in Biloxi. Removed to France in 1707, but in 1717 returned to Louisiana with the title of general commander. Removed to France in 1723 following some difficulties, he was dismissed on April 9, 1726. Appointed governor of Louisiana on July 25, 1732, he held this post until the arrival of his successor, the Marquis de Vaudreuil-Cavagnal, May 10,

1743. Returned to France he was made captain of the ship on January 1, 1745. He retired on February 18, 1746, with a pension of 3000 livres on the Royal Treasury and 1800 livres on the Navy. His funeral was in Paris on May 7, 1768, at the age of 88 years. Knight of Saint-Louis on September 20, 1717, with permission to carry the cross until it could be received. (Mazas, II, 114).

35 – *Charles, Marquis de BEAUHARNOIS*, son of François de Beauharnois, seigneur de la Boische, and Marguerite-Françoise Pyvart de Chastullé. After entering the navy in 1691, he was captain of the ship since April 23, 1798 [sic], when he was appointed governor of Canada on January 10, 1726. Made chief wing officer January 14, 1741. Left the governorship on September 19, 1747, was promoted lieutenant general on January 1, 1748, and died in Paris on June 12, 1749. Had married in 1716, Renée Pays, widow of Pierre Hardouineau, but had no children. Knight of Saint-Louis on June 28, 1718, commander ad honores on March 29, 1732, and Grand Cross on March 25, 1738.

53 – *Pierre-Jacques de TAFFANEL, Marquis de la Jonquière.* Son of [*Jean*] de Taffanel de la Jonquière and Catherine de Bonnes, born around 1685 in Graulhet in the Tarn. Entered the navy in 1697, he was made captain of ships in 1731 and squadron leader in 1746. Appointed in this last year governor of Canada, he left for his government with a fleet, but after having supported the famous battle on May 14, 1747, against Admiral Anson, he was captured and taken to England. Liberated by the peace of Aix-la-Chapelle in 1748, he was finally able in 1749 to go to Canada to fill his post, which had been filled by an interim post by Mssr. de la Galissonnière. Died at Quebec on March 17, 1752. Had married, on June 3, 1721, Marie-Angelique de la Valette, a family of the Parliament of Toulouse. Knight of Saint-Louis on December 23, 1721, and honorary commander on April 15, 1750, he obtained, on June 1, 1751, the pension of 2000 livres on the vacant order by the death of Mssr. de l'Etanduère. (Mazas, II, 159).

67 – *Pierre de RIGAUD de Vaudreuil-Cavagnal*, son of Philippe de Rigaud de Vaudreuil and Louise-Elisabeth de Joybert; born at Quebec on November 22, 1698. Ensign in Canada on June 16, 1708, marine officer in 1711, lieutenant on May 28, 1712, captain on June 2, 1715, major of the troops on April 23, 1726, governor of Three Rivers on April 1, 1733, governor of Louisiana July 1, 1742, and finally governor of Canada since July 10, 1755, until the end of French rule. Removed to France after the capitulation, he was put in the Bastille because of the Bigot case, but soon acquitted. Died in Paris on August 4, 1778. Had married in 1742, probably in Paris before leaving for Louisiana, Jeanne-Charlotte, daughter of Jacques-Alexis Fleury Deschambault and Marguerite de Chavigny, widow of François Le Verrier de Rousson. Knight of Saint-Louis on March 25, 1730, commander on May 15, 1757, and honorary Grand Cross on February 16, 1759.

79 – *Charles LEMOYNE, second baron of Longueuil*, son of Charles LeMoyne, first baron of Longueuil, and his first wife, Claude-Elisabeth Souart, born in Montreal on October 20, 1687. Marine at Rochefort January 6, 1706, lieutenant in Canada on June 28, 1713, and captain on May 13, 1719. Appointed major of Montreal on April 1, 1733, lieutenant of the king in Three Rivers on May 1, 1743, and finally governor of Montreal on February 15, 1749. Died in Montreal on January 17, 1755. He married at Saint-Ours on April 29, 1720, Catherine-Charlotte, daughter of Louis-Joseph Le Gouès de Grais and Marguerite Le Gardeur de Tilly. Knight of Saint-Louis on May 20, 1734. (Mazas, II, 133).

87 – *François-Pierre de RIGAUD de Vaudreuil*, son of Philippe de Rigaud de Vaudreuil and Louise-Elisabeth de Joybert; born and raised in Montreal on February 8, 1703, solemnly baptized on June 29, 1704. Ensign *en pied* in Canada in 1712, lieutenant on June 2, 1720, captain on June 12, 1724, major of Three Rivers in May 1741, lieutenant of the king in Quebec City on February 15, 1748. Governor of Three Rivers May 1, 1749, last governor of Montreal from May 1, 1757 to 1760. Removed to France after capitulation, he re-

Coulon de Villiers

tired in 1762. Died at his château de Collier, in the Loir-et-Cher, August 24, 1779. Had married at Quebec, May 5, 1755, Louise, daughter of Joseph Fleury de la Gorgendière and Claire Joliet. Knight of St. Louis on March 25, 1738. (Mazas, II, 134).

89 – *Ange, Marquis DUQUESNE Menneville*, son of Alexandre DuQuesne Mônier, squadron leader, and Ursule Poissel, born in Toulon around 1702. Entered the navy in 1714, he was captain of the ship since August 25, 1749, when he was appointed governor of New France, January 1, 1752. Having obtained his recall April 1, 1755, he returned to France and resumed his service in the navy. He was a squadron leader in 1759. Retired in 1776, he died at Anthony (Seine) on September 17, 1778. Knight of Saint-Louis on May 13, 1738, he was promoted commander in 1758. (Mazas, I, 582).

90 – *Roland-Michel BARRIN de la Galissonnière*. Son of Roland Barrin de la Galissonnière and Catherine Bégon, born in Rochefort on November 11, 1693. Ensign in the navy in 1710, he became captain of the ship in 1738. He was commissioner general of the artillery at Rochefort when, in June 1747 the king charged him to replace the governor of Canada, Mssr. de la Jonquière, who was a prisoner in England. Moved to France after the return of Mssr. de la Jonquière, he was named on December 15, 1749, one of the commissioners to delimit the boundaries of Acadia. Chief of squadron in 1750 and lieutenant-general of armies of the sea in 1756, he distinguished himself the same year by his glorious naval victory over Admiral Byng. Died in Nemours soon after, October 26, 1756. Had married in 1713 Marie Antoinette Catherine de Lauzon. Knight of Saint-Louis in 1738, commander in 1752, he obtained the expectation of Grand Cross on October 19, 1756, a few days before his death.

94 – *Pierre-Joseph CÉLORON de Blainville*, son of Jean-Baptiste Céloron de Blainville and Hélène Picoté de Belestre, born in Montreal on December 29, 1693. Ensign on July 1, 1715, lieutenant on February 5, 1731, Captain on March 25, 1738. Died in Montreal on April 12, 1759. He married, first in Montreal on December 30, 1724, Ma-

rie-Madeleine, daughter of Maurice Blondeau and Suzanne Charbonnier; she died in 1733. He married second in Montreal on October 13, 1743, Catherine, daughter of François Eurry de la Pérelle and Charlotte Aubert de la Chesnaye; she died in 1797 religious at the Gray Nuns. Knight of Saint-Louis on May 17, 1741. (Rep. Arch. of Can., 1904, p 289).

101 – *Paul-Joseph LeMoyne, chevalier de Longueuil*, son of Charles LeMoyne, first Baron of Longueuil, and Claude-Elisabeth Souart, born in Longueuil on September 19, 1701. After serving in France as a lieutenant in the Normandy Regiment, he served in the troops of Canada and became lieutenant on January 8, 1726, captain April 11, 1727, major of Quebec in February 1748 and governor of Three Rivers May 1, 1757. Removed to France after the capitulation, he was in charge of the command of Canadian officers stationed in Touraine. Died in Port-Louis, Morbihan, on May 12, 1778. He married at Quebec, October 19, 1728, Marie-Geneviève, daughter of Pierre-Jacques Joybert and Marie-Anne Bécard de Grandville; she died in 1766. Knight of Saint-Louis on April 24, 1744. (Mazas, II, 144).

111 – *Nicolas-Antoine Coulon de Villiers*, son of Nicolas-Antoine Coulon de Villiers and Angélique Jarret de Verchères, born in Contrecoeur on June 25, 1708. Ensign on March 23, 1732, lieutenant on March 20, 1734, captain on April 24, 1744, and major at Three Rivers on February 15, 1748. Died in Montreal on April 3, 1750. He had married Madeleine-Marie-Anne, daughter of Pierre-Thomas Tarieu de Lanaudière, Sieur de la Pérade, and Madeleine Jarret de Verchères, widow of Richard Testu de la Richardière. Knight of Saint-Louis on January 31, 1748, during a stay in France, according to letters of instruction to Mssr. de Beauharnois, former governor of Canada.

113 – *Jean-Baptiste-Nicolas-Roch de Ramezay*, son of Claude de Ramezay and Marie-Charlotte Denys de la Ronde, born in Montreal on September 4, 1708. Ensign May 7, 1720, Lieutenant on April 23, 1726, Captain on March 20, 1734, major of Quebec on May 1, 1757.

Coulon de Villiers

Died in Blaye (Gironde) on May 7, 1777. Had married in Three Rivers, on December 6, 1728, Louise, daughter of René Godefroy de Tonnancour and Marguerite Ameau. Knight of Saint-Louis on February 15, 1748, according to the letters of instruction to Mssr. de la Galissonnière.

119 – *Nicolas-Joseph de NOYELLES*, son of Joseph de Noyelles and Marguerite Boidoux, born in Crécy, diocese of Meaux, circa 1694. Ensign in Canada on May 5, 1710, lieutenant on February 11, 1721, captain on August 1, 1733, major of Three Rivers in June 1751, lieutenant of the king of the same city on January 1, 1759. Died in Rochefort on August 16, 1761. Had married in Montreal on August 8, 1718, Marie-Charlotte, daughter of Charles Petit de Livilliers and Madeleine Gauthier de Varennes. Knight of Saint-Louis on May 1, 1749, according to letters of instruction to Mssr. de la Jonquière.

126 – *Jacques LE GARDEUR de Saint-Pierre*, son of Jean-Paul Le Gardeur de Saint-Pierre and Marie-Josephte Le Neuf de la Vallière. Officer of the troops of Canada, he was made ensign *en second* in 1724, ensign *en pied* in 1733, lieutenant on May 17, 1741, and captain on February 15, 1748. After the death of La Vérendrye, he was charged to continue in his place the discovery of the West Sea. Killed at the battle of the Blessed Sacrament on September 8, 1755. He married at Quebec, October 27, 1738, Marie-Josephte, daughter of Charles Cuillimin and Françoise Lemaitre La Morille; she died in 1768. Knight of Saint-Louis April 15, 1750, according to the orders of the king addressed to Mssr. de la Jonquière. (Mazas, II, 157).

127 – *Louis de LACORNE, dit Lacorne the eldest*, son of Jean-Louis de Lacorne and Marie Pécaudy de Contrecoeur, born in Montreal on June 24, 1696. After having served twelve years in France, particularly in Royal-La-Marine, he returned to Canada and was made an ensign *en pied* on March 22, 1732, lieutenant on April 1, 1733, and captain on April 24, 1744. Withdrawn on January 1, 1758. Died in Terrebonne on April 2, 1762. Had married in Montreal on Sep-

tember 1, 1740, Elisabeth, daughter of Claude de Ramezay and Marie-Charlotte Denys de la Ronde. Knight of Saint-Louis on April 1, 1751, according to the letters of instruction to Mssr. de la Jonquière.

128 – *Claude-Antoine de BERMEN de Martinière*, son of Claude de Bermen, seigneur de la Martinière, and his second wife, Marie-Anne Cailleteau, born in Quebec City on July 12, 1700. Officer of the troops of Canada, he was there made ensign *en second* on May 5, 1722, ensign *en pied* April 12, 1727, lieutenant March 20, 1734, and captain May 1, 1743. Commander for the king in Acadia from May 24 to July 28, 1754, he retired on March 15, 1755, and died at Quebec on December 24, 1761. He married, by contract passed in Montreal on March 18, 1729, Catherine Parsons, who had been taken captive to Canada in 1704. Knight of Saint-Louis on April 1, 1751, according to the king's orders addressed to Mssr. de la Jonquière.

129 – *Paul-Louis DAZEMARD de Lusignan*, son of Paul Dazemard de Lusignan and Jeanne Baby. Born in Champlain on November 19, 1691. Ensign in Martinique on March 18, 1721, he returned to Canada in the same capacity on June 1, 1724, was promoted lieutenant on April 1, 1735, and captain on April 17, 1744. Died in Québec on September 4, 1764. Married in Montreal on January 8, 1732, Madeleine-Marguerite, daughter of François-Marie Bouat and Madeleine Lambert Dumont. Knight of Saint-Louis on May 15, 1752, according to the letters of instruction to Governor DuQuesne (Mazas, II, 162).

134 – *Pierre-Paul MARIN de la Malgue*, son of Charles Marin de la Malgue and Marie-Madeleine Niquet, born in Montreal on March 19, 1692. Ensign on March 22, 1732, lieutenant on May 17, 1741, captain on February 15, 1748. Died at Fort Duquesne [*sic: Le Boeuf*] on October 29, 1753. Married in Montreal on March 21, 1718, Marie-Josephte, daughter of Joseph Guyon-Després and Madeleine Petit-Boismorel. Knight of Saint-Louis on April 1, 1753, according to the letters of instruction to Governor DuQuesne.

Coulon de Villiers

144 – *Jacques-Pierre DANEAU de Muy*, son of Nicolas de Muy and Marguerite Boucher, born in Boucherville on October 7, 1695. Ensign *en second* on June 1, 1724, ensign *en pied* on April 1, 1733, lieutenant on May 17, 1741, and captain February 15, 1748. Died in Detroit May 20, 1758. Married in Montreal on January 30, 1725, Louise-Geneviève, daughter of François-Madeleine-Fortuné Ruette d'Auteuil and Marie-Anne Juchereau. Knight of Saint-Louis on April 1, 1754, according to the letters of instruction to Governor DuQuesne.

149 – *Jean-Daniel DUMAS*, born February 24, 1721, in Montauban, today in the department of Tarn-et-Garonne. Made second lieutenant of grenadiers in the regiment of Agenois on August 26, 1742, then lieutenant on April 4, 1743, he was captain reformed in the regiment of Condé since October 18, 1747, when, on April 15, 1750, he was destined to serve in Canada's troops as captain. When Mssr. de Beaujeu was killed at the battle of Monongahela on July 9, he took the command in his place and secured the victory. Appointed major of Quebec on May 1, 1757, he was promoted on January 1, 1759, major general and inspector of the troops of Canada. Removed to France after the capitulation, he obtained the rank of colonel on March 27, 1761, was appointed governor of the islands of France and Bourbon on May 1, 1766, was promoted on February 29, 1768, brigadier of infantry, recalled in France on July 3 the same year, and made maréchal de camp[272] March 1, 1780. Knight of Saint-Louis March 17, 1756, according to the King's orders addressed to the Marquis de Vaudreuil. (Mazas, II, 169).

151 – *Michel-Jean-Hugues PEAN*, son of Jacques-Hugues Péan de Livaudière and Marie-Françoise Pécaudy de Contrecoeur, born in Saint-Ours on June 18, 1723. Ensign *en second* on March 25, 1738, ensign *en pied* on April 27, 1742, aide-major[273] at Quebec on May 12, 1745, with rank of captain on June 14, 1750. Removed to France after 1760, he was involved in the Canadian affair, put in the Bastille and sentenced to restitution. Married in Québec City on January 3, 1746, Angelique, daughter of Nicolas-Marie Renaud de Avesnes des Méloizes and Angélique Chartier de Lotbinière. Knight of Saint-

Louis on March 17, 1756, according to letters of instruction to Mssr. de Vaudreuil.

152 – *Claude-Pierre PECAUDY de Contrecoeur*, son of François-Antoine Pécaudy de Contrecoeur and Jeanne de Saint-Ours, born in Contrecoeur on January 26, 1706. Ensign *en second* on April 20, 1729, ensign *en pied* on April 13, 1734, lieutenant April 27, 1742, Captain February 15, 1748, retired January 1, 1759. Remained in Canada after the capitulation, he died in Montreal December 15, 1775. Had married first in Boucherville January 10, 1729, Madeleine, daughter of René Boucher de la Perrière and Françoise Mailhot, second in Montreal on September 9, 1768, Marguerite, daughter of Louis Haincque de Puygibault and Marie-Marguerite Gauthier de Varennes. Knight of Saint-Louis on March 17, 1756, according to letters of instruction to Mssr. de Vaudreuil.

154 – *Pierre-Jean-Baptiste-François-Xavier LE GARDEUR de Repentigny*, son of Jean-Baptiste-René Le Gardeur de Repentigny and Marie-Catherine Juchereau de Saint-Denys, born in Montreal on May 24, 1719. Officer in the troops from Canada, he was made ensign *en second* on March 9, 1734, ensign *en pied* April 10, 1742, and lieutenant on February 15, 1748. That same year he was embroiled in the unfortunate accident made famous by the legend of the Golden Dog;[274] he killed the merchant Jacquin Philibert during a quarrel. It was thought wiser, after he obtained his letters of grace in April 1749, to transfer him to the troops of Ile Royale where he was named captain on April 15, 1750. Returned to the troops of Canada May 1, 1757, he accomplished until the end of the Seven Years' War several brilliant actions, which have been falsely attributed by most historians to his brother, the Chevalier Louis de Repentigny. Removed to France after the capitulation, he entered in February 1769, with the approval of the king, in the service of the company of the Indies as major general of the troops of India and major of the Place de Pondicherry. Appointed May 2, 1774, governor of Mahé, he died there in 1776. He married in Montreal, January 30, 1753, Catherine-Angelique, daughter of Pierre Payen de Noyan and Catherine

d'Ailleboust Manthet. Knight of Saint-Louis on May 1, 1757, according to the King's orders addressed to the Marquis de Vaudreuil. (Mazas, II, 172).

155 – *Christophe SABREVOIS de Sermonville*, son of Jacques-Charles de Sabrevois and Jeanne Boucher; born at Boucherville on February 26, 1701. Ensign *en second* in 1732, ensign *en pied* on April 1, 1733, lieutenant on May 17, 1741, aide-major in Montreal on May 12, 1745, with captain's commission on February 15, 1748. Removed to France after 1760, he retired to Touraine where he still lived in 1779. Had married in Montreal, August 16, 1731, Agathe, daughter of Joseph Hertel de Saint-François and Catherine Philippe. Knight of Saint-Louis on May 1, 1757, according to letters of instruction to Mssr. de Vaudreuil. (Mazas, II, 172).

157 – *Antoine de LACORNE la Colombière*, son of Jean-Louis de Lacorne and Marie Pécaudy de Contrecoeur, born in Contrecoeur on December 1, 1708. Ensign *en second* on April 1, 1733, ensign *en pied* on April 1, 1739, lieutenant on February 15, 1748, captain April 1, 1753. Removed to France in 1761, he retired to Loches where he died September 23, 1780. Had married in Montreal, November 6, 1744, Marguerite, daughter of Charles Petit de Livilliers and Madeleine Gauthier de Varennes, widow of Louis-Joseph-Marie Rocbert de la Morandière. Knight of Saint-Louis on May 1, 1757, according to letters of instruction to Mssr. de Vaudreuil. (Mazas, II, 172).

156 – *François LE MERCIER*, son of Nicolas-François Le Mercier and Charlotte Le Rebours, born in Caudebec, Normandy, on December 29, 1722. Ensign *en second* in the Canadian troops in 1743, he was appointed artillery assistant in 1748, was sent to Metz the following year to improve his artillery, and on April 15, 1750, on his return, he was appointed lieutenant of the new gunboat-bombardiers company. Captain of the same company in 1753, he was made commander of the artillery in Canada on March 19, 1757. Returned to France after the capitulation, he was involved in the Bigot case and was imprisoned for some time in the Bastille. He then retired to Lisieux, where he died a little before the end of the eighteenth century.

The Knights of Saint-Louis

After renouncing the Reformed religion and being baptized at the bishopric of Quebec on November 12, 1757, he married at Sainte-Foye three days later on the 15th, Françoise, daughter of René Boucher de la Bruère and Louise-Renée Pécaudy de Contrecoeur. Knight of Saint-Louis on May 1, 1757, according to the king's orders addressed to Mssr. de Vaudreuil. (Mazas, II, 172).

159 – *Louis COULON de Villiers*, son of Nicolas-Antoine Coulon de Villiers and Angélique Jarret de Verchères, born in Verchères on August 10, 1710. Ensign *en second* on March 20, 1734, ensign *en pied* in 1741, lieutenant on February 15, 1748, and captain April 1, 1753. Died at Quebec on November 2, 1757. He was the vanquisher of Washington at Fort Necessity, known as "Grand Villiers." He married in Montreal, December 29, 1755, Amable, daughter of Louis Prud'homme and Louise Marin. Knight of Saint-Louis on May 1, 1757, according to letters of instruction to Mssr. de Vaudreuil.

166 – *Pierre-Roch de SAINT-OURS des Chailions*, son of Jean-Baptiste de Saint-Ours des Chaillons and Marguerite Le Gardeur de Repentigny, born in Quebec City on February 17, 1712. Ensign *en second* on April 1, 1733, ensign *en pied* March 25, 1738, lieutenant April 2, 1744, Captain February 15, 1748. Remaining in Canada after the capitulation, he became a member of the Legislative Council and died in Montreal on September 24, 1782. He married at Quebec, June 30, 1745, Charlotte, daughter of Louis-Henry Deschamps de Boishébert and Louise-Geneviève de Ramezay. Knight of Saint-Louis on January 1, 1759, according to the letters of instruction to Mssr. de Vaudreuil.

167 – *Luc de LACORNE, dit Lacorne Saint-Luc*, son of Jean-Louis de Lacorne and Marie Pécaudy de Contrecoeur, born in Montreal in 1711. Ensign *en second* on April 1, 1735, ensign *en pied* on April 27, 1742, lieutenant February 15, 1748, captain March 15, 1755. Legislative counselor under the English regime, he died in Montreal on October 4, 1784. He had married first in Montreal on December 10,

Coulon de Villiers

1742, Marie-Anne, daughter of Jean-Baptiste Hervieux and Catherine Magnan; she died in 1753. He married second in Montreal on September 3, 1757, Marie-Josephte, daughter of Charles Guillimin and Françoise Lemaitre La Morille, widow of Jacques Le Gardeur de Saint-Pierre. He married third in Montreal on April 9, 1774, Marguerite, daughter of Pierre de Boucherville and Marguerite Raimbault. Knight of Saint-Louis on January 1, 1759, according to the letters of instruction to Mssr. de Vaudreuil. (Mazas, II, 174).

169 – *Gaspard-Joseph* CHAUSSEGROS *de Léry*, son of Gaspard Chaussegros de Léry and Marie-Renée Le Gardeur de Beauvais, born in Quebec City on July 20, 1721. Served first as an engineer, became ensign *en second* in 1742 and ensign *en pied* in 1748, left the engineers in 1750, was lieutenant on April 1, 1751, and captain on May 14, 1757. Removed to France in 1761, he returned soon after. Member of the Legislative Council of Canada, he died in Quebec City on December 11, 1797. He married in Quebec City on September 24, 1753, Louise, daughter of François Martel de Brouage and Louise-Madeleine Mariauchau d'Esgly; she died in 1793. Knight of Saint-Louis on January 1, 1759. (Mazas, H, 175).

175 – *François* COULON *de Villiers*, known as le Chevalier de Villiers, son of Nicolas-Antoine Coulon de Villiers and Angélique Jarret de Verchères, born about 1712. After having served some time in Canada as a cadet, he was made an ensign in Louisiana in 1736, lieutenant in 1746, and was made captain in the course of the year 1757. Died in New Orleans on May 22, 1794. Had married first before 1740, Elisabeth Groston of Saint-Ange-Bellerive; second Madeleine, daughter of Paul Marin and Jeanne-Josephte Guyon-Després; third Genevieve [*Énault*] de Livaudais. He had been made Knight of Saint-Louis on September 7, 1759, but having, that same year, been made prisoner near Fort Niagara with Captain Aubry, he did not return to France until 1761, wherefore on March 27, new orders to receive him were sent to Count de la Serre. (Mazas, II, 176).

178 – *Jacques-François LE GARDEUR de Croisille de Courtemanche*, son of Charles Le Gardeur de Croisille and Marie-Anne-Geneviève Robineau, born in Cap-de-la-Madeleine on December 11, 1710. Ensign *en second* on March 20, 1736, ensign *en pied* on May 31, 1743, lieutenant on February 15, 1748, and captain on March 17, 1755. Removed to France after the capitulation in 1761, he returned to Canada in 1763, spent about three years there, remarried, and retired for good from the country in 1767 to live in Loches, in Touraine, where he died on May 3, 1777. He married in Montreal, April 26, 1737, Marie-Louise, daughter of Pierre de Saint-Ours and Hélène Céloron de Blainville; she died in 1765. He married second in Montreal on September 29, 1766, Marie-Madeleine, daughter of François Duplessis-Fabert and Geneviève-Catherine Pelletier; she died in Loches in 1787. Knight of Saint-Louis on February 8, 1760, according to the king's orders addressed to Mssr. de Vaudreuil. (Mazas, II, 179).

196 – *Philippe-Ignace AUBERT de Gaspé*, son of Pierre Aubert de Gaspé and Angélique Le Gardeur de Tilly, born in Saint-Antoine de Tilly, on April 5, 1714. Ensign *en second* in Canada on April 1, 1739, ensign *en pied* May 12, 1745, lieutenant on May 1, 1749, and Captain on March 17, 1756. Died in Saint-Jean-Port-Joli on January 28, 1787. Had married at Quebec, June 30, 1745, Marie-Anne, daughter of Nicolas-Antoine Coulon de Villiers and Angélique Jarret de Verchères. He was appointed Knight of Saint-Louis on March 24, 1761, but he was never received and, until the end, could only say to himself "admitted to the order of Saint-Louis."

197 – *Joseph-Michel LE GARDEUR de Montesson*, son of Charles Le Gardeur de Croisille and Marie-Anne-Geneviève Robineau, born in Bécancour on December 30, 1716. Officer in the Canadian troops, he was made ensign *en second* in 1742, ensign *en pied* on February 15, 1748, lieutenant on April 1, 1753, and Captain on May 1, 1757. Removed to France in 1761, he returned to Canada in 1763. He was imprisoned by the Americans at Fort Saint-Jean in 1775 and died shortly afterwards in Bristol, Pennsylvania, and was buried in Phil-

adelphia. On October 25, 1745, he married Claire-Françoise, daughter of Pierre Boucher de Boucherville and Charlotte Denys de la Ronde, widow of Jean-Baptiste Pommereau. Knight of Saint-Louis on March 27, 1761, according to the king's orders addressed to the Count de la Serre, Governor of the Invalides.[275]

199 – *Michel MAREY or MAREST de la Chauvignerie*, son of Louis Marey de la Chauvignerie and Catherine Joly, born in Montreal on September 5, 1704. Ensign *en second* on May 17, 1741, ensign *en pied* on February 15, 1748, lieutenant on March 15, 1755, captain February 1, 1760. Removed to France after the capitulation. Had married in Verchères, August 16, 1740, Marie-Josephte, daughter of Paul-François Raimbault and Marie-Catherine Du Verger d'Aubusson. Knight of Saint-Louis on March 27, 1761, according to the letters of instruction to the Count de la Serre, Governor of the Invalides. Mssr. de la Chauvignerie having not been in Paris, new orders to receive him were despatched on April 10, 1761, to Mssr. Dupin de Bellugard, commander of the navy at Rochefort.

201 – *Paul LEBORGNE*, born in France. Ensign *en second* in Canada in 1744, ensign *en pied* on May 23, 1749, lieutenant on April 1, 1753, captain on January 1, 1759. Removed to France after the capitulation, he was named, January 4, 1766, lieutenant in the corps of volunteers from Africa to Goree. He was still living in 1789, 72 years old. Knight of Saint-Louis on March 27, 1761, according to the letters of instruction to Mssr. de Chastelroger, chief of squadron, commander of the navy at Brest.

206 – *Pierre Odet de PIERCOT de Bailleul, dit Bailleul Canut*, son of Louis Odet de Piercot, sieur de Bailleul, and Marie-Anne Trottier, born in Montreal on March 12, 1724. Ensign *en second* on April 15, 1750, ensign *en pied* March 15, 1755, and lieutenant January 1, 1759. Removed to France after the capitulation, he still lived in Paris in 1789, retired captain. Had married in Quebec City on January 17, 1757, Charlotte-Thérèse, daughter of Louis Denys de la Ronde and Marie-Louise Chartier de Lotbinière. Knight of St. Louis March 27,

1761, according to the letters of instruction to the Count de la Serre, while he was still a lieutenant.

209 – *Antoine-Gabriel* BENOIST, known as le Chevalier Benoist, son of Gabriel Benoist and Francoise de Trevet, born in Paris on October 5, 1715. Moved to Canada in 1735, as a cadet *à l'aiguillette*, he was made an ensign *en second* April 1, 1741, and ensign *en pied* on April 1, 1745, served as aide-major in 1747 and 1748, was promoted lieutenant on May 1, 1749, and finally captain on May 1, 1757. Removed to France in 1761, he returned in Canada to seek his family in 1763 and returned to France definitively in 1764. Died in Paris on January 23, 1776. Had married in Montreal, November 11, 1743, Marie-Louise, daughter of Jacques Le Ber de Senneville and Marie-Louise Miray de l'Argenterie. Knight of Saint-Louis in March 1761, he was received into the Order on the 29th of the same month by Count de la Serre, Governor of the Invalides.

215 – *Jean-Baptiste-Philippe* TESTARD *de Montigny*, son of Jacques Testard de Montigny and Marie-Anne Laporte de Louvigny, born in Montreal on June 16, 1724. Ensign *en second* on May 31, 1743, ensign *en pied* on February 15, 1748, lieutenant on April 1, 1753, captain May 1, 1757. Removed to France after the capitulation, he retired to Blois and died there on November 4, 1786. Had married in Montreal, on October 28, 1748, Charlotte, daughter of Julien Trottier des Rivières and Louise-Catherine Raimbault. Knight of Saint-Louis on August 8, 1762, according to the letters of instruction to the Comte de Roquefeuil, chief of squadron, commander of the navy at Brest.

A greater number of young Canadians than are generally thought, especially sons of officers who had been too young to take part in the defense of their country, wanted at least, after the capitulation, to still serve their old flag and entered the army or the navy of France. Many of them provided a good career and some became Knights of Saint-Louis. Of these I have so far discovered only thirty-eight whose quality has been proven to me, but I know at least the double of which I am morally sure that they have achieved the same honor, but that I did not think I had the right to inscribe here for want of definite proof.

11 – *Alexandre-René DAGNEAU Douville*, son of Alexandre Dagneau Douville and Marie Coulon de Villiers, born in Cataracoui (Kingston) about 1736. After having served in Canada with his father as a cadet, he was named ensign in the troops of the Martinique. Having become lieutenant-colonel of infantry, he was governor of the islands Saint-Martin and Saint-Barthélémy until 1784 when these islands were ceded to Sweden. He retired on this occasion. Had married at Guadeloupe, May 28, 1764, Marie-Félicité Ricord. Knight of Saint-Louis on June 20, 1774. (Rep Arch of Can, 1905, I, 405).[276]

ENDNOTES

NOTES TO PREFACE AND INTRODUCTION

[1] Alberts's 1965 book, *The Most Extraordinary Adventures of Major Robert Stobo*, provides great detail of a protagonist other than George Washington regarding the battle of Fort Necessity at Great Meadows. In an attempt to provide some background of Louis Coulon de Villiers, he perpetuated an historical error, which Gosselin had corrected (albeit in French) sixty years earlier, when he misattributed Nicolas-Antoine's victory at Grand Pré to the younger Villiers brother. Further, Alberts mistakenly made Louis the half-brother of Jumonville, perhaps confused by the difference in names.

The Fort Ligonier Association's 1993 publication *War for Empire in Western Pennsylvania* provides no background of the Villiers brothers. They continue the error that Louis was perhaps only the half-brother of Jumonville. The authors mention the Jumonville affair, Fort Necessity, Fort Granville, and Major Grant's capture, yet neglect to provide any background of Jumonville or Louis and fail to mention François at all.

Dr. Peyser in 1999 wrote a pamphlet, *Ambush and Revenge*, in which he provides two outstanding essays detailing the careers of Jumonville and Louis. He corrects some of Gosselin's mistakes, including providing primary source documentation verifying that Louis, not François, was the brother wounded in the 1733 fight with the Sauk and Meskwaki. However, the printing was limited, and few historians have taken note of this work.

In 2000, Dr. Anderson, in his 878-page tome, *Crucible of War*, devoted 75 pages to the events that precipitated the French and Indian War, including the Jumonville affair and the sacking of Fort Necessity. Framed through the lense of Washington – the father of his country, Anderson provides little detail—less than a page—on the backgrounds of Jumonville and Coulon de Villiers. Short shrift when considering that Louis was the only adversary to compel Washington's signature on a surrender document.

Dr. Axelrod's 2007 book, *Blooding at Great Meadows*, provides greater detail of the Jumonville affair and Fort Necessity than perhaps any previous work. He, too, writes with a Washington-centric perspective with almost no discussion at all regarding the Villiers brothers.

Dr. Dickerson wrote a dissertation in 2011, *Diplomats, Soldiers, and Slaveholders*, that provides the most in-depth look at the life of Jumonville and the Villiers family. She quotes from François's 1777 petition but does not identify Damonville as the name of the unknown Villier brother killed along with his father and brother-in-law. She also makes no mention that it was Louis who was wounded in that same 1733 La Baye affair.

Misencik, in his 2014 book, *George Washington and the Half-King*, writes perhaps the most balanced view of the Jumonville and Fort Nessecity affairs, providing great detail of the many Frenchmen and Indians who played key roles in the lead up to both battles. Unfortunately, again, the background and detail of the Villiers brothers is lacking. We learn only that Jumonville has an "undistinguished military career," and that Louis is "perhaps the most distinguished warrior of the family." Misencik repeats that Louis is only a half-brother of Jumonville.

[2] Photograph courtesy the Archives de Montréal, Pièce P0817.

NOTES TO CHAPTER I. HEAD OF THE FAMILY

[3] Louis-Hector de Callière, or Callières, see page 157 for his Knight of Saint-Louis biography.

[4] Charles LeMoyne, first baron of Longueuil, Baron de Longueuil, see page 158 for his Knight of Saint-Louis biography.

[5] This reference is the *Registre des Insinuations*, which is translated literally as the *Register of Insinuations*. It has sometimes been translated as the *Registry of Inscriptions* or the *Gift Register*. It was an official record, required by law, and kept by the colonial government of New France to record gifts and donations between the elite families of Canada, Illinois, and Louisiana, particularly at the sealing of a marriage contract. The full title of this reference, which Gosselin unfortunately does not provide, likely is *Registre des insinuations de la prévôté de Québec*. It may also have been the *Registre des insinuations ecclésiastiques, Archives de l'Archevêché de Québec*. It also could be a reference to the *Registre des Insinuations du Conseil Souverain*.

[6] Philippe de Rigaud de Vaudreuil, Marquis de Vaudreuil, see page 158 for his Knight of Saint-Louis biography.

[7] Claude de Ramezay, see page 159 for his Knight of Saint-Louis biography.

[8] Jérôme Phélypeaux de Pontchartrain, served as the Secrétaire d'État de la Marine from 1699 to 1715. He was born in March 1674 and died February 8, 1747. Fort Pontchartrain in Detroit and Lake Pontchartrain in Louisiana were named for his father, Louis Phélypeaux de Pontchartrain. Charles Frostin, *Les Pontchartrain, ministres de Louis XIV : Alliances et réseau d'influence sous l'Ancien Régime* (Rennes, France: Presses universitaires de Rennes, 2006), 15-67.

[9] Étienne de Villedonné was esquire, captain in the colonial regular troops, and commandant at Fort St. Joseph, 1722 – 1726. He was born in Paris, *circa* 1666 and died in Quebec, May 12, 1726. Yves F. Zoltvany, "Villedonné, Étienne de," in *Dictionary of Canadian Biography* (hereafter cited as *DCB*), vol. 2, accessed May 21, 2017, http://www.biographi.ca/en/bio/villedonne_etienne_de_2E.html.

[10] Dickerson explains the typical inheritance in New France when a man died leaving a widow and children, where the former retained half the land and the latter split the other half. Of the children's portion, the eldest

son received half and the other children split the remainder. Dickerson, *Diplomats, Soldiers, and Slaveholders*, 17. A letter of enumeration dated Jan. 12, 1737, (BAnQ Québec, E1, S4, SS3, P256) details the living heirs of François Jarret de Verchères and provides an indication of how his property was dispersed to his widow and children:

> Confession and enumeration of Christophe-Hilarion Dulaurent (Du Laurent), in the name and as attorney of Lady Madeleine d'Ailleboust de Manthet, wife of Jean-Baptiste Jarret de Verchères, lieutenant in the troops of the detachment of Marines, commander at post of Michillimakinac, owner of half of the stronghold of Verchères, both in his name as eldest son and heir of François Jarret de Verchères, as Louis Jarret de Verchères, Joseph Jarret de Pouligny, Marie-Madeleine Jarret de Verchères, wife of Pierre-Thomas Tarieu de La Pérade (LaPérade), for the children of the late Angélique Jarret de Verchères, widow of Nicolas-Antoine Coulon de Villiers, and for Marguerite Jarret de Verchères, wife of Léon Levreau de Langy (Levrault de Langis) , which confession and enumeration is made for said fief of Verchères.

[11] Robert Groston de Saint-Ange was an officer in the colonial regular troops in the Illinois country. He was born at Châtillon-sur-Seine, diocese of Langres, province of Champagne, the son of Jean Groston and Marie Rebourceau. In 1692, he married Marguerite Crevier; she died in 1707. He later married Élisabeth, daughter of François Chorel de Saint-Romain, dit d'Orvilliers, and Marie-Anne Aubuchon. Saint-Ange died before June 1740. Saint-Ange cooperated with Nicolas-Antoine Coulon de Villiers, the father, in the 1730 siege of the Meskwaki. In 1740, his daughter married François Coulon de Villiers. Walter B. Douglas, "The Sieurs de St. Ange," *Transactions of the Illinois State History Society for the year 1909*, pub. 14 (Springfield, IL: State Journal Co., State Printers, 1910), 135-146.

[12] The Siege of the Fox occurred in present day McLean County, Illinois; Rhett Felix, "Siege of the Fox (Mesquakie)," *McLean County Museum of History*, accessed May 1, 2017, http://www.mchistory.org/research/fox-fort-site.php.

[13] Nicolas-Joseph de Noyelles de Fleurimont, see page 164 for his Knight of Saint-Louis biography.

[14] Charles Beauharnois de la Boische, Marquis de Beauharnois, see page 160 for his Knight of Saint-Louis biography.

[15] Jean-Frederic Phélypeaux, Count of Pontchartrain and Maurepas, minister of the Navy to Louis XV administering the navy, including the Troupes de Marine, the colonies and seaborne trade. Rule, "Jean-Frederic Phelypeaux, comte de Pontchartrain et Maurepas," 365-377.

[16] Jacques Testard de Montigny, see page 159 for his Knight of Saint-Louis biography.

[17] Jacques Legardeur de Saint-Pierre, see page 164 for his Knight of Saint-Louis biography.

[18] Gilles Hocquart was financial commissary and intendant of New France, born 1694 in the parish of Sainte-Croix, Mortagne-au-Perche, France, third of 14 children of Jean-Hyacinthe Hocquart and Marie-Françoise Michelet Du Cosnier. He married Aug. 23, 1750, Anne-Catherine de La Lande in Brest, France; the marriage was childless. He died April 1, 1783, at Paris. Hocquart served as Intendant of New France from 1729 to 1748. Donald J. Horton, "Hocquart, Gilles," in *DCB*, vol. 4, accessed May 21, 2017, http://www.biographi.ca/en/bio/hocquart_gilles_4E.html.

[19] Jean-Baptiste-René Legardeur de Repentigny was born on June 15, 1695, at Montréal. He married Marie-Catherine Juchereau de Saint-Denys in 1718. He was serving as commandant of Michilimackinac when he was killed with Coulon de Villiers on Sept. 16, 1733, at the Sauk village near La Baye. Association des familles Le Gardeur de Repentigny et de Tilly "Descendance de Jean-Baptiste-René Le Gardeur de Repentigny et de Marie-Catherine Juchereau de Saint-Denys" Salaberry-de-Valleyfield, Québec, accessed May 21, 2017, http://www.derepentigny.org/html/genealogie_1_gp_dr.html.

[20] Roy, "La Noblesse des Coulon de Villiers," 246-250.

NOTES TO CHAPTER II.
CHILDREN OF NICHOLAS ANT. COULON DE VILLIERS

[21] Din, "François Coulon de Villiers," 352.

[22] Ibid.

[23] Ibid.

[24] Ibid.

[25] Charles-Pierre Legardeur de Villiers was born in 1637 in Quebec, married first Marie Macard in 1663 and second Jeanne de Matras in 1669, and died 1684. He had one daughter by his second marriage, Marie-Charlotte Legardeur. François Marchi, "Sieur Charles Legardeur de Villiers (1637 - 1684)," *Généalogie Québec*, accessed May 21, 2017, http://genealogiequebec.info/testphp/info.php?no=63062.

[26] Din, "François Coulon de Villiers," 353.

[27] Archives nationales d'outre-mer (hereafter cited as ANOM), France, COL C11A, vol. 74, fol. 142. Pierre-Joseph Céloron de Blainville, see page 162 for his Knight of Saint-Louis biography.

[28] Pierre Du Jaunay was a Jesuit priest and missionary. He was born at Vannes, France, on either Aug. 11, 1704, or Aug. 10, 1705. He entered

the Jesuit order in Paris, and, following his ordination, he sailed for Canada in 1734. He ministered to the Ottawa Indians for nearly 30 years. Fr. Du Jaunay died on July 16, 1780, at Quebec. David A. Armour, "Du Jaunay, Pierre," in *DCB*, vol. 4, accessed Jan. 1, 2018, http://www.biographi.ca/en/bio/du_jaunay_pierre_4E.html.

29 Jacques Legardeur de Saint-Pierre, see page 164 for his Knight of Saint-Louis biography.

30 Daniel-Hyacinthe-Marie Liénard de Beaujeu was an officer in the colonial regular troops, seigneur, and entrepreneur. He was born Aug. 9, 1711, at Montreal, the son of Louis Liénard de Beaujeu and Thérèse-Denise Migeon de Branssat, and was killed in action near Fort Duquesne, July 9, 1755. Beaujeau kept a detailed journal during the 1746 – 1747 campaign in Acadia that climaxed at Grand Pré. Malcolm MacLeod, "Liénard de Beaujeu, Daniel-Hyacinthe-Marie," in *DCB*, vol. 3, accessed May 21, 2017, http://www.biographi.ca/en/bio/lienard_de_beaujeu_ daniel_hyacinthe_marie_3E.html.

NOTES TO CHAPTER III.
NICOLAS-ANTOINE COULON DE VILLIERS, THE SON

31 Louis-François de la Faye was a Sulpician priest and founder of the first boys' school at Montreal. He was born 1657 in Paris. He entered the order as a sub-deacon in 1684, was in New France the following year, and was consecrated a priest in Canada on Sept. 26, 1688. He served in various parishes in the Montreal area from 1691 to 1728. Fr. De la Faye died on July 6, 1729, at Montreal. Jean-Marc Paradis, "La Faye, Louis-François de," in *DCB*, vol. 2, accessed Jan. 1, 2018, http://www.biographi.ca/en/bio/la_faye_louis_francois_de_2E.html.

32 Joseph Jarret de Verchères de Pouligny was Angélique's youngest brother, born 1695, died on Sept. 27, 1753. He stood as godfather to his nephews, Nicholas-Antoine and Joseph (Jumonville) Coulon de Villers. See Roy, *La famille Jarret de Verchères*, 24.

33 Charles Beauharnois de la Boische, Marquis de Beauharnois, see page 160 for his Knight of Saint-Louis biography.

34 The Saulteaux were a branch of the Ojibwe tribe. Saulteaux was a French word meaning "people of the rapids," which referred to this band's former location at Sault Ste. Marie. They were also sometimes called Anishinaabe.

35 Peyser, *Ambush and Revenge*, 22.

36 Alexandre Dagneau Douville was an officer in the colonial regular troops, interpreter, and fur-trader. He was born in April or May 1698 at Sorel, Quebec, the son of Michel Dagneau Douville and Marie Lamy. In 1730, he married Marie, daughter of Nicolas-Antoine Coulon de Villiers

and Angélique Jarret de Verchères. Dagneau Douville died in 1774 at Verchères, Quebec. Donald Chaput, "Dagneau Douville, Alexandre," in *DCB*, vol. 4, accessed May 21, 2017, http://www.biographi.ca/en/bio/dagneau_douville_alexandre_4E.html.

[37] Jean-Baptiste-Nicolas-Roch de Ramezay, see page 163 for his Knight of Saint-Louis biography.

[38] Claude-Antoine de Bermen de La Martinière, see page 165 for his Knight of Saint-Louis biography.

[39] Jacques-Pierre Daneau de Muy, see page 166 for his Knight of Saint-Louis biography.

[40] Paul-Louis Dazemard de Lusignan, see page 165 for his Knight of Saint-Louis biography.

[41] ANOM, France, COL C11A, vol. 75, fol. 174-181v. An English translation of Beauharnois's letter is provided in *Collections of the State Historical Society of Wisconsin*, vol, 17, 360-366.

[42] Richard Testu de La Richardière was a navigator, naval officer, and port captain of Quebec. Born on April 15, 1681, at L'Ange-Gardien, Quebec, he was the son of Pierre Testu Du Tilly, a merchant, and Geneviève Rigault. He married first on July 22, 1709, at Quebec Marie Hurault, and secondly on Oct. 17, 1727, also at Quebec Madeleine-Marie-Anne Tarieu de La Pérade. De La Richardière died on Oct. 24, 1741, at Quebec without children. James S. Pritchard, "Testu de La Richardière, Richard," in *DCB*, vol. 3, accessed May 21, 2017, http://www.biographi.ca/en/bio/testu_de_la_richardiere_richard_3E.html.

[43] Joseph de Fleury de La Gorgendière was a merchant, seigneur, and an agent-general in Canada for the Compagnie des Indes. He was born April 9, 1676, at Quebec, the son of Jacques-Alexis de Fleury Deschambault and Marguerite de Chavigny de Berchereau. He married on May 11, 1702, Claire, daughter of Louis Jolliet. La Gorgendière died May 1, 1755, at Quebec. Andrew Rodger, "Fleury de La Gorgendière, Joseph de," in *DCB*, vol. 3, accessed Jan. 2, 2018, http://www.biographi.ca/en/bio/fleury_de_la_gorgendiere_joseph_de_3E.html.

[44] Pierre-Thomas Tarieu de la Pérade was an officer in the colonial regular troops and a seigneur. He married the celebrated Marie-Madeleine Jarret de Verchères in Sept. 1706. He outlived his wife by nearly ten years. Tarieu de La Pérade was buried at Sainte-Anne-de-la-Pérade on Jan. 26, 1757. André Vachon, "Jarret de Verchères, Marie-Madeleine," *DCB*, vol. 3, accessed Jan. 2, 2018, http://www.biographi.ca/en/bio/jarret_de_vercheres_marie_madeleine_3E.html.

[45] Joseph-André-Mathurin Jacrau was a parish priest, procurator of the seminary of Quebec, and promoter of justice in the diocesan tribunal. He was born about 1698 in the diocese of Angers, France. He is known to have prepared the nominal census of Quebec and its suburbs which was begun on Sept. 15, 1740. Jacrau died July 23, 1772, in Quebec. Honorius Provost, "Jacrau, Joseph-André-Mathurin," in *DCB*, vol. 4, accessed Jan.

2, 2018, http://www.biographi.ca/en/bio/jacrau_joseph_andre_mathurin_4E.html.

⁴⁶ Pierre-Roch de Saint-Ours des Chaillons, see page 169 for his Knight of Saint-Louis biography.

⁴⁷ Ignace-Philippe Aubert de Gaspé. His name is sometimes shown as Philippe-Ignace. See page 171 for his Knight of Saint-Louis biography.

⁴⁸ Jean-Baptiste-Nicolas-Roch de Ramezay, see page 163 for his Knight of Saint-Louis biography.

⁴⁹ Daniel-Hyacinthe-Marie Liénard de Beaujeu, see note 30.

⁵⁰ Jean-Baptiste-Louis-Frédéric de La Rochefoucauld de Roye, Marquis de Roucy, Duc d'Anville, was a naval officer, He was born on Aug. 17, 1709, the son of Louis de La Rochefoucauld, Marquis de Roye, lieutenant-general of the galleys, and Marthe Ducasse. He married on Feb. 28, 1732, Marie-Louise-Nicole de La Rochefoucauld, by whom he had a son and two daughters. Duc d'Anville died Sept. 27, 1746, at Chebucto, Halifax, Nova Scotia, and was buried on George Island in the port of Halifax, then at Louisbourg, Île Royale, Cape Breton Island, and finally in France. Étienne Taillemite, "La Rochefoucauld de Roye, Jean-Baptiste-Louis-Frédéric de, Marquis de Roucy, Duc d'Anville," in *DCB*, vol. 3, accessed May 21, 2017, http://www.biographi.ca/en/bio/la_rochefoucauld_de_roye_jean_baptiste_louis_frederic_de_3E.html.

⁵¹ Arthur Noble was a merchant and a military officer. Family tradition indicates that he was born at Enniskiller, County Fermanagh, Ulster, Ireland, and came to the English colonies circa 1720 with two brothers. He was commissioned Feb. 5, 1745, by Governor Shirley, a Lieutenant Colonel of the Second Massachusetts Regiment, also serving as Captain of the 2d Company. Noble was killed at Grand Pré, Nova Scotia, Jan. 31, 1747. Goold, *Col. Arthur Noble, of Georgetown*, 114-136.

⁵² Pierre Maillard, who was sometimes called Pierre-Antoine-Simon, was priest of the Missions Étrangères and a missionary. He was born about 1710 in France, in the diocese of Chartres, and died Aug. 12, 1762, in Halifax, Nova Scotia. Micheline D. Johnson, "Maillard, Pierre," in *DCB*, vol. 3, accessed May 21, 2017, http://www.biographi.ca/en/bio/maillard_pierre _3E.html.

⁵³ Pierre-Jean-Baptiste-François-Xavier Legardeur de Repentigny, see page 167 for his Knight of Saint-Louis biography.

⁵⁴ Cadet Lusignan was the youngest son of Paul-Louis Dazemard de Lusignan, see note 204.

⁵⁵ Louis de La Corne, Chevalier de La Corne, see page 164 for his Knight of Saint-Louis biography.

⁵⁶ Henri-Marie Dubreil de Pontbriand was the sixth bishop of Quebec. He was born in Vannes, France, probably in Jan. 1708, the son of Joseph-Yves Dubreil, Comte de Pontbriand, captain of coastguards in the bishopric of Saint-Malo, and Angélique-Sylvie Marot de La Garaye. Msgr. de Pontbriand died June 8, 1760, at Montreal. Jean-Guy Lavallée, "Dubreil

de Pontbriand, Henri-Marie," in *DCB*, vol. 3, accessed May 21, 2017, http://www.biographi.ca/en/bio/dubreil_de_pontbriand_henri_marie_3E.html.

⁵⁷ Roland-Michel Barrin de La Galissonnière, marquis de La Galissonnière, see page 162 for his Knight of Saint-Louis biography.

⁵⁸ Jacques-Pierre de Taffanel de La Jonquière, see page 160 for his Knight of Saint-Louis biography.

⁵⁹ François Bigot was the financial commissary of Île Royale and intendant of New France. He was baptized on Jan. 30, 1703, in the parish of Saint-André, Bordeaux, France, the son of Louis-Amable Bigot and Marguerite Lombard. Bigot died on Jan. 12, 1778, at Neuchâtel, Switzerland. J. F. Bosher and J.-C. Dubé, "Bigot, François (d. 1778)," in *DCB*, vol. 4, accessed May 21, 2017, http://www.biographi.ca/en/bio/bigot_francois_1778_4E.html.

⁶⁰ Jean-François Gaultier was a physician and naturalist. He was born Oct. 6, 1708, at La Croix-Avranchin, department of Manche, France, the son of René Gaultier and Françoise Colin. Gaultier died on July 10, 1756, in Quebec. Bernard Boivin, "Gaultier, Jean-François," in *DCB*, vol. 3, accessed May 21, 2017, http://www.biographi.ca/en/bio/gaultier_jean_francois_3E.html.

Notes to Chapter IV. Joseph Coulon De Villiers

⁶¹ Joseph Jarret de Verchères de Pouligny, see note 32.

⁶² Antoine-Louis Rouillé, Count of Jouy, was born in Paris on June 7, 1689, and died in Neuilly on Sept. 20, 1761. He was Secretary of State of the Navy (1749-1754) and then French Minister of Foreign Affairs (1754-1757). Christy L. Pichichero, *The Military Enlightenment: War and Culture in the French Empire from Louis XIV to Napoleon* (Ithaca: Cornell University Press, 2017), 35.

⁶³ Edouard Richard, *Supplement to Dr. Brymner's Report on Canadian Archives*, 25.

⁶⁴ Pierre-Paul Marin de La Malgue, see page 165 for his Knight of Saint-Louis biography.

⁶⁵ Jean-Baptiste-Nicolas-Roch de Ramezay, see page 163 for his Knight of Saint-Louis biography.

⁶⁶ Corlar is a French reference to the city of Schenectady, New York, see Charlevoix, *History and General Description of New France*, vol. 5, 166. Peyser lists French names for Schenectady as Corlac, Corlear, and Corlar, see *On the Eve of Conquest*, 52.

⁶⁷ Louis de La Corne, Chevalier de La Corne, see page 164 for his Knight of Saint-Louis biography.

⁶⁸ O'Callaghan, ed., *Colonial History of New York*, 164 and 168. Joseph Hertel de Saint-François was a cadet with the colonial regular troops.

He was born on Oct. 19, 1732, at Saint-François-du-Lac, Quebec, the eldest son Joseph Hertel de Saint-François and Suzanne Blondeau. He was fifteen years old when he was killed in June 1748 while serving under Villiers de Jumonville. The *Seasonal Papers,* vol. 5, records that Cadet Hertel's father related the details of his son's death in a July 1748 letter to the Minister:

> Killed in his sixth incursion into the enemy's country. The Abenakis, who were most conversant with the facts as to his fate assured me in the presence of Rev. Père Aubry, that being unwilling to abandon an Iroquois comrade who was killed beside him and whom he could not remove from the field of battle, though the risk was pointed out to him, he received a gunshot wound in the upper part of left thigh, under which he merely stooped. He then sprung up again and fired at his enemy, and while the blood flowed freely from his wound, attempted to reload his weapon. While so doing he received a second wound in the body and fell to the ground. Shortly afterwards he was heard to cry out, like one who has received a dangerous wound, and then he uttered a smothered cry, which he was unable to finish. Inasmuch as he was surrounded at the time by English Indians, the Abenakis conclude that his head was cut off at that moment, for the enemy shouted their death cry over him.

[69] Roland-Michel Barrin de La Galissonnière, marquis de La Galissonnière, see page 162 for his Knight of Saint-Louis biography.

[70] Peyser, *Ambush and Revenge,* 4.

[71] Charles Beauharnois de la Boische, see page 160 for his Knight of Saint-Louis biography.

[72] Jean-Baptiste-Marie Blaise Des Bergères de Rigauville was an officer in the colonial regular troops. He was born Oct. 28, 1720, at Berthier-sur-Mer, Quebec, the son of Nicolas Blaise de Bergères de Rigauville, commandant of Fort Niagara, and Marie-Françoise Viennay-Pachot, widow of Alexandre Berthier. He married on Nov. 7, 1751, at Fort-de-la-Présentation, Ontario, Louise-Suzanne Céloron, daughter of Louis-Jean-Baptiste Céloron and Suzanne Piot de Langloiserie. Rigauville was captured on Nov. 3, 1775, during the American invasion of Quebec while serving as a militia officer. He died in captivity in Bristol, Pennsylvania, on Oct. 30, 1776. "Jean-Baptiste-Marie Blaise des Bergères de Rigauville," *Assemblée nationale du Québec,* accessed Jan. 3, 2018, http://www.assnat.qc.ca/fr/patrimoine/anciens-parlementaires/blaise-des-bergeres-de-rigauville-jean-baptiste-marie-939.html.

[73] Charles LeMoyne de Longueuil, second Baron de Longueuil, see page 161 for his Knight of Saint-Louis biography.

74 Peyser, *Ambush and Revenge*, 5. Peyser's source for this information was a letter from Bigot to the minister on May 8, 1752.

75 The Belle-Riviere comprised the Ohio and Allegheny Rivers. It translates literally as the Beautiful River. The French name may have had its origins from the Lenape tribe who called the Allegheny River the oolikhana or beautiful stream.

76 Ange Duquesne de Menneville, Marquis Duquesne, see page 162 for his Knight of Saint-Louis biography.

77 Claude-Pierre Pécaudy de Contrecoeur, see page 167 for his Knight of Saint-Louis biography.

78 Robert Dinwiddie was the Lieutenant Governor of the Royal Colony of Virginia from 1751 to 1758. He was born in 1692 and died in 1770. Dinwiddie was also a share holder in the Ohio Company of Virginia that sought to settle land along the southern portion of the Ohio River. John H. Zimmerman, "Robert Dinwiddie," *George Washington's Mount Vernon*, accessed Jan. 3, 2018, http://www.mountvernon.org/digital-encyclopedia/article/robert-dinwiddie/

79 Jacques Le Gardeur de Saint-Pierre, see page 164 for his Knight of Saint-Louis biography.

80 François-Marc-Antoine Le Mercier, see page 168 for his Knight of Saint-Louis biography.

81 Washington did not begin to construct a fort at Great Meadows until after the Jumonville affair. Up to that point the Virginia colonials were only encamped at Great Meadows. On May 30, 1754, two days after attacking the Jumonville party, Washington wrote in his journal, "Began to raise a Fort with small Pallisadoes, fearing that when the French should hear the news of that Defeat, we might be attacked by considerable Forces." Twohig, *George Washington's Diaries*, 52.

82 Pierre-Jacques Druillon de Macé was an officer in the colonial regular troops. He was baptized Sept. 9, 1727, in the parish of Saint-Solenne at Blois, France, the son of Pierre-Jacques Druillon, lieutenant-general for the bailiwick of Blois, and Marie Bachaddelebat. He married in 1769 Marie-Anne Petit de Thoizy at Blois. Druillon died there June 26, 1780. He was wounded and captured by George Washington during the Jumonville affair. F. J. Thorpe, "Druillon de Macé, Pierre-Jacques," in *DCB*, vol. 4, accessed May 21, 2017, http://www.biographi.ca/en/bio/druillon_de_mace_pierre_jacques_ 4E.html.

83 Historians accept that only one Candian escaped from the Jumonville party and returned to Fort Duquesne, as reported by Contrecoeur to Duquesne on June 2, 1754: "One of the Party, *Monceau* by Name, a *Canadian*, made his Escape;" *A Memorial Containing a Summary View of Facts*, 120.

84 For the Washington quotes that Gosselin provides, I have quoted the English translation of Washington's journal from *A Memorial, Containing A Summary View of Facts*, 148 and 151.

85 Gaspard-Joseph Chaussegros de Léry, see page 170 for his Knight of Saint-Louis biography.

86 Tanaghrisson, Tanacharisson, or Thaninhison was known by the British as the Half-King and was their primary ally among the Seneca in the Ohio valley. Léry's journal entry details an account that Tanaghrisson was born a Catawba, or flathead, and was captured as a child and later adopted by the Senaca. He was the leading chief among the Mingo warriors in the Ohio, with authority over them, but with no authority to make treaties on behalf of the Iroquois confederacy, thus, the English title Half-King. William A. Hunter, "Tanaghrisson," in *DCB*, vol. 3, accessed May 23, 2017, http://www.biographi.ca/en/bio/tanaghrisson_3E.html.

87 Léry, *Journal of Chaussegros de Léry*, 19.

88 Jean-Pierre Bachoue de Barraute. Fauteux, "Quelques officiers de Montcalm," 525-529, records of him :

> Was a captain in the 2nd battalion of Béarn when he embarked at Brest on *L'Opiniâtre*, April 8, 1755. He was made lieutenant in 1732, and captain in 1739. On July 16, 1747, he was made Knight of Saint-Louis, after Mazas who named him on this occasion Mssr. de Barante....
>
> He took part in the battle of Ste-Foy April 28, 1760, and came out unscathed; it was only on May 12 that he received at the camp of Quebec the mortal wound. His case seemed at first not serious. On May 13, the Chevalier de Lévis announced the news to Mssr. de Vaudreuil in these terms: "Mssr. Barod was wounded yesterday slightly with a bomb burst," and the 15th, he writes again: "Mssr. Barod well enough, from his injury, there is no accident." The wounded man was none the less seriously affected and died on May 21, 1760, at the General Hospital.

89 The Régiment of Béarn was established in 1684 and recruited from the Béarn province of France. At the onset of hostilities in the Americas, the regiment was sent to New France in June 1755. See Summers and Chartrand, "History of Le Regiment de Bearn."

90 François de Lévis, Duc de Lévis, was an army officer. He was born Aug. 20, 1719, at the Château d'Ajac, near Limoux, France, son of Jean de Lévis, Baron d'Ajac, and Jeanne-Marie de Maguelonne. The Marquis de Lévis died Nov. 26, 1787, at Arras, France. W. J. Eccles, "Lévis, François de, Duc de Lévis," in *DCB*, vol. 4, accessed May 21, 2017, http://www.biographi.ca/en/bio/levis_francois_de_4E.html.

91 Nicolas-René Berryer, Count de La Ferrière, seigneur de Ravenoville, near Valognes, was a French magistrate and politician born in Paris on March 24, 1703. He served as lieutenant-general of police (1747-1757), Secretary of State of the Navy (1758-1761), and Keeper of the Seals of France (1761-1762) during the reign of Louis XV. He married in 1738

Catherine-Madeleine, daughter of Gabriel Jorts, seigneur de Fribois, and Catherine Marguerite de Vougny. Berryer died at Versailles on Aug. 15, 1762. Père Anselme de Guibours, *Histoire de la Maison royale de France*, vol. 9, part 2 (Paris: Editions du Palais Royal, Première réimpression, 1968), 467-468.

[92] Pierre de Rigaud de Vaudreuil de Cavagnial, Marquis de Vaudreuil, see page 161 for his Knight of Saint-Louis biography.

[93] The spelling of the last name in the source document is *Baraute*.

[94] Roy, "La Descendance de Coulon de Jumonville," 256-259.

[95] Roy spelled the last name *Barraute* in his quote; Gosselin spelled the name *Barrante* quoting the same text. The source that both authors cite spelled it *Baraute*. Fauteux, "Quelques officiers de Montcalm," 528, "The name of our officer is written in various ways in the documents of the time. The extract from the boarding journal at Brest, says Barotte; Barot, Baraute, and even Barod are read elsewhere in the Letters of the Chevalier de Lévis."

[96] Ibid.

[97] Gallifet, "Villiers de Jumonville. Capitaine tué au Canada. 1775, pension pour ses filles," *Library and Archives Canada* (Aug. 12, 1775); Fauteux, "Quelques officiers de Montcalm," 527.

NOTES TO CHAPTER V. LOUIS COULON DE VILLIERS

[98] Pierre Odet de Piercot de Bailleul, dit Bailleul Canut, see page 172 for his Knight of Saint-Louis biography.

[99] "Troupes des colonies, Canada et Ile Royale," *Compagnies détachées 1737-1771*, Library and Archives Canada, Online MIKAN no. 2460249, Nov. 1751, and no. 2460273, Oct. 1754, accessed May 20, 2017, http://collectionscanada.gc.ca/pam_archives/index.php?fuseaction= genitem.displayItem&rec_nbr=2460273&lang=eng&rec_nbr_list= 2460273. These rolls are described as, "The present state of the troops maintained by his majesty in Canada."

[100] Louis Audet-Pierrecot (or Louis-Odet Piercot), Sieur de Bailleul, was an officer in the colonial regular troops. He was born at Bourg-Beaudoin, France, about 1674, the son of Pierre de Piercot and Marie-Anne Guillemette. He immigrated to Quebec, Canada, in 1696 and there married his first wife, Madeleine Chrétien, on June 19, 1702. He married his second wife, Marie-Anne Trottier, daughter of Catherine Lefebvre and Sieur Antoine Trottier des Ruisseaux, on Feb. 14, 1712, in Quebec; they had seven children. In addition to being Louis Coulon de Villiers's godfather, his son, Pierre Odet de Piercot de Bailleul, dit Bailleul Canut, served under Coulon de Villier's command at the Battle of Fort Necessity. Audet-Pierrecot died

on Dec. 8, 1738, in Verchères, Quebec. François Marchi, "Louis Audet Pierrecot de Bailleul (1674 - 1738)," *Généalogie Québec*, accessed May 21, 2017, http://genealogiequebec.info/testphp/info.php?no=16106.

[101] Peyser, *Letters from New France*, 210.

[102] Peyser, *Ambush and Revenge*, 17, 22 & 27. Peyser provides a copy of the original certificate and his own translation with the following notation, "Attestation of Surgeon Major Joseph Benoist, Montreal, June 10, 1734, AN Col., C11A61:214. I am grateful to Joseph G. Piroch, M.D. of Foxburg, Pennsylvania for his analysis of Benoist's description of the wound, permitting me to translate it into modern colloquial English."

[103] Charles Beauharnois de la Boische, see page 160 for his Knight of Saint-Louis biography.

[104] Gilles Hocquart, see note 18.

[105] Peyser, *Letters from New France*, 150.

[106] Jacques-Pierre Daneau de Muy, see page 166 for his Knight of Saint-Louis biography.

[107] Pierre-Joseph Céloron de Blainville, see page 162 for his Knight of Saint-Louis biography.

[108] Paul LeBorgne, see page 172 for his Knight of Saint-Louis biography.

[109] Céloron de Blainville, "Celoron's Journal," 14-15.

[110] Jacques-Pierre de Taffanel de La Jonquière, see page 160 for his Knight of Saint-Louis biography.

[111] Jacques-François Le Gardeur de Croisille de Courtemanche, see page 171 for his Knight of Saint-Louis biography.

[112] Claude-Pierre Pécaudy de Contrecoeur, see page 167 for his Knight of Saint-Louis biography.

[113] Daniel-Marie Chabert de Joncaire, sieur de Clausonne, was an officer in the colonial regular troops, an Indian agent, and an interpreter. He was baptized on Jan. 6, 1714, at Repentigny, Quebec, the son of Louis-Thomas Chabert de Joncaire and Marie-Madeleine Le Gay de Beaulieu. He married Marguerite-Élisabeth-Ursule Rocbert de La Morandière on Jan. 19, 1751, at Montreal. Joncaire Chaber, as he signed his name, constructed little Niagara fort or Fort du Portage, about a mile and a half above the falls. Its purpose was to intercept furs that might otherwise be traded with the British at Oswego. He commanded at the new post and was subsequently given a monopoly on the portage traffic. Chabert was among the officers who signed the surrender of Fort Niagara in 1759. Joncaire Chaber was buried July 5, 1771, at Detroit. In collaboration with Walter S. Dunn Jr, "Chabert de Joncaire de Clausonne, Daniel-Marie," in *DCB*, vol. 4, accessed January 4, 2018, http://www.biographi.ca/en/bio/chabert_de_joncaire_de_clausonne_daniel_marie_4E.html.

[114] Peyser, *Letters from New France*, 210. This letter is provided in its entirety in appendix I.

115 François-Josué de La Corne, Sieur Dubreuil, was baptized on October 7, 1710. He was commanding at Kaministiquia as ensign in 1743, and was recommended for a lieutenancy in that year, the rank he held at the time of his death. He was the son of Jean-Louis de La Corne de Chaptes and a brother of Louis de La Corne, Chevalier de La Corne and Luc de La Corne. La Corne died October 18, 1753, in Quebec after becoming seriously ill during Paul Marin de La Malgue's 1753 expedition to the Ohio valley. François-Josué de La Corne is sometimes erroneously listed as a Knight of Saint-Louis; the recipient was a nephew of the same name. Pease and Jenison, *Illinois on the Eve of the Seven Years' War 1747-1755*, 224.

116 Ibid.

117 Ange Duquesne de Menneville, Marquis Duquesne, see page 162 for his Knight of Saint-Louis biography.

118 Gaspard-Joseph Chaussegros de Léry, see page 170 for his Knight of Saint-Louis biography.

119 Paul-Joseph LeMoyne de Longueuil, Chevalier de Longueuil, see page 163 for his Knight of Saint-Louis biography.

120 Joseph-Michel Le Gardeur de Croisille et de Montesson, see page 171 for his Knight of Saint-Louis biography.

121 Joseph-Dominique-Emmanuel LeMoyne de Longueuil, was an army and militia officer, a seigneur, and politician. He was born April 2, 1738, in the seigneury of Soulanges, Quebec, the son of Paul-Joseph LeMoyne de Longueuil, known as the Chevalier de Longueuil, and Marie-Geneviève Joybert de Soulanges. De Longueuil died Jan. 19, 1807, in Montreal, Lower Canada. Gérald Pelletier, "Le Moyne de Longueuil, Joseph-Dominique-Emmanuel," in *DCB*, vol. 5, accessed May 21, 2017, http://www.biographi.ca/en/bio/le_moyne_de_longueuil_joseph_dominique_emmanuel_5E.html.

122 Michel-Jean-Hugues Péan, see page 166 for his Knight of Saint-Louis biography.

123 Léry, *Journal of Chaussegros de Léry*, 17-18.

124 Claude-Antoine Drouet de Carqueville was born in 1715. He served as an ensign in the campaigns of 1746–1747 when he led groups of Indians against British posts near Fort St. Frédéric and Saratoga on the New York frontier. He married Marguerite de Couagne in Montreal in 1747. Drouet de Carqueville died of wounds received during the Battle of the Monongahela and was buried at Fort Duquesne. Preston, *Braddock's Defeat*, 135, 147, 156, 264 & 345.

125 François-Marc-Antoine Le Mercier, see page 168 for his Knight of Saint-Louis biography.

126 James Mackay was born about 1718 in Sutherland, Scotland. He served in Ogelthorpe's regiment in the Georgia Colony during the War of Jenkins' Ear, and then commanded one of two British Independent companies stationed in the colony of South Carolina as a captain in the British regulars. He was ordered on May 4, 1754, to the Virginia colony with his

company to aide in the Expedition to the Ohio. He linked up with George Washington at Great Meadows in early June and fought at Fort Necessity. His was the first signature on the capitulation signed on July 3. Mackay died in 1785 in Alexandria, Virginia. Harden, "James Mackay, of Strathy Hall," 85, 94 & 96.

127 La rivière Malengueulée, Mal-engueulée, or Manangaîlé were French spellings for the Monongahela River, which was derived from an Amerindian word for "the banks that collapse."

128 François Bigot, see note 59.

129 This likely is a reference to François-Clément Boucher de la Perrière. He was an officer in the colonial regular troops. Born on April 23, 1708, at Montreal, Quebec, he was the son of René Boucher de Perrière and Marie-Francoise Mailhot. He married on Jan. 21, 1737, at Montreal Charlotte Pécaudy de Contrecoeur, daughter of Antoine de Pécaudy and Jeanne Saint-Ours. Boucher de la Perrière may have been a Knight of Saint-Louis, as Fauteux wrote:

> There is still Francois Clement Boucher de la Perriere who died at the General Hospital of Quebec on September 17, 1759, after being mortally wounded at the head of his company at the Battle of the Plains of Abraham. His act of burial in the register of the General Hospital says the Chevalier de Saint-Louis. Despite this prima facie case, and despite his glorious death, I firmly believe that François-Clément Boucher de la Perrière never had the cross, and that is why I thought I should omit him in the Knights' List of Canada.

130 Antoine-Gabriel-François Benoist, see page 173 for his Knight of Saint-Louis biography. Benoist was appointed in 1752 commandant of Fort of the Lake of the Two Mountains, and the following year he was sent to participate in Paul Marin de La Malgue's expedition to the Ohio valley. In 1754, he was posted to command Fort de La Présentation; he replaced Alexandre Dagneau Douville at Fort Presque Isle in 1755. Étienne Taillemite, "Benoist, Antoine-Gabriel-François," in *DCB*, vol. 4, accessed Jan. 8, 2018, http://www.biographi.ca/en/bio/benoist_antoine_gabriel_francois_4E.html.

131 Major General William Shirley was a 61-year-old British officer when he led his campaign in 1755 – 1756 following General Braddock's defeat.

132 Pierre de Rigaud de Vaudreuil de Cavagnial, Marquis de Vaudreuil, see page 161 for his Knight of Saint-Louis biography.

133 Louis-Joseph de Montcalm, Marquis de Montcalm, was seigneur of Saint-Veran, Candiac, Tournemine, Vestric, Saint-Julien, and Arpaon, Baron de Gabriac, and a lieutenant-general. He was born at Candiac, France, Feb. 28, 1712, the son of Louis-Daniel de Montcalm and Marie-

Thérèse-Charlotte de Lauris de Castellane. He served as maréchal de camp from 1755 to 1759. Montcalm died at Quebec Sept. 14, 1759, after he was mortally wounded during the retreat from the Plains of Abraham. W. J. Eccles, "Montcalm, Louis-Joseph de, Marquis de Montcalm," in *DCB*, vol. 3, accessed May 21, 2017, http://www.biographi.ca/en/bio/ montcalm_louis_ joseph_de_3E.html.

134 Jacob Van Braam was born April 1, 1729, at Bergen Op Zoom, Netherlands. He served with Lawrence Washington on the 1741 Carthagena Expedition in the War of Jenkins' Ear. He served as a Virginia colonial captain during George Washington's 1754 expedition to the Ohio valley. In addition to his native Dutch, he spoke some French and English and served as a translator during the surrender of Fort Necessity. He was widely blamed by both Washington and Dinwiddie for mistranslating "l'assassinat" and unwittingly, or worse, purposefully, causing Washington to admit in writing that he was responsible for assassinating Jumonville. Van Braam was held as a prisoner in Montreal until that city was captured by the British in 1760. He was tried for treason in Virginia but acquitted due to the rain-soaked and ink-smudged surrender document and his poor English skills. Rather than being convicted, he was awarded £500 and 9,000 acres of land as compensation for his six years of captivity and recommended for promotion to major. Van Braam died Aug. 7, 1792, at Charleville-Mézières, France. Nolan, Kiera E. "Lawrence Washington." In The Digital Encyclopedia of George Washington, http://www.mount vernon.org/digital-encyclopedia/article/jacob-van-braam/.

135 Robert Stobo, was a Virginia colonial military officer. He was born in Glasgow, Scotland, on Oct. 7, 1726, the son of William Stobo, a well-to-do merchant. He was given as a hostage by George Washington to Louis Coulon de Villiers at Fort Necessity. Coulon de Villiers interacted with Stobo while that officer was confined at Fort Duquesne through the remainder of July and later when he was confined in Montreal. De Villiers was later called to testify in Stobo's trial, in which the latter was convicted of spying and sentenced to death. The death sentence was never carried out, and Stobo later escaped captivity and eventually returned to Virginia where he was hailed as a hero and promoted to major. Stobo died a bachelor on June 19, 1770, at Chatham, England. See Alberts, *The Most Extraordinary Adventures of Robert Stobo*, and Stobo, *Memoirs of Major Robert Stobo of the Virginia Regiment*.

136 Luc de La Corne, also known as La Corne Saint-Luc, see page 169 for his Knight of Saint-Louis biography.

137 François-Pierre de Rigaud de Vaudreuil, see page 161 for his Knight of Saint-Louis biography.

138 François Marie Peyrenc de Moras, served as Secretary of State of the Navy, or Minister of the Marine, from 1757 to 1758. For six months he served the dual role of France's controller general of finances, enabling

him to approve all military expenses he deemed necessary. A. J. B. Johnston, *Endgame 1758: The Promise, the Glory, and the Despair of Louisbourg's Last Decade* (University of Nebraska Press, 2007), 115 – 116.

139 Christophe Sabrevois de Sermonville, see page 168 for his Knight of Saint-Louis biography.

140 Antoine de La Corne la Colombière, see page 168 for his Knight of Saint-Louis biography.

141 Pierre-Jean-Baptiste-François-Xavier Legardeur de Repentigny, see page 167 for his Knight of Saint-Louis biography.

142 François-Charles de Bourlamaque was a French army officer and governor of Guadeloupe. He was born in 1716 at Paris, France.

> In 1756 the court of Versailles reinforced New France and sent out new commanders for the troops there. The Marquis de Montcalm was promoted major-general (maréchal de camp) and dispatched to take command of the regular force; the Chevalier de Lévis was made brigadier and second in command. Bourlamaque, who was still at this time captain and adjutant (capitaine aide-major) in the Régiment du Dauphin, was commissioned as colonel of infantry in Canada (11 March 1756) and thus became third in command. At the same time he received the cross of Saint-Louis.
>
> Bourlamaque played a prominent part in the campaign of 1757 on the Lac Saint-Sacrement (Lake George) front. In the spring he was placed in command on this frontier. When the main French army invested Fort William Henry (also called Fort George; now Lake George, N.Y.) in the first week of August he was again charged by Montcalm with the direction of the siege. The place surrendered on the 9th, the capitulation being followed by an Indian massacre of prisoners. Montcalm was unable to follow up the victory, and the season ended with Bourlamaque standing on the defensive at the head of Lake Champlain with two regular battalions, working on the fort at Carillon (Ticonderoga, N.Y.)

Bourlamaque died the night of June 23–24, 1764, at Guadeloupe. C. P. Stacey, "Bourlamaque, François-Charles de," in *DCB*, vol. 3, accessed May 21, 2017, http://www.biographi.ca/en/bio/bourlamaque_francois_charles_de_3E.html.

143 François de Lévis, Duc de Lévis, see note 90.

144 Jean-Félix Récher was a parish priest and author of a diary of events at Quebec from 1757 to 1760. He was born in 1724, likely in the diocese of Rouen, France. Récher died March 16, 1768, in Quebec. Jean-

Pierre Asselin, "Récher, Jean-Félix," in *DCB*, vol. 3, accessed Jan. 8, 2018, http://www.biographi.ca/en/bio/recher_jean_felix_3E.html.

[145] Fauteux, "Quelques officiers de Montcalm," 524-525.

[146] Jean-Bernard Bossu was a French officer, adventurer, explorer and author. He was born on Sept. 29, 1720, at Baigneux-Les-Juifs, France. His works include: *Nouveaux Voyages aux Indes Occidentales*, Paris, 1768; *Nouveaux voyage dans l'Amérique septentrionale*, Amsterdam, 1777; *Nouveaux Voyages en Louisiane 1751–1768*, Paris, 1994.

NOTES TO CHAPTER VI. FRANÇOIS COULON DE VILLIERS

[147] See note 99, and the text that it annotates, regarding Chev. Villiers on the rolls of Canadian troops.

[148] Charles Beauharnois de la Boische, see page 160 for his Knight of Saint-Louis biography.

[149] Gilles Hocquart, see note 18.

[150] Peyser, *Ambush and Revenge*, 22; Peyser, *Letters from New France*, 210; Din, "François Coulon de Villiers," 352.

[151] Ibid, 353. François wrote in 1777, "In the year 1736, I was appointed sublieutenant in Louisiana."

[152] Jean-Baptiste LeMoyne de Bienville, see page 159 for his Knight of Saint-Louis biography.

[153] Jacques-Pierre Daneau de Muy, see page 166 for his Knight of Saint-Louis biography.

[154] Din, "François Coulon de Villiers," 352. Peyser, *Ambush and Revenge*, 23.

[155] Jean-Baptiste-Philippe Testard de Montigny, see page 173 for his Knight of Saint-Louis biography.

[156] Jean-Victor Varin de La Marre was commissary and controller of the Marine, subdelegate of the intendant, and councillor of the Conseil Supérieur of Quebec. He was born Aug. 14, 1699, at Niort, France, the son of Jean Varin de La Sablonnière, an infantry officer. Varin died sometime between 1780 and 1786, probably at Malesherbes, France. André Lachance, "Varin de La Marre, Jean-Victor," in *DCB*, vol. 4, accessed May 21, 2017, http://www.biographi.ca/en/bio/varin_de_la_marre_jean_victor_4E.html.

[157] Claude-Pierre Pécaudy de Contrecoeur, see page 167 for his Knight of Saint-Louis biography.

[158] Pierre de Rigaud de Vaudreuil de Cavagnial, Marquis de Vaudreuil, see page 161 for his Knight of Saint-Louis biography.

[159] James Mackay, see note 126.

[160] Din, "François Coulon de Villiers," 353-354.

[161] Jean-Daniel Dumas, see page 166 for his Knight of Saint-Louis biography.

162 Louis Billouart de Kerlérec was the French governor of Louisiana from 1753 to 1763. He was born on June 26, 1704, at Quimper, France, the son of Guillaume Billouard de Kerelec, sieur de Kervasegan, and Louise de Lansulyen. He married March 1, 1738, in the chapel of the Bot in Quimerch, Marie Josèphe du Bot de Loc'hant. Kerlérec died Sept. 9, 1770, at Paris, France. Donald J. Lemieux, "Louis Billouart, Chevalier de Kerlerec: Colonial Governor, 1753-1763," *The Louisiana Governors: From Iberville to Edwards* (Baton Rouge, LA: Louisiana State University Press, 1990), Joseph G. Dawson III, ed., 33-36.

163 Jean Jacques Macarty Mactigue was born in 1708 in France to a family of Irish military refugees; his father was Theodore Macarty. He was a cadet in the Black Musketeers in 1722 and came to Louisiana in 1732. He was a captain of engineers in 1735, the same year he married Françoise Trépaginer. At the onset of the French and Indian War, Macarty was a major and commandant of the Illinois at Fort de Chartres. He was received as a Knight of Saint-Louis by Bienville on July 16, 1750. He is not listed in Fauteux's *Les Chevaliers* because his service was in Louisiana, not Canada. Macarty died on April 20, 1764, at New Orleans. McCarthy, "The Chevalier Macarty Mactigue," 41-57.

164 George Croghan was a trader, frontiersman, Indian agent, and interpreter. He emigrated to Pennsylvania around 1741 and quickly established himself as a successful fur trader on that colony's frontier. He had established a number of fortified positions in western Pennsylvania, Fort Shirley being one. Croghan died on Aug. 31, 1782, at Passyunk, Pennsylvania. Joshua J. Jeffers, "George Croghan," *George Washington's Mount Vernon*, accessed Jan. 8, 2018, http://www.mountvernon.org/digital-encyclopedia/article/george-croghan/.

165 Eschenmann identifies the village as Kittanning. He further indicates that the Loups (Wolves) were the Munsee, who were a subtribe of the Lenape, originally residing near the Delaware, but relocated to the Ohio by the mid-18th century. Eschenmann, *Indians Indians*, 7.

166 Din, "François Coulon de Villiers," 354-355.

167 Louis-Joseph de Montcalm, Marquis de Montcalm, see note 133.

168 Louis-Charles-Marie de la Bourdonnaye de Montluc was a relative of Montcalm. Of this individual, Montcalm recorded, "We arrived at Rennes on the 18th, where Mssr. de la Bourdonnaye, my brother-in-law, had gone from his land to see me. Mssr. de la Bourdonnaye de Montluc, President of the Parliament of Brittany, could not have made us more welcome with the honors of the city." Louis-Joseph Marquis de Montcalm de Saint-Véran, *Journal du marquis de Montcalm*, 21.

169 Charles-Philippe Aubry, (c. 1720-1770) was a captain during the Seven Years' War. He and François Coulon de Villiers's careers and fates were linked during much of the war. He was made a Knight of Saint-Louis in 1761 after he and François were released from captivity and returned to France. He was not listed in Fauteux's *Les Chevaliers*, likely because he

was assigned to Louisiana, not Canada. Aubry went on to serve as the last governor of Louisiana under French possession and was instrumental in transferring the colony to Spanish rule. He assisted O'Reilly in restoring order following the 1768 insurrection and identified leaders of the rebellion, which made him unpopular with French New Orleanians. Aubry died Feb. 17, 1770, in a shipwreck off Bordeux, France, while returning home from Louisiana. Carl A. Brasseaux, "Charles Phillipe Aubry: Colonial Governor, 1765-1766," *The Louisiana Governors: From Iberville to Edwards* (Baton Rouge, LA: Louisiana State University Press, 1990), Joseph G. Dawson III, ed., 41-43.

[170] James Grant was a British major defeated at the Battle of Fort Duquesne in 1758 where he was taken prisoner. He was born in 1720, the second son of Lieutenant Colonel William Grant of Ballindalloch. He served as ensign 1st Royal Regiment 1741; captain 1744; major 77th Foot 1757; lieutenant colonel 40th Foot 1760; Governor of East Florida 1763-73; colonel 1772; colonel 55th Foot 1775 – 1791; major general (in America) 1776; major general 1777; lieutenant general 1782; colonel 11th Foot 1791 until his death; and general 1796. Grant died April 13, 1806. Edith Lady Haden-Guest, "Grant, James (1720-1806), of Ballindalloch, Banff.," *The History of Parliament: British Political, Social & Local History*, accessed Feb. 17, 2018, http://www.historyofparliamentonline.org/volume/1754-1790/member/grant-james-1720-1806.

[171] Pierre Pouchot de Maupas was a military engineer, an officer in the French regular troops, and author of *Mémoires sur la dernière guerre de l'Amérique septentrionale*. He was born April 8, 1712, at Grenoble, France, the son of an impoverished merchant. Pouchot died May 8, 1769, on Corsica. Peter N. Moogk, "Pouchot, Pierre," in *DCB*, vol. 3, accessed May 21, 2017, http://www.biographi.ca/en/bio/pouchot_pierre_ 3E.html.

[172] François-Marie Le Marchand de Lignery was an officer in the colonial regular troops. He was born Aug. 24, 1703, in Montreal, the son of Constant Le Marchand de Lignery and Anne Robutel de La Noue. De Lignery died July 28, 1759. C. J. Russ, "Le Marchand de Lignery, François-Marie," in *DCB*, vol. 3, accessed May 21, 2017, http://www.biographi.ca/en/bio/le_marchand_de_lignery_ francois_marie_3E.html.

[173] John Prideaux was a British brigadier general during the French and Indian War. Born in Devonshire in 1718, he was the second son of a baronet, Sir John Prideaux, and the grandson of a viscount. He accepted a lieutenant's commission in the British army on July 17, 1739, and served as regimental adjutant at the Battle of Dettingen, July 27, 1743. He was colonel of the 55th Foot October 20, 1758. Prideaux was killed on July 19, 1759, at Fort Niagara when he was struck by a British mortar being test fired in the camp. Emerson, *The Niagara Campaign of 1759*, 37.

[174] Sir William Johnson, First Baronet, was a British colonial officer and superintendent of the northern Indians. He was born about 1715, the first son of Christopher Johnson of Smithtown, Ireland, and Anne Warren.

He received a royal commission in Feb. 1756 as "Colonel of... the Six united Nations of Indians, & their Confederates, in the Northern Parts of North America" and "Sole Agent and Superintendent of the said Indians." In 1759, Johnson was second in command under Prideaux, and assumed command when the latter officer was killed. With a contingent of almost 1,000 Indians, Johnson effectively ambushed a French force under Le Marchand de Ligneris leading to the surrender of Fort Niagara and denying that important portage route to the Canadians. Johnson died on July 11, 1774, at Johnstown, New York. Julian Gwyn, "Johnson, Sir William," in *DCB*, vol. 4, accessed Jan. 9, 2018, http://www.biographi.ca/en/bio/johnson_william_4E.html.

175 Din, "François Coulon de Villiers," 355-356.

176 McDermott, "Groston de Saint-Ange, Robert." See note 11 for details of Robert Groston de Saint-Ange.

177 Pierre-Paul Marin de La Malgue, see page 165 for his Knight of Saint-Louis biography.

178 Arthur Noble, see note 51.

NOTES TO CHAPTER VII. THE DAMSELS DE VILLIERS

179 Alexandre Dagneau Douville, see note 36.

180 Pierre-Philippe d'Aubrespy de La Farelle, is described by Fauteux, "Quelques officiers de Montcalm," 523, in the following detail:

> Captain in the 2nd battalion of Béarn, he embarked in Brest on the Leopard, in April 1755. Lieutenant in 1735, he had been made captain in 1746.
>
> He was 34 years old when he married, in Montreal, on April 23, 1759, Marie-Louise, 25 years old, daughter of Alexandre Dagneau Douville, captain in the Marine troops and Marie Coulon de Villiers. In the marriage certificate, he is known as Knight of Saint-Louis, son of Sieur Claude d'Aubrespy, Ecr., Knight, former battalion commander and Catherine de la Farelle, of Notre-Dame de Montpellier parish.
>
> Member of the council of war, September 13, 1759, Sieur Aubrespy concluded the most honorable capitulation possible, given the lack of food.
>
> The Sieur d'Aubrespy was still alive in 1777; On January 4 of that same year, the President of the Council of Marine wrote to him that he put before the King his request for a pension for his wife in consideration of his father and his ancestors in Canada, but that he cannot do anything for the moment.
>
> Sometimes his name is written Obrespy.

> According to Georgel, Armorial of Lorraine, a family of Aubrespy de Courcelles, which is probably related to that of our Canadian officer, has the following blazon:
> "Azure three towers of gold terrassée of the same."

[181] Peyser, *Letters from New France*, 210.

[182] Alexandre-René Dagneau Douville, see page 174 for his Knight of Saint-Louis biography.

[183] Drolet, *Genealogical Tables of the Quebec Noblesse*, 45.

[184] Jean-Daniel Dumas, see page 166 for his Knight of Saint-Louis biography.

[185] Hunter, *Forts on the Pennsylvania Frontier*, 122-123.

[186] Claude Marin de La Perrière was a trader. He was baptized Oct. 28, 1705, at Montreal, the son of Charles-Paul de Marin de La Malgue and Louise Lamy. Marin died before Sept. 28, 1752. David A. Armour, "Marin de La Perrière, Claude," in *DCB*, vol. 3, accessed May 21, 2017, http://www.biographi.ca/en/bio/marin_de_la_perriere_claude_3E.html.

[187] Joseph d'Amours, Sieur de Plaine, was a navigator, sailor, merchant, and ship owner. He was born in 1698, the illegitimate son of Bernard D'Amours, Sieur de Plaine, and Marie St-Etienne de la Tour, the widow of the late governor of Acadia, Alexandre LeBorgne of Belle-Isle. He was named captain of ship in 1732 and established a shipowner's trade. He married first Catherine de Monbrun on July 29, 1735; she died in Dec. 1752. His second wife was Madeleine Coulon de Villiers. D'Amours died in February 1768; Madeleine, thrice a widow, died three years later. D'Amours, *Mathieu D'Amours, Sieur de Chaufour et ses descendants*, 151-158.

[188] Ignace-Philippe Aubert de Gaspé, see page 171 for his Knight of Saint-Louis biography.

[189] Bellin, "Partie Occidentale de la Nouvelle France ou du Canada."

NOTES TO APPENDICES

[190] Nicolas-Antoine Coulon de Villiers, letter dated 1733, *Collections of the State Historical Society of Wisconsin*, vol. 17, edited by Reuben G. Thwaites, 113-118, hereafter cited as *Wisconsin Historical Collections*.

[191] Le Rocher is a large sandstone butte that overlooks the Illinois River. Today it is known as Starved Rock based on American Indian tradition that relates an engagement, circa 1770, in which some Peoria Indians were trapped on the rock without food or water when they came under attack by a war party of Potawatomi Indians and suffered starvation. Forty years before this engagement, the French referred to the landmark simply as The Rock.

192 Nicolas-Joseph de Noyelles de Fleurimont, see page 164 for his Knight of Saint-Louis biography.

193 Robert Groston de Saint-Ange, see note 11.

194 Beauharnois and Hocquart, letter dated Nov. 11, 1733, *Wisconsin Historical Collections*, 188-191.

195 Edmunds and Peyser's source for this information was a letter from Beauharnois to the Franch minister dated July 1, 1733. Edmunds and Peyser, *The Fox Wars*, 175-176.

196 Beauharnois, letter dated Oct. 5, 1734, *Wisconsin Historical Collections*, 200-204.

197 Grignon, "Seventy-Two Years' Recollections of Wisconsin," *Wisconsin Historical Collections*, 204-206.

198 Charles-Michel Mouet de Langlade was a fur-trader, an officer in the colonial regular troops, and an Indian department employee. He was baptized May 9, 1729, at Michilimackinac (now Mackinaw City, Mich.), the son of Augustin Mouet de Langlade, a prominent trader, and Domitilde, sister of Nissowaquet. He married on Aug. 12, 1754, at Michilimackinac Charlotte-Ambroisine, daughter of René Bourassa, dit La Ronde, and they had two daughters. He also had a son Charles by an earlier liaison with an Ottawa woman. Langlade died during the winter of 1800 – 1801 at La Baye (Green Bay, Wis.). Of note, Grignon indicates that his grandfather, Charles Langlade, took an active role in the French reprisals against the Sauk. Grignon mistakenly places this event in the year 1746 when Langlade would have been seventeen years old. However, Langlade was less than five in September 1733. Paul Trap, "Mouet de Langlade, Charles-Michel," in *DCB*, vol. 4, accessed May 21, 2017, http://www.biographi.ca/en/bio/mouet_de_langlade_charles_michel_ 4E.html.

199 O'Callaghan, "Battle of Minas," 106-108.

200 Jean-Baptiste-Nicolas-Roch de Ramezay, see page 163 for his Knight of Saint-Louis biography.

201 Louis de La Corne, Chevalier de La Corne, see page 164 for his Knight of Saint-Louis biography.

202 Colonel Arthur Noble, see note 51.

203 Captain Edward How was an English councilman at Annapolis Royal, Nova Scotia. He was born circa 1702 in the New England provinces. At Grand-Pré he served as commissary officer under Arthur Noble. Though severly wounded in the battle of Grand-Pré, he recovered and continued his service for the British colony in Nova Scotia. How was killed in October 1750 near the Missaguash River. Detailing his death, Governor Cornwallis wrote on Nov. 27, 1750, "LeCorne sent one day a flag of truce by a French officer to the water side, a small river that parts their people from our troops. Capt. How and the officer held a parley for some time across the river. How had no sooner taken leave of the officer than a party that lay *perdue* fired a volley at him and shot him through the heart." Nova Scotia Historical Society, *Collection of the Nova Scotia Historical Society*,

for the years 1879-80, vol. 2 (Halifax: Morning Harold Office, 1881), 24-26.

[204] Lusignan was the youngest son of Paul-Louis Dazemard de Lusignan and had been a cadet since 1740. Writing in October 1747, Cadet Lusignan described his wounds:

> That the same winter it had been deemed advisable by the Commanders to strike at a detachment of 500 Englishmen who had withdrawn to Les Mines, I was among those who were detached for this expedition under the command of Monsieur Coulon de Villiers; that having been chosen by the said Sieur de Coulon to be of his brigade composed of 50 men, I was wiped off the attack of an enemy guard house by three discharges, and that wishing to enter with sword in hand although wounded in the right arm by a shot fired at me from behind my shoulder, I received a second which broke my thigh and of which I remain lame for all my life: I think it useless, My Lord, that I have the honor of maintaining Your Greatness with all that I have suffered since these great wounds; it must be sufficient to consider that this action, which has taken place in the coldest winter and in the abundance of snow and ice, does not offer very mild relief to a man wounded as dangerously as I had been. I was in the woods 60 leagues from the general camp where I had to be carried on a stretcher destitute of all help.

Imprimerie de L.-J. Demers & Frère, *Documents Inédits sur le Canada et l'Amerique* (Quebec: Imprimerie de L.-J. Demers & Frère, 1889), 76-77.

[205] Captain Benjamin Goldthwait or Goldthwiate was born Nov. 5, 1704, at Boston. He served from 1744 – 1746 as captain of the fourth company of Col. Waldo's Second Massachusetts Regiment. He served as second in command under Arthur Noble in the expedition to Minas and later served as a colonel during the French and Indian War. Goldthwait died at Medford, Massachusetts, in 1761. Robert G. Carter, *Record of the Military Service of Colonel Benjamin Goldthwaite, a Provincial Soldier*, 1910, 1-2.

[206] Wikimedia Commons contributors, "File:WCJefferys Battle of Grand Pre.png," Wikimedia Commons, the free media repository, https://commons.wikimedia.org/w/index.php?title=File:WCJefferys_Battle_of_Grand_Pre.png&oldid=252992210 accessed June 10, 2018. After consulting with the Anthony Allen of the CWJefferys.ca website, if appears the Wikimedia citation is incorrect. The correct citation likely may be: C. W. Jefferys, "The fight of Grand Pre, February 11, 1747," from *The land of Evangeline: Nova Scotia, annotated guide*, by Parker (Cambridge, Mass., University Press, 1925), p. 48.

[207] Mallet, "Washinton et Coulon de Viliers," 60-61; A. Coté et Cie, *Collection de manuscrits contenant lettres, mémoires, et autres documents historiques relatifs a la Nouvelle-France, recueillis aux Archives de la Province de Québec, ou copiés a l'étanger* (Quebec : A. Coté et Cie, 1884), vol. 3, 521.

[208] Dumas, *La Regence et Louis XV*, 278-280.

[209] Jumonville Glen, the site of Washington's ambush of Jumonville's party, was more than five miles from the site of Washington's camp at Great Meadows. Moreover, Washington did not begin construction of his fort of necessity until after—and in consequence of—the death of Jumonville. See note 81.

[210] Moreau, *A Memorial, Containing a Summary View of Facts, with their Authorities*, 117-118.

[211] Coulon de Villiers, "The Journal of Louis Coulon de Villiers," *Moreau De Saint-Méry Collection*, ANOM, France, vol. 14 of sub-series F3, fol. 52-60. According to the Archives nationales d'outre-mer, the Moreau Collection of Saint-Méry is not a series of archives, but a collection created during the last years of the Ancien Régime and during the Revolution by Louis-Médéric Moreau de Saint-Méry (1750-1819), Creole of Martinique, former advisor to the Superior Council of Santo Domingo.

[212] Claude-Pierre Pécaudy de Contrecoeur, see page 167 for his Knight of Saint-Louis biography.

[213] Coulon de Villiers chose to use the word "Sauvage" rather than "Indien" to denote his native allies. That was the accepted word choice by French officers in New France in the mid-18th century. He capitalized Sauvage, using it as a proper noun. A literal translation would be "Savages" rather than "Indians." Of note is that Chattin's 1756 English translation in *A Memorial Containing a Summary View of Facts* also translated Sauvage as Indian, and more recent translations, such as in Peyser's *Letters from New France* also translate Sauvage as Indian. In Beauharnois's two letters from 1733 (appendix B) and 1734 (appendix C) Thwaites used the literal translation "savage."

[214] François-Marc-Antoine Le Mercier, see page 168 for his Knight of Saint-Louis biography.

[215] Indian name for the Canadian Great Father, the governor of New France.

[216] Likely a reference to the Munsee (the Wolf clan), a subtribe of the Lenape, who originally lived on the Delaware River, but moved to the Susquehanna and later the Ohio River by the mid-18th Century. Eschenmann, *Indians Indians*, 7. This could also be the Mahican or Mohican, an eastern Algonquin tribe also called Loups (wolves) by the French.

[217] Paul-Joseph LeMoyne de Longueuil, see page 163 for his Knight of Saint-Louis biography.

[218] Coulon de Villiers used the phrase *Coureurs Sauvages*, which translates literally as Savage couriers or runners. Chattin translated this

sentence as, "I began, from that instant, to send out some *Indians* to range about by land, to prevent being surprised;" *A Memorial Containing a Summary View of Facts*, 174. Peyser translated it as "I began from that moment on to have Indian Scouts on land to avoid any surprise;" *Letters from New France*, 201. According to Boyer's 1751 French-English dictionary, the contemporary French translation of scout was *un coureur d'armé*.

[219] In the Drucour version from the *Moreau De Saint-Méry Collection*, it states six or eight arpents. Gosselin's version clearly states seven or eight. An arpent is about 190 feet, thus Coulon de Villiers planned to camp about 1,100 to 1,500 feet above the fork of the Monongahela and the Youghiogheny Rivers.

[220] Likely a Seneca chief from the town of Sonontouan on the Scioto River.

[221] In 1751, the French word "hangard" translated as coach house or cart house. In his 1757 translation, Chattin left the word "hangard" untranslated. More modern translations use the word "warehouse." The modern version of the word is hangar in both French and English. This was the Ohio Company's fortified storehouse at Red Stone Creek. I have chosen the word "storehouse," as that is how William Trent, who constructed the building, referred to it.

[222] A band of Algonquian from the Lake Huron area.

[223] Coulon de Villiers makes no mention of burying the remains, but a Canadian militiaman in his command, J. C. Bonin, recorded in his memoirs, "we found ourselves at the place where Sieur Jumonville was killed; there were still four corpses whose scalps were removed; they were buried, and we made a general prayer, after which the commander DeVilliers spoke to the Indians, on the place of the assassination of his brother and on the vengeance which he hoped to draw with their help; they promised to help him well." The author of the original manuscript identified himself only by the initials J. C. B. Casgrain posited that the author may have been Mssr. Bonnefons, but provided some doubt to this identification. Rene Chartrand in 1993 demonstrated that the initials were most likely those of Joseph-Charles Bonin, dit Jolicoeur. Casgrain, *Voyage au Canada dans le Nord de l'Amérique*, 106; Pierre Bonnin, "Les livres de Pierre Bonin," *Fondation littéraire Fleur de Lys*, accessed Jan. 15, 2018, https://manuscritdepot.com/a.pierre-bonin.4.htm

[224] Fascines are bundles of wood or brush tied together and used to shore up trenches and ramparts or create visual obstructions.

[225] Pierre Odet de Piercot de Bailleul, dit Bailleul Canut, see page 172 for his Knight of Saint-Louis biography.

[226] Jacob Van Braam, see note 134.

[227] Robert Stobo, see note 135.

[228] James Mackay, see note 126.

229 Coulon de Villiers wrote the word "Panis." Gosselin transcribed the word "Pany." Chattin in his 1756 translation also wrote "Pany" and annotated that it was the name of an Indian. Peyser translated the word as Pawnee and annotated that it was an Indian slave of a French officer. According to Riddell in "The Slave in Canada," 264, "The name Pani or Panis, anglicized into Pawnee, was used generally in Canada as synonymous with 'Indian Slave' because these slaves were usually taken from the Pawnee tribe." In an extract of Coulon de Villiers's journal held in the ANOM in France, this line is written "le Panis du M. Péan," or "the Indian slave of Mssr. Péan." ANOM, France, COL C11A, vol. 99, fol. 496.

230 Michel Marey or Marest de la Chauvignerie, was the commandant at Chiningué or Logstown in 1754; see page 172 for his Knight of Saint-Louis biography. Also, see Hunter, *Forts on the Pennsylvania Frontier*, 35.

231 Peyser, *Letters from New France*, 209-210.

232 Pierre-Joseph Céloron de Blainville, see page 162 for his Knight of Saint-Louis biography. Céloron served as the town-major of Detroit immediately following his 1749 expedition of the Ohio River. He was made town-major of Montreal in 1753.

233 Jacques-Pierre de Taffanel de La Jonquière, see page 160 for his Knight of Saint-Louis biography.

234 Charles LeMoyne de Longueuil, second Baron de Longueuil, see page 161 for his Knight of Saint-Louis biography.

235 Ange Duquesne de Menneville, Marquis Duquesne, see page 162 for his Knight of Saint-Louis biography.

236 Gosselin does not mention that Louis's eldest sister Marie, and her husband, Alexndre Dagneau Douville, had a son, but clearly that is implied here when Louis mentions his nephew was wounded while serving as a cadet at the battle of Fort Necessity. According to Drolet, *Genealogical Tables of the Quebec Noblesse*, there were two sons from this marriage, Alexandre-René (1736-1789) and Joseph (1739-1756). See page 85-86. See page 174 for Alexandre-René's Knight of Saint-Louis biography.

237 Dawson, "The 'Jumonville' of Thomas and Washington," 201-203.

238 François Coulon de Villiers, circa 1760. This image is available from the Bibliothèque et Archives nationales du Québec under the reference number P560, S2, D1, P206; available from *Wikimedia Commons*, accessed April 11, 2017, https://commons.wikimedia.org/wiki/File:Fran%C3%A7ois_Coulon_de_Villiers.jpg.

239 Din, "François Coulon de Villiers," 351-357.

240 According to Din, the petition of François Coulon de Villiers is attached to Bernardo de Gàlvez to José de Gàlvez, No. 28, New Orleans, March 21, 1777, Archivo General de Indias, Santo Domingo, Leg. 2547.

241 Din provides a notation indicating that an alcalde ordinario was a municipal judge. John Bach McMaster in his 1914 work, *A History of the*

People of the United States, from the Revolution to the Civil War, 19-20, provided the following lengthy explanation of the Alcalde of New Orleans:

> The Alcalde formed part of a municipal government as strange to an American as the city and its people. Over New Orleans and its dependencies in Spanish days presided a Cabildo, or City Council of six hereditary Regidors; two Alcaldes, a Procureur-General, a Secretary, and the Governor of the Province. Five of the Regidors held offices of great weight. One was known as Alferez Royal, and bore the royal banner; another was Alcalde Mayor Provincial; another, Alguazil Mayor; a fourth, Depository-General; a fifth, Receiver of penas de camara, or fines for the use of the royal treasury. The Governor presided over the Cabildo, and met it in the City Hall on Friday of each week and on the first day of each new year. At the weekly meetings such business was done as concerned the city and the province. At the new year meeting the Cabildo chose two Judges or Alcaldes Ordinary, the Procureur-General, and a Mayordome de propres, or manager of rents and city taxes. The Alcaldes were judges of civil and criminal law; never appeared in public without their wands of office; visited the prisons each Friday, examined the prisoners, and set free such debtors as seemed fit subjects of mercy. Each night one of the Alcaldes, with the Alguazil Mayor and the Scrivener, walked the streets of the city to see that the laws were obeyed and that peace and quiet prevailed. Three times each year, on the eves of Christmas, of Easter, and of Pentecost, the Governor went the rounds of the prisons with the Alcaldes, and never failed to set some petty criminals free. The authority of the Alcaldes spread over the city and five leagues around it. At this limit the rule of the Alcalde Mayor Provincial began. Before him came every offender who had done his deed out of the bounds of New Orleans, or the villages; or, having done it in the city or the villages, fled for refuge to the country. And woe to the criminal who, friendless and rankless, came before this Alcalde! For him justice was speedy and sure. If he had reviled the Saviour or the Blessed Virgin, his property was confiscated and his tongue cut out. If he had vilified the King or the Queen, or any member of the Royal Family, half his property was taken and he was well flogged. If he had stolen the sacred vessels from a holy place, or had robbed a traveller on the King's highway, or had murdered a fellow-creature, or assaulted a woman, he was given over to the Alguazil to be put to death with every

mark of shame. The property of the ravisher was given to the victim. The murderer was dragged to execution at the tail of a horse. False witnesses were exposed to public shame and banished. Adulterers were given over to the injured husband to do with as he would. But if he put the man to death he must the woman also.

242 Alexander O'Reilly, known as Bloody O'Reilly, was born to an upper-class Irish family in 1722. Following his father's lead, he joined the Spanish infantry at the age of ten. O'Reilly became the second Spanish governor of Louisiana in 1768 after Ulloa was ejected by New Orleanians. Mizell-Nelson, Catherine "Alejandro O'Reilly," *KnowLouisiana.org Encyclopedia of Louisiana*, edited by David Johnson, Louisiana Endowment for the Humanities, 2010–. Article published February 25, 2013. http://www.knowlouisiana.org/entry/oreilly-alejandro.

243 Parkman, *A Half-Century of Conflict*, 328, confirmed the estimate of 800 dead recording the killed as "two hundred of their warriors besides six hundred of their women and children." Edmunds and Peyser, *The Fox Wars*, 156, placed the number at 500: 200 warriors and 300 women and children. François's father recorded, "more than 200 warriors were killed." Villiers to Beauharnois, Sep. 23, 1730, in *Wisconsin Historical Collections*, vol. 17, 117. Nicolas-Antoine Coulon de Villiers's interpreter, Jean-Baptiste Reaume, provided the following list of Meskwaki casualties: "It was said that there were 500 killed, namely: 200 men and 300 women and children. Three hundred women and children were taken prisoner." Reaume was likely Edmund and Peyser's source. Lenville J. Stelle, "History and Archaeology: New Evidence of the 1730 Mesquakie (Renard, Fox) Fort," Champaign, IL: Center for Social Research, Parkland College, 1992, accessed Feb. 15, 2018, http://virtual.parkland.edu/lstelle1/len/center_for_social_research/Fox_Fort/ idotfx.htm.

244 This is a reference to the Battle of Les Mines or Grand Pré.

245 As shown in chapter II, Pierre Lespiney Coulon de Villiers died of illness a month before the Battle of Les Mines.

246 This is a reference to Antoine du Verger d'Aubusson born in 1664 in France. He was married to Marie-Jeanne Jarret de Verchères, sister of François Coulon de Villiers's mother, Angélique. Marie-Jeanne was already a widow at the hands of the Iroquois when she married Antoine in 1689. According to Roy in his *La famille Jarret de Verchères*, "Mssr. Du Verger d'Aubusson was kidnapped and massacred by the Iroquois in 1691 two years after his marriage." Like the exploits of Angélique's sister, Madeleine de Verchères, who single handedly saved the French stronghold at Verchères, the family accounts of the death of Antoine du Verger d'Aubusson clearly made a great impression on the Coulon de Villiers brothers growing up, as both events occurred when Angélique Jarret de Verchères was a young girl of seven or eight years old and more than a decade before

she married Nicolas-Antoine Coulon de Villiers in 1705 or 1706. André Vachon, "Jarret de Verchères, Marie-Madeleine," *DCB*, vol. 3, accessed May 21, 2017, http://www.biographi.ca/en/bio/jarret_de_vercheres_marie_madeleine _ 3E.html.

247 Anderson, *Crucible of War*, 62-63, states of Washington's strength the morning of July 3, 1754, "only three hundred of the four hundred men at Fort Necessity were fit for duty."

248 Washington had nine swivel guns. Designed for naval vessels to sweep the decks of enemy ships at close range, the swivel guns at Fort Necessity could fire grape shot or a half pound solid shot ball with an effective range at an aimed point target of about 30 yards. National Park Service, "Historic Weapons Program," *Fort Necessity National Battlefield*, updated Aug. 19, 2016 and accessed Jan. 15, 2018, https://www.nps.gov/fone/planyourvisit/historic-weapons-program.htm

249 Anderson, *Crucible of War*, 65, records Washington's casualties as "thirty killed and seventy wounded."

250 Charles-Philippe Aubry, see note 169.

251 Din provided the following footnote: "François Coulon de Villiers gives a poor description of events of 1758. In the fall of that year, English general John Forbes marched at the head of 6,000 troops toward Fort Duquesne. Before he arrived, the Indian allies deserted the French. Bereft of support and with few soldiers, the French blew up the fort on November 24, 1758, and left." De Villiers was accurate in his description of the events of Sept. 14, 1758, wherein French and Indian forces under him and Aubry engaged Major James Grant near the outpost of Loyalhanna while the British were building what became known as Fort Ligonier (see note 252). A third of the British force was killed, wounded, or captured, including Major Grant, who was sent to Canada. Anderson, *Crucible of War*, 272. See note 170 for a description of James Grant.

252 According to MacDonald, *Lives of Fort de Chartres*, 99 & 212, De Villiers's description of the fight at Royal Fort Annon is actually a reference to Loyalhanna. The post was established as part of Forbes's 1758 campaign to seize Fort Duquesne serving as the final link in a chain of fortifications and located just 50 miles from that French citadel on the Belle-Riviere. Forbes later renamed Loyalhanna after his superior officer, Sir John Ligonier. Anderson, *Crucible of War*, 272.

253 Jean-Jacques-Blaise d'Abbadi was born at Château d'Audoux in 1726. He was one of three officers that King Louis XV sent to govern Louisiana in 1763. He served as director-general until 1765 when he died in New Orleans of a stroke on Feb. 4. Carl A. Brasseaux "Jean Jacques Blaise d'Abbadie," *The Louisiana Governors: From Iberville to Edwards* (Baton Rouge, LA: Louisiana State University Press, 1990), Joseph G. Dawson III, ed., 37-40.

254 Ancestry.com, *Sons of the American Revolution Membership Applications, 1889-1970* (Louisville: National Society of the Sons of the American Revolution), SAR Membership: 97783.

255 Walter B. Douglas, "The Sieurs de St. Ange," *Transactions of the Illinois State History*, 136. See note 11 for biography of Robert Groston de St-Ange.

256 Ekberg and Person, *St. Louis Rising*, 36.

257 Ibid., 155.

258 Cleary, *The World, the Flesh, and the Devil*, 146-147. William C. Breckenridge, in his notes to Primm's "History of the 'Chanson de L'Année du Coup," 301, provides another view of the dissolution of this marriage:

> After forgiving [*Madame de Volsey's*] desertion of him in 1772 and taking her back, de Volsey was finally forced to divorce her on account of her flagrant misconduct with René Kiercereau dit Renaud. This proceeding for a dissolution of his marriage ties was begun before Governor Cruzat on September 11th, 1777, and a decree was granted him on August 21st, 1779, by Governor de Leyba. This was the first divorce case in St. Louis.

259 *S.A.R. Membership Applications*, 97783.

260 Pierre-Paul Marin de La Malgue, see page 165 for his Knight of Saint-Louis biography.

261 *S.A.R. Membership Applications*, 75988.

262 Huchet de Kernion, "Coulon de Jumonville and de Villiers Family," 228.

263 Oeil-de-Boeuf is a circular window, noted in 17th- and 18th-century French architecture.

264 Prie-Dieux is a type of prayer desk primarily intended for private devotional use.

265 Louis, also called Louis D'or, was a gold coin circulated in France before the Revolution. The franc and livre were silver coins that had shrunk in value to such an extent that by 1740 coins of a larger denomination were needed.

266 Latin for *Louis the Great instituted 1693.*

267 Latin for *Wars and the reward of virtue.*

268 Alexei Nikolaevich Romanov, "Ordre de Saint-Louis," *Wikimedia Commons*, color sketch version, accessed Jan. 6, 2018, https://commons.wikimedia.org/wiki/ File:Ordre_de_Saint-Louis_GTColl.jpg

269 Officers in Canada holding the title of "reformed" in front of their rank received only half-pay. Douglas in his essay, "The Sieurs De St. Ange," 137, explained that, "The King seemed to have the idea that money was a superfluity with his American officers. They were dignified by being called *officiers reformès*, instead of half pay officers."

270 Guards of the Navy or *Gardes de la Marine* were gentlemen chosen and maintained by the King in the ports to learn the service of the navy and make them officers. Nicolas Viton de Saint-Allais, *Dictionnaire encyclopédique de la noblesse de France*, vol. 1 (Paris: Valade, Imprimeur du Roi, 1816), 410.

271 A lieutenant of the king was the commanding officer of a place of war in the absence of the governor. His position in the hierarchy precedes that of the major.

272 Maréchal de camp was a general officer rank used by the French Army until 1848. The rank originated from the older rank of sergeant major general. Sergeant major general was third in command in an army, after the general and the lieutenant general.

273 The aide-major was an officer whose function was to assist the major in the command of a troop corps or the administration of a city.

274 William Kirby, *The Chien d'or. The Golden Dog; a Legend of Quebec*, New York: R. Worthington, 1878.

275 From its opening in 1698 under King Louis XIV, the Hotel des Invalides in Paris was run by governors until 1792.

276 Alexandre-René Dagneau Douville may have been the cadet wounded in the foot at the Battle of Fort Necessity while serving under his uncle, le Grand Villiers. See page 133 and note 236.

Bibliography

Alberts, Robert C. 1965. *The Most Extraordinary Adventures of Major Robert Stobo*. Boston: Houghton Mifflin Company.

Andreson, Fred. 2000. *Crucible of War: The Seven Years' War and the Fate of the Empire in British North America, 1754-1766*. New York: Vintage Books.

Baudry, P.-J.-U. 1888. "Un Vieux Fort Français." In *Mémoires et Comptes Rendus de la Société Royale Du Canada pour l'Année 1887*, 93-114. Montréal: Dawson Frères, Libraires-Éditeurs.

Beauharnois. 1743. *Canada-Correspondance Générale*. Vol. 79. Ottawa, October 20. 233.

—. 1741. "List of proposed promotions among the troops." *Canada-Correspondance Générale: M. de Beauharnois, Governor General--M. Hocquart, Intendant*. Vol. 75. Ottawa, October 30. 312.

—. 1740. "Promotions and Appointments in the Army." *Canada-Correspondance Générale: M. de Beauharnois, Governor General--Other Officials of the Colony*. Vol. 74. Ottawa, November 4. 37.

—. 1733. "Villiers and Repentigny have been killed at La Baie." *Canada-Correspondance Générale: Beauharnois, Governor General. Hocquart, Intendant*. Vol. 59. Ottawa, November 11. 37.

Beauharnois, and Hocquart. 1733. "Events which have happened at the post of La Baie, commanded by Villiers." *Canada-Correspondance Générale: Hocquart, Intendant and other Functionaries of the Colony*. Vol. 60. Ottawa, November 11. 134.

Bossu, Jean Bernard. 1768. *Nouveaux voyages aux Indes Occidentales; : contenant une relation des differens peuples qui habitent les environs du grand fleuve Saint-Louis, appellé vulgairement le Mississippi; leur religion; leur gouvernement; leurs murs; leurs guerres & leur commerce*. Paris: Chez le Jay.

Bourlamaque, François-Charles de. 1891. *Lettres de M. de Bourlamaque au Chevalier de Lévis*. Edited by Henri-Raymond Casgrain. Québec: Imprimerie de L.-J. Demers Frère.

Boyer, Abel. 1751. *The Royal Dictionary Abridged. I. French and English II. English and French*. London: Messrs. Innys, Brotherton. Accessed April 30, 2017.

Brymner, Douglas. 1889. *Report on Candian Archives, 1888*. Ottawa: Printed by Maclean, Roger & Co.

Casgrain, Henri-Raymond, ed. 1890. *Lettres de la Cour de Versailles au Baron de Dieskau, au Marquis de Montcalm et au Chevalier de Lévis*. Québec: Imprimerie de L.-J. Demers & Frère.

—. 1871. *Philippe Aubert de Gaspé*. Quebec: Atelier Typographique de Léger Brousseau.

—. 1895. *Relations et journaux de différentes expéditions faites durant les années 1755-56-57-58-59-60*. Quebec: Imprimerie de L.-J. Demers & Frère.

—. 1894. *Une seconde Acadie: L'Ile Saint-Jean - Ile du Prince-Edouard sous le régime français*. Quebec: Imprimerie de L.-J. Demers & Frère.

—. 1887. *Voyage au Canada dans le Nord de l'Amérique septentrionale fait depuis l'an 1751 à 1761 par J. C. B*. Québec: Imprimerie Léger Brousseau.

Céloron de Blainville, Pierre Joseph. 1921. "Céloron's Journal." In *Expedition of Celoron to the Ohio country in 1749*, by Charles B. Galbreath, edited by Reb. A. A. Lambing, 12-77. Columbus: F. J. Heer Printing Co.

Charlevoix, Pierre-François-Xavier de. 1902. *History and General Description of New France*. Translated by John G. Shea. London: Francis P. Harper.

Choiseul, duc de Etienne-François. 1904. *Mémoires du duc de Choiseul, 1719-1785*. Paris: Plon-Nourrit et cie.

Cleary, Patricia. 2011. *The World, the Flesh, and the Devil: A History of Colonial St. Louis*. Columbia: University of Missouri Press.

Coulon de Villiers, Louis. 1754. *The Journal of Louis Coulon de Villiers*. Edited by Guy Berthiaume. September 6. Accessed March 31, 2017. http://www.bac-lac.gc.ca/eng/discover/exploration-settlement/new-france-new-horizons/Documents/Warfare/journal-coulon-devilliers.pdf.

D'Amours, Albert. 1974. *Mathieu D'Amours, Sieur de Chaufour et ses descendants*. Charlebourg: Les pères Eudistes.

Daniel, François. 1867. *Le Vicomte C. de Léry, Lieutenant-Général de l'Empire Français, Ingénieur en Chef de la Grande Armée, et sa Famille*. Montréal: Eusebe Senécal, Imprimeur-Éditeur.

Daniel, François. 1867. *Supplement A L'Histoire Des Grandes Familles Francaises Du Canada*. Vol. 2, in *Nos Gloires Nationales: ou, Histoire des Principales Familles du Canada*, 379-418. Montréal: Eusebe Senécal, Imprimeur-Éditeur.

Dawson, Henry B., ed. 1862. "The 'Jumonville' of Thomas and Washington." *The Historical Magazine, and Notes and Queries Concerning the Antiquities, History and Biography of America*, July: 201-203.

De Villier, Gladys LaGrange. 1993. *The De Villiers: the Epic of a Noble Family of France, Canada and Louisiana*. Saint Martinville: G. L. de Villiers.

Dickerson, Christina. 2011. *Diplomats, Soldiers, and Slaveholders: The Coulon de Villiers Family in New France*. Dissertation, Nashville: Vanderbilt University.

Din, Gilbert C. 2000. "François Coulon de Villiers: More Light on an Illusive Historical Figure." *Louisiana History: The Journal of the Historical Association* 41 (3): 345-357.

Drolet, Yves. 2009. *Genealogical Tables of the Quebec Noblesse from the 17th to the 19th Century*. Montreal: Société Généalogique Canadienne-Française.

Dumas, Alexandre. 1857. *La Regence et Louis XV*. Paris: Dufour, Mulat et Bou-langer, Éditeurs.

Duquesne. 1754. *Canada-Correspondance Générale*. Vol. 99. Ottawa, October 10. 275.

Dussieux, Louis Étienne. 1862. *Le Canada sous la domination française, d'après les Archives de la Marine et de la Guerre* . Paris: Jaques Lecoffre.

Edmunds, R. David, and Joseph L. Peyser. 1993. *The Fox Wars: The Mesquakie Challenge to New France*. Norman: University of Oklahoma Press.

Ekberg, Carl J., and Sharon K. Person. 2015. *St. Louis Rising: The French Regime of Louis St. Ange de Bellerive.* Chicago: University of Illinois Press.

Emerson, George Douglas. 1909. *The Niagara campaign of 1759.* Buffalo: Buffalo Association of the Society of Colonial Wars.

Eschenmann, Hayes R. 1992. *Indians Indians.* Shippensburg, PA: Whipporwill Publications.

Fauteux, Aegidius. 1940. *Les Chevaliers de Saint-Louis en Canada.* Montreal: Les Éditions des Dix.

—. 1951. "Quelques officiers de Montcalm." *Revue d'histoire de l'Amérique française,* March: 521-529.

Ferland, Jean Baptiste Antoine. 1865. *Cours d'Histoire du Canada.* Québec: Augustin Coté, Editeur-Imprimeur.

Galissonnière. 1747. *Canada-Correspondance Générale.* Vol. 87. Ottawa, November 3. 218.

Gallifet, Louis. 1775. "Villiers de Jumonville. Capitaine tué au Canada. 1775, pension pour ses filles." *Library and Archives Canada.* August 12. Accessed December 24, 2017. http://collectionscanada.gc.ca/ourl/res.php?url_ver=Z39.88-2004&url_tim=2017-12-24T13%3A21%3A56Z&url_ctx_fmt=info%3Aofi%2Ffmt%3Akev%3Amtx%3Actx&rft_dat=3053895&rfr_id=info%3Asid%2Fcollectionscanada.gc.ca%3Apam&lang=eng.

Gaspé, Philippe Aubert de. 1877. *Les Anciens Canadiens.* Québec: Augustin Coté.

—. 1866. *Mémoires.* Ottawa: G. E. Desbarates, Imprimeur-Éditeur.

Goold, William. 1881. *Col. Arthur Noble, of Georgetown. Fort Halifax. Col. William Vaughan, of Matinicus and Damariscotta: Papers Read Before the Main Historical Society.* Portland: Stephen Berry.

Gosselin, Amédée Edmond. 1906. *Notes sur la Famille Coulon de Villiers.* Lévis: Bulletin des Recherches Historiques.

Grave, Victor-Eugène, and Adrien Maquet. 1881. *Supplément au Nobiliaire et armorial du comté de Montfort-l'Amaury.* Versailles: Imp. de Autlet.

Grignon, Augustin. 1857. *Seventy-two Years' Recollections of Wisconsin.* Vol. iii, in *Third Annual Report and Collections of the State Historical Society, of Wisconsin, for the year 1856*, edited by Wm. R. Smith, 197-295. Madison: Calkins & Webb, Printers.

Harden, William. 1917. "James Mackay, of Strathy Hall, Comrade in Arms of George Washington." *The Georgia Historical Quarterly* I (2): 77-98.

Hocquart. 1747. *Canada-Correspondance Générale*. Vol. 89. Ottawa, October 9. 15.

Huchet de Kernion, George Campbell. 1931. "Coulon de Jumonville and de Villiers Family." In *Old Families of Louisiana*, edited by Stanley C. Arthur, 221-229. New Orleans: Clearfield Company, Inc.

Hunter, William A. 1960. *Forts on the Pennsylvania Frontier, 1753-1758*. Harrisburg: The Pennsylvania Historical and Museum Commission.

Jonquiere, and Bigot. 1750. *Canada-Correspondance Générale*. Vol. 95. Ottawa, October 2. 40.

Kerallain, René de. 1896. *La jeunesse de Bougainville et la Guerre de sept ans*. Paris.

Législature de Québec. 1884. *Collection de manuscrits contenant lettres, mémoires, et autres documents historiques relatifs à la Nouvelle-France : recueillis aux archives de la province de Québec, ou copiés à l'étranger* . Québec: Imprimerie A. Coté.

Léry, Joseph Gaspard Chaussegros de. 1940. *Journal of Chaussegros de Léry*. Edited by Sylvester K. Stevens and Donald H. Kent. Harrisburg: Pennsylvania Historical Commission.

Lévis, François Gaston, and Henri-Raymond Casgrain. 1889. *Lettres du Chevalier de Lévis concernant la Guerre du Canada (1756-1760)*. Montreal: C. O. Beauchemin & Fils.

Liénard de Beaujeu, Daniel-Hyacinthe-Marie. 1889. *Journal de la Campagne du Détachment de Canadá a l'Acadie et aux Mines, en 1746-47*. Vol. 2, in *Collection de Documents Inédits sur le Canada et l'Amerique Publiés par Le Canada-Français*, 16-75. Quebec: Imprimerie de L.-J. Demers & Frère.

MacDonald, David. 2016. *Lives of Fort de Chartres: Commandants, Soldiers, and Civilians in French Illinois, 1720-1770*. Carbondale: Southern Illinois University Press.

Mallet, M. Edmond. 1906. "Washington et Coulon de Villiers." *Bulletin de la Société Historique Franco-Américaine* 17-66.

Mazas, Alex. 1860. *Histoire de l'Ordre de Saint-Louis, Depuis son Institution en 1693 jusqu'en 1830*. Vol. 2. Paris: Firmin Didot Frères, Fils et Cie.

McCarthy, William P. 1968. "The Chevalier Macarty Mactigue." *Journal of the Illinois State Historical Society* 61 (1): 41-57.

McMaster, John Bach. 1914. *A History of the People of the United States, from the Revolution to the Civil War*. Vol. 3. New York: D. Appleton and Company.

Montcalm de Saint-Véran, Louis-Joseph Marquis de. 1895. *Journal du Marquis de Montcalm Durant ses Campagnes en Canada de 1756 à 1759*. Edited by H.-R. Casgrain. Québec: Imprimerie de L.-J. Demers & Frère.

Moreau, Jacob Nicolas, trans. 1757. *A Memorial, Containing A Summary View of Facts with their Authorities, In Answer to the Observations sent by the English Ministry to the Courts of Europe*. Philadelphia: James Chattin.

O'Callaghan, Edmund B., ed. 1858. *Documents Relative to the Colonial History of the State of New York*. Albany: Weed, Parsons and Company, Printers.

O'Callaghan, Edmund B. 1855. *Battle of Minas*. Vol. 9, in *The New England Historical and Genealogical Register*, by New England Historic-Genealogical Society, 105-112. Boston: Samuel G. Drake.

Parkman, Francis. 1892. *A Half-Century Of Conflict*. Vol. 1. Boston: Little, Brown, and Company.

—. 1885. *Montcalm and Wolfe*. Vol. 1. London: MacMillan and Co.

Pease, Theodore C., and Ernestine Jenison, . 1940. *Illinois on the Eve of the Seven Years' War, 1747-1755*. Vol. 3. Springfield, IL: Illinois State Historical Library.

Peyser, Joseph L. 1999. *Ambush and Revenge: George Washington's Adversaries in 1754, Ensign Joseph Coulon de

Jumonville and Captain Louis Coulon de Villiers . Dunbar: Stefano's Printing.

—. 1997. *On the Eve of Conquest: The Chevalier de Raymond's Critique of New France in 1754*. East Lansing: Michigan State University Press.

Peyser, Jospeh L., ed. 1993. *Letters from New France: The Upper Country 1686-1783*. Translated by Joseph L. Peyser. Chicago: University of Illinois.

Pouchot, Pierre. 1781. *Mémoires sur la dernière guerre de l'Amérique septentrionale, entre la France et l'Angleterre*. Vol. 1. Yverdon: F.B. de Félice.

Preston, David L. 2015. *Braddock's Defeat: The Battle of the Monongahela and the Road to Revolution*. New York: Oxford University Press.

Primm, Wilson. 1914. "History of the 'Chanson de L'Année du Coup'." *Missouri Historical Society Collections*, 295-302.

Richard, Édouard-Émery. 1901. *Supplément du Rapport du Docteur Brymner Archives Canadiennes, 1899*. Ottawa.

Riddell, William Renwick. 1920. "The Slave in Canada." Edited by Garter G. Woodson. *The Journal of Negro History* (The Association for the Study of Negro Life and History, Inc.) 5: 261-377.

Roy, Pierre-Georges. 1908. *La famille Jarret de Verchères*. Lévis.

—. 1931. *Les Petites Choses de Notre Histoire* . Lévis: Pierre-Georges Roy.

Rule, John C. 1965. "Jean-Frederic Phelypeaux, comte de Pontchartrain et Maurepas: Reflections on His Life and His Papers." *The Journal of the Louisiana Historical Association* 6: 365-377.

Sargent, Winthrop. 1856. *The History of an Expedition Against Fort DuQuesne in 1755; under Major-General Edward Braddock, Generalissimo of H. B. M. Forces in America*. Philadelphia: J. B. Lippincott & Co.

Stobo, Robert. 1854. *Memoirs of Major Robert Stobo of the Virginia Regiment*. Edited by Neville B. Craig. Pittsburgh: John S. Davidson.

Sulte, Benjamin. 1902. "Le Titre de Chevalier." Edited by Pierre-Georges Roy. *Reserches Historiques; Bulletin d'Archéologie, d'Histoire, de Biographie, de Bibliographie, de Numismatique, etc., etc.* 8: 36.

Summers, James L., and Rene Chartrand. n.d. *History and Uniform of Le Regiment de Bearn, 1755-1760.* Accessed April 7, 2017. http://www.militaryheritage.com/bearn.htm.

Tanguay, Cyprien. 1887. *Dictionnaire Genealogique des Familles Canadiennes Depuis la Foundation de la Colonie Jusqu'a Nos Jours.* Vols. 2, 3 &4. Montréal: Eusebe Senécal & Fils, Imprimeurs-Éditeurs.

Thomas, Antoine Léonard. 1759. *Jumonville : Poëme .* Paris.

Thwaites, Reuben G., ed. 1906. *Collections of the State Historical Society of Wisconsin.* Vol. xvii. Madison: State historical Society of Wisconsin.

Thwaites, Reuben G., ed. 1900. *The Jesuit Relations and Allied Documents : Travels and Explorations of the Jesuit Missionaries in New France, 1610-1791 : The Original French, Latin, and Italian Texts, with English Translations and Notes.* Vol. 70. Cleveland: Burrows Brothers.

Twohig, Dorothy, ed. 1999. *George Washington's Diaries: An Abridgment.* Charlottesville: University of Virginia Press.

Valfons, Charles de Mathei, Camille Régis Mathei de la Calmette Valfons, and Georges Maurin. 1906. *Souvenirs du marquis de Valfons, vicomte de Sebourg, 1710-1786.* Paris: Émile-Paul.

Villiers du Terrage, Marc de. 1904. *Les Dernières Années de la Louisiane Française; le Chevalier de Kerlérec, d'Abbadie--Aubry, Laussat.* Edited by E. Guilmoto. Paris: Libraire Orientale & Américaine.

Winsor, Justin, ed. 1887. *Narrative and Critical History of America.* Boston: Houghton, Mifflin and Company.

Index

Abenaki: 119, 183-n.68.
Acadia: 11, 19, 26, 27, 33, 34, 50, 51, 84, 132, 144, 157, 159, 162, 165, 179-n.30, 196-n.187.
Aix-la-Chapelle: 160.
Algonquin or Algonkin: 54, 119, 125, 199-n.216.
Allegheny River: xi, 184-n.75.
Ameau, Marguerite: 164.
Anson, George; First Lord of the Admiralty: 160.
Aspiran, France: 86.
Attakapas; Louisiana colony: 148.
Aubert de Gaspé, Genevieve; daughter of Ignace-Philippe: 87.
  Ignace: 87.
  Ignace-Philippe: 25, 65, 87, **171**, 181-n.47, 196-n.188.
  Louis-Ignace: 87.
  Marie-Anne-Angélique: 87.
  Marie-Anne-Joseph: 87.
  Marie-Catherin: 87.
  Philippe: 3-n.iv, 11, 65, 87.
  Pierre: 171.
  Pierre-Ignace: 87.
Aubert de la Chesnaye, Charlotte: 163.
Aubry, Charles Philippe: 78, 79, 80, 81, 145, 170, **193-n.169**, 204-n.250.
  Père: 183-n.68.
Aubuchon, Marie-Anne: 177-n.11.
Audet-Pierrecot or Odet de Piercot, Louis, sieur de Bailleul: 49, 172, **186-n.100**.
Avice, Colombe: 64.
  Gabriel-Amateur-Louis: 64.
  Louise-Françoise-Catherine: 64.
  Marie-Amable: 64.
  Marie-Pétronille-Rose: 64.
  Michel-Marie-Charles, chevalier de Montgon de Surimeau: 63-64.
Avice de la Carte, Charles-Antoine-Jean: 64.

Baby, Jeanne: 165.
Bachaddelebat, Marie: 184-n.82.
Bachoie de Barraute, Pierre-Jean: 42, 43, 44, 45, 46, **185-n.88**.
Baie Verte, New Brunswick: 29.
Baigneux-Les-Juifs, France: 192-n.146.
Bailleul: see Audet-Pierrecot or Piercot de Bailleul.
Ballindalloch, Scotland: 194-n.170.
Bareges, Hautes-Pyrénées, France: 30.
Barrin de La Galissonnière, Roland: 162.
  Roland-Michel, Marquis de La Galissonnière: 30, 34, 160, **162**, 164, 182-n.57, 183-n.69.
Bastille, Paris, France: 161, 166, 168.
Beaubassin, Acadia: 19, 26, 27, 29, 84, 108, 110.
Beauharnois de la Boische, Charles de, Marquis de Beauharnois: 8, 9, 16, 17, 22, 23, 24, 26, 35, 50, 51, 70, 71, 92, **160**, 163, 177-n.14, 179-n.33, 180-n.41, 183-n.71, 187-n.103, 192-n.148, 197-n.194 - n.196, 199-n.213, 203-n.243; letters: 97-100, 101-104.
  François de, seigneur de la Boische: 160.
Beaujeu: see Liénard de Beaujeu.
Bécancour, Quebec: 171.
Bécard de Grandville, Marie-Anne: 163.
Bégon, Catherine: 162.
Belle-Isle, now Detroit, Michigan: 43, 196-n.187.
Belle-Riviere: xi, 36, 37, 38, 40, 41, 51, 53, 57, 58, 73, 77, 78, 112, 115, 117, 121, 122, 124-n.i, 128, 132, 137, **184-n.75**, 184-n.78, 193-n.165, 204-n.252.
Benedictines of Villarceaux: 46.
Benoist, Joseph: 49, 187-n.102.

Coulon de Villiers

Benoist or Benoît, Antoine-Gabriel: 58, **173**, 189-n.130.
   Gabriel: 173.
Bergen Op Zoom, Netherlands: 190-n.134.
Berger, Jean-Baptiste; captured by Washington: 113.
Bermen de La Martinière, Claude de: 165.
   Claude-Antoine de: 23, **165**, 180-n.38.
Berryer, Nicolas-René, Count of La Ferrière, seigneur de Ravenoville: 42, 45, **185-n.91**.
Berthier, Alexandre: 183-n.72.
Berthier-sur-Mer, Quebec: 183-n.72.
Bienville: see LeMoyne de Bienville.
Bigot, François: 31, 57, 161, 168, **182-n.59**, 184-n.74, 189-n.128.
   Louis-Amable: 182-n.59.
Billouard de Kerelec, Guillaume, sieur de Kervasegan: 192-n.162.
Billouart de Kerlérec, Louis, Chevalier de Kerlérec: 20, 74-n.ii, 75, 76, 77, 78, 81, **193-n.162**.
Blaise de Bergères de Rigauville, Nicolas: 183-n.72.
   Jean-Baptiste-Marie: 35, **183-n.72**.
Blaise de d'Abbadie, Jean-Jacques: see d'Abbadie.
Blaye, Gironde; France: 164.
Blois, Charles; killed with Jumonville: 113.
Blois, France: 173, 184-n.82.
Blondeau, Marie-Madeleine: 162-160.
   Maurice: 163.
   Suzanne: 183-n.68.
Boidoux, Marguerite: 164.
Bonin, Joseph Charles, dit Jolicoeur: 200-n.223.
Bonnes, Catherine de: 160.
Bonvouloir, Augustin; captured by Washington: 113.
Bordeux, France: 194-n.169.
Boschenry de Drucour, Augustin de: 117, 198-n.219.
Bossu, Jean-Bernard: 65, 74, 191-n.146.
Boston, Massachusetts: 37, 41.
Bot de Loc'hant, Marie Josèphe du: 192-n.162.
Bouat, François-Marie: 165.
   Madeleine-Marguerite: 165.
Boucher, Jeanne: 168.
   Marguerite: 166.
Boucher de Boucherville, Claire-Françoise: 172.
   Pierre: 172.
   René-Amable; cadet: 113, 125-n.i.
Boucher de la Bruère, Françoise: 169.
   René: 169.
Boucher de la Perrière, François-Clément: 58, 59, **189-n.129**.
   Madeleine: 167.
   René: 167, 189-n.129.
Boucherville, Marguerite: 170.
   Pierre de: 170.
Boucherville, Quebec: 113, 166, 167, 168.
Bourassa, Charlotte-Ambroisine, dit La Ronde: 197-n.198.
   René: 197-n.198.
Bourdonnaye: see La Bourdonnaye de Montluc.
Bourlamaque, François-Charles de: 61, **191-n.142**.
Braddock, Edward; British major general: 58, 60, 135, 140, 189-n.131.
Brandy Pot Island, Pot-à-l'Eau-de-Vie, Quebec: 26, 26-n.v.
Bristol, Pennsylvania: 171, 183-n.72.
Brown, Joseph; captured by Washington: 113.
Buisson, Délie: 150.
Byng, John; Admiral: 162.
Cacapon River: 86.
Cahokia, Caokias, Kaokia, Kaoquia, Kaôquias: 24, 93, 95.
Cailleteau, Marie-Anne: 165.

Index

Callières, Jacques de: 157.
  Louis-Hector de: 11, **157**, 176-n.3.
Candiac, France: 189-n.133.
Canon: 150.
Cap-de-la-Madeleine, Quebec: 171.
Caron; killed with Jumonville: 113.
Casgrain, Henri-Raymond: 3-n.iv, 11, 25, 28, 79, 200-n.223.
Catawba, Flathead, Teste Plate, Testes plates, Teteplates, Tette platte: 40, 185-n.86.
Caudebec, Normandy, France: 168.
Causse, Bernard: 30.
Céloron, Louise-Suzanne: 183-n.72.
  Louis-Jean-Baptiste: 183-n.72.
Céloron de Blainville, Hélène: 171.
  Jean-Baptiste: 162.
  Pierre-Joseph: 18, 51, 132, 133, **162-163**, 171, 178-n.27, 187-n.107, 201-n.232.
Chabert de Joncaire, Daniel-Marie, sieur de Clausonne: 52, **187-n.113**.
  Louis-Thomas: 187-n.113.
Chadakoin: see Chautauqua portage.
Champlain, Quebec: 165.
Charbonnier, Suzanne: 163.
Charles III; King of Spain: 17, 18, 47, 71, 72, 73, 80, 81, 142, 143, 202-n.241.
Chartier de Lotbinière, Angélique: 166.
  Marie-Francoise: 158.
  Marie-Louise: 172.
Chasteloger: see De Mercerel van Chasteloger.
Château d'Ajac, Limoux, France: 185-n.90.
Chateaugué, or Châteauguay, Quebec: 51.
Chateauverdun, Marie de: 159.
Chaussegros de Léry, Gaspard: 170.
  Gaspard-Joseph: 40, 53, 54, 55, 124-n.i, **170**, 184-n.85, 185-n.86, 188-n.118.
Chautauqua portage, Chatakuin, Chadakoin, Chatocoin; now in western New York: 40, 51, 53-n.iii, 55.
Chauvignerie: see Maray de la Chauvignerie.
Chavigny de Berchereau, Marguerite de: 161, 180-n.43.
Chesne de Vauve, Marie Maixende de: 64.
Chickasaw, Chicacha, Chicachas, Chikachas, Chikachau, Chis, Chiskachias, Chy, Tchikachas, Tchikakas: 18, 24, 50, 71; war with: 23, 33, 72, 144.
Chikagon; now Chicago, Illinois: 23.
Chiningué, aka Logstown; now Baden, Pennsylvania: 36, 201-n.230.
Chippewa, Anishinaabe, Ojibwa, Ojibwe, Saulteurs, Saulteux, Sauteurs, Sauteux: 95, 97, 98, 99, 179-n.34.
Chorel de Saint-Romain, Élisabeth: 177-n.11.
  François, dit d'Orvilliers: 177-n.11.
Chrétien, Madeleine: 186-n.100.
Colin, Françoise: 182-n.60.
Collet; captured by Washington: 113.
Commagère, Délie: 150.
Conocoheague Creek: 86.
Contrecoeur, Quebec: 4, 15, 21-n.i, 33-n.i, 70, 163, 167, 168.
Contrecoeur: see Pécaudy de Contrecoeur.
Corlar, aka Corlac, Corlear, Corlar, or Schenectady, New York: 34, 182-n.66.
Couagne, Marguerite de: 188-n.124.
Coulon, Guillaume, squire, sieur de Chanteraine: 12.
  Nicolas, sieur de Villiers and Chanterenne: 12.
  Nicolas: 12.

217

Coulon de Villiers

Raoul-Guillaume, sieur de Villiers: 12.
Coulon de Jumonville, Charlotte-Amable; daughter of Jumonville: 42-46.
Coulon de Villiers, Charles-François: 16, 17, 84.
   Charlès-Marie-Hucher; son of Jean-Marc: 149.
   Charles-Philippe Jumonville: 82, 150.
   Damonville: 15, 16, **17**, 84, 101, 105, **144**, 175-n.1.
   Felix; son of Jean-Marc: 149.
   Firmin; son of Jean-Marc: 149.
   François, le Chevalier de Villiers: xi, 15, 16, 26, 47, 49-n.iii, **69-84**; 1777 petition: 15, 17, 18, 47, 62, 71, 72, 73, 80, 81, 84, **142-147**, 175-n.1; avenging Jumonville: 47, 65, 73-74, 77, 83, 145; captivity: 79, 80, 81, 146, 193-n.172; Chickasaw war: 72, 144; confusion with Louis: **48**, 49, 70, 71, 72, 73, 175-n.1, 192-n.147; death: 81-82, 84; descendants: 148-150; Fort Duquesne: 75, 78, 145-146, 204-n.251 & n.252; Fort Granville: 65, 74-77, 78-n.iv, 82, 145; Fort Niagara: 79, 146; knight of Saint-Louis: 76, 77, 78, 81, 143, 144, 146, **170**; known as le Chevalier: 48, 52, 69, 70, 141, 193-n.169; marriage and children: 82-83, **148-150**, 177-n.11; New Orleans alcalde: 143, 147; not wounded by Sauk: 71, 72, 175-n.1; regarding Damonville: 15, 16, 17, 144; regarding Lespinay: 18, 19, 144; signature: 66.
   François-Louis; son of François: 148-149.
   Hypolite-Etienne; son of Jumonville: 42, 44.
   Isabelle or Elisabeth; daughter of François: 148.
   Jean-François; son of Jean-Marc: 149.
   Jean-Marc; son of François: 149.
   Joachime; daughter of François: 148.
   Joseph; first son of Jumonville: 42, 44.
   Joseph; second son of Jumonville: 42, 44.
   Joseph, sieur de Jumonville: xi, 15 17, 18, **33-46**, 48, 175-n.1, 179-n.32, 184-n.81, n.82 & n.83; Acadia: 26, 34, 51, 183-n.68; avenged: xi, 1, 25, 28, 47, 54, 56, 65, 66, 73-74, 75, 77, 82, 83, 140, 145; Chickasaw war: 33, 72; Contrecoeur's order: **115-116**; Contrecoeur's summons: 38-39, **112-113**; Fort Duquesne: 36-39; in France: 35; killed: 39-41, 47, 54-55, 84, 113, **114**, **125-n.1**, 128, 132, 137-139, 145, 190-n.134, 199-n.209, 200-n.223; marriage and children: 42-46; Poem: 134-140; signature: 35.
   Joseph; son of François: 148.
   Louis, le Grande Villiers: xi, 15, 16, 17, **47-68**, 85, 86, 175-n.1, 186-n.100, 201-n.236; Articles of Capitulation: 56, 68, 127-129, 131; avenging Jumonville: 47, 65, 66, 73, 83, 118, 119, 120, 121, **127**, **129**, 139, 140, 145, 200-n.223; Céloron de Blainville's 1749 expedition: 51; Chickasaw War: 50; confusion with François: 22, **48**, 49, 70, 71, 72, 73, 175-n.1, 186-n.99, 192-n.147; death: 61-62; Fort Miami: 51-53, 133; Fort Necessity: 54, 55, 56, 60; Fort Niagara: 58, 59; Fort William Henry: 60-61; Journal of 1754 campaign: 56, 57, **117-130**; knight of Saint-Louis: 57, 58, 59, 61, 62, 132, **169**; marriage

218

and children: 62-63; signature: 67-68; wounded by Sauk: **49-50**, 100, **133**, 187-n.102.
Louis; son of Jean-Marc: 149.
Louise: 62-63.
Madeleine-Angélique; wife of Charles-Thomas de Gannes Falaise: 16, 31, **88**.
Manuel; son of Jean-Marc: 149.
Marguerite; wife of Pierre de Gannes Falaise: 16, **88**.
Marie; wife of Alexandre Dagneau Douville: 14-15, 69, **85-86**, 97-n.i, 174, 179-n.36.
Marie-Anne; wife of Ignace-Philippe Aubert de Gaspé: 16, 25, 65, **87**, 171.
Marie-Anne-Catherine; daughter of Jumonville: 42, 44.
Marie-Jean; daughter of Jean-Marc: 149.
Marie-Joseph-Hugues; daughter of Jean-Marc: 149.
Marie-Madeleine; wife of François Duplessis-Faber, Claude Marin de La Perrière, and Joseph Damoiris: 14-15, 69, 85, **86-87**, 196-n.187.
Marie-Suzanne; daughter of Jean-Marc: 149.
Marie-Suzanne-Alice; wife of Jose-Ignace Cruzat: 83, 149.
Marie-Victoire; daughter of Jean-Marc: 149.
Nicolas-Antoine; the father: xi, **3-13**, 22, 23, 33, 34, 49, 50, 69, 70, 71, 72, 73, 82, 84, 147, 175-n.1; death: 9, 98, 103-104, 106, 144; marriage and children: 4, 14-16, 163, 169, 170, 171; Sauk-Meskwaki fight: 7-8, **97-107**, 144; siege of Meskwaki: 9-10, **92-96**, 144, 177-n.11, 203-n.243; signature: 6.
Nicolas-Antoine; the son: xi, 14, 15, 16, 17, 18, **21-32**, 35, 47, 51, 52, 69, 71, 72, 73, 171-n.1;
Chickasaw war: 23-24; death: 31, 84; Grand Pré: 25-29, 31, 32, 83, **108-111**, 132, 144, 198-n.204; knight of Saint-Louis: 30, **163**; marriage and children: 24, 31; Sauk-Meskwaki fight: 22-23, 70, 97, 97-n.ii, 98, 103; siege of Meskwaki: 8, 22, 96; signature: 23; wound: 29-30, 31, 84.
Pierre, Lespiney: xi, 16, **17-19**; Acadia: 19; Chickasaw war: 18; death: 19, 84, 144, 203-n.245; signature: 18.
Therese: 14, 16.
Count de la Serre: see d'Azemard de Panat.
Courtemanche: see LeGardeur de Croisille de Courtemanche.
Crécy, France: 164.
Crevier, Marguerite: 177-n.11.
Crisafy, Antoine de: 157, 155.
Cruzat, Francisco Zavier; lieutenant governor of Upper Louisiana: 205-n.258.
John William: 2, 16-n.ii, 20-n.i, 30-n.iv, 66, 81-n.ii, 82-n.i & n.iii, 83, 141.
Jose-Ignace: 83, 149.
Cuillimin, Charles: 164.
Marie-Josephte: 164.
D'Ailleboust Manthet, Catherine: 167-168.
Madeleine: 175-n.10.
D'Abbadie, Jean-Jacques-Blaise: 146, **204-n.253**.
D'Acosta, Delia; aka Marie Louise Clara de Acosta, wife of Charles-Philippe Jumonville Coulon de Villiers: 150.
Dagneau Douville, Alexandre: 17, 22, 71, **85-86**, 97, 98, 100, 179-n.36, 189-n.130, 195-n.182 & n.183, 201-n.236.
Alexandre-René: **85-86**, 133, **174**, 196-n.182, 201-n.236, 206-n.276.

219

Coulon de Villiers
> Joseph: **85-86**, 133, 201-n.236.
> Louise-Angelique: 86.
> Marie-Louise; wife of Pierre-Philippe d'Aubrespy de Lafarelle: 85, 86.
> Michel: 179-n.36.

Daillebout, Sieurs: 99.
Damonville: see Coulon de Villiers, Damonville.
Damours des Chauffours, Marguerite: 159.
> Mathieu: 159.

D'Amours or Damours, Bernard, sieur de Plaine: 196-n.187.
> Joseph, sieur des Plains: 87, 196-n.187.

Daneau de Muy, Jacques-Pierre: 23, 26, 51, **166**, 180-n.39, 187-n.106, 192-n.153.
> Nicolas: 166.

Daniel, François: 3-n.iv, 32, 67, 68-n.i, 87.
D'Aubigné, Françoise, Marquise de Maintenon, aka Madame de Maintenon, second wife of King Louis XIV: 45.
D'Aubrespy, Claude: 195-n.180.
D'Aubrespy de Lafarelle, Pierre-Philippe: 85, **195-n.180**.
Dazemard de Lusignan, cadet: 29, 30, 109, 181-n.54, **198-n.204**.
> Paul: 165.
> Paul-Louis: 23, **165**, 180-n.40, 181-n.54, 198-n.204.

D'Azemard de Panat, François, Count de la Serre: 81, 170, 172, 173.
De Fleury de la Gorgendiere, Charlotte: 87.
De Gannes de Falaise, Charles-Thomas: 31, 88.
> Charlotte: 88.

De Gannes de Falaise, Gabrielle: 88.
> Marguerite-Angélique: 88.
> Marguerite-Anne: 88.
> Marie-Anne: 88.
> Marie-Antoinette: 88.
> Pierre: 16, 88.

De Leyba, Don Fernando; governor of Upper Louisiana: 205-n.258.
De Mercerel van Chasteloger, Charles-Auguste-Hyacinthe: 172.
De Muy: see Daneau de Muy.
De Velie: see Coulon de Villiers, Nicholas-Antoine, the father.
De Villiers, Balthazar Ricard: 142, 143.
Denys de la Ronde, Charlotte: 172.
> Charlotte-Thérèse: 172.
> Louis: 172.
> Marie-Charlotte: 159, 163, 165.
> Pierre: 159.

Deroussel; killed with Jumonville: 113.
Des Musseaux: 99.
Deschamps de Boishébert, Charlotte: 169.
> Louis-Henry: 169.

Detroit, now Michigan: see Fort Detroit.
Devonshire, England: 194-n.173.
D'Hozier, Louis-Philippe; judge-at-arms of the nobility of France: 13, 45-46.
Dinwiddie, Robert; lieutenant governor, Colony of Virginia: 36, 41, 184-n.78, 190-n.137.
Domitilde: 197-n.198.
Drouet de Carqueville, Claude-Antoine: 55, **188-n.124**.
Drucour: see Boschenry de Drucour.
Druillon, Pierre-Jacques: 184-n.82.
Druillon de Macé, Pierre-Jacques; ensign captured by Washington: 38, 113, 125-n.i, **184-n.82**.
Du Jaunay, Pierre; Jesuit priest: 18, **178-n.28**.
Du Verger d'Aubusson, Marie-Catherie: 172.
Dubreil, Joseph-Yves, Comte de Pontbriand: 181-n.56.

Index

Dubreil de Pontbriand, Henri-Marie: 30, **181-n.56**.
Duc d'Anville: see La Rochefoucauld de Roye.
Ducasse, Marthe: 181-n.50.
Ducharme; captured by Washington: 113.
Duchâtelet, Joseph; captured by Washington: 113.
Ducros, Rodolphe Joseph: 150.
Dumas, Alexandre: 114.
   Jean-Daniel: 74, 75, 86, **166**, 192-n.161, 196-n.184.
Dupin de Bellugard: 172.
Duplessis-Faber, François; cadet: 9, 17, 86, 99, 101, 105, 144.
   Geneviève: 86.
   François: 171.
Duplessis-Fabert, Marie-Madeleine: 171.
Dupuy: 150.
Duquesne de Menneville, Ange, Marquis Duquesne: 36, 38, 39, 42, 53, 55, 56, 57, 58, 133, **162**, 165, 166, 184-n.76 & n.83, 188-n.117, 201-n.235; letter to Contrecoeur regarding Dinwiddie's request: 37.
DuQuesne Mônier, Alexandre: 162.
Dusablé; cadet captured by Washington: 113.
Énault de Livaudais, Marie Geneviève; 3rd wife of François Coulon de Villiers: 82, 83, 149, 170.
Enniskiller, County Fermanagh, Ulster; Ireland: 181-n.51.
Eurry de la Pérelle, Catherine: 163.
   François: 163.
Fauteux, Aegidius: xii, 46, 63, 81, 151, 157, 157-n.i, 189-n.129, 193-n.163, 194-n.169.
Ferland, Jean Baptiste Antoine: 9, 14, 68.
Fily, Laurent: 107.
Flathead: see Catawba.
Fleitas: 150.

Fleury de la Gorgendière, Joseph: 162.
   Louise: 162.
Fleury Deschambault, Jacques-Alexis: 161, 180-n.43.
   Jeanne-Charlotte: 161.
Folles Avoines: see Menominee.
Fontenelle, Marie Genevieve de: 148.
Fort Carillon, now Ticonderoga: 59, 60, 191-n.142.
   Chouaguen, aka Fort Oswego; now Oswego, New York: 24, 59, 187-n.113.
   Cumberland, now Cumberland, Maryland: 75, 86, 145.
   de Chartres, Illinois district; near present day Prairie Du Rocher, Illinois: 7, 20, 74, 77, 83, 148, 193-n.163.
   de La Presentation, now Ogdensburg, New York: 119.
   Detroit, aka Fort Pontchartrain du Détroit; now Detroit, Michigan: 51, 93, 132, 166, 176-n.8, 187-n.113.
   du Portage, aka Fort Little Niagara; now Niagara County, New York: 187-n.113.
   Duquesne, now Pittsburgh, Pennsylvania: 36, 54, 55, 56, 58, 60, 74, 75, 76, 78, 86, 112, 117, 121, 122, 124-n.i, 128, 145, 165, 179-n.30, 184-n.82, 189-n.124, 190-n.135, 194-n.170, 204-n.251 & n.252.
   Frontenac, aka Cataracoui or Cataraqui, now Kingston, Ontario: 86, 172.
   George, Ontario; Quebec: 62, 191-n.142.
   Granville, now Lewistown, Pennsylvania: xi, 25-n.iv, 32, 65, **74-76**, 77, 78-n.iv, 82, 145, 175-n.1.
   La Baye, now Green Bay, Wisconsin: 9, 22, 33, 49, 71, 97, 99-n.i,

101, 103, 105, 175-n.i, 179-n.19, 197-n.198.
Le Boeuf, now Waterford, Pennsylvania: 36, 40, 41, 83, 115, 121, 165.
Ligonier: see Loyalhanna.
Machault, now Franklin, Pennsylvania: 79.
Miami, now Maumee, Ohio: 51, 52, 53, 83, 84.
Michilimackinac, now Mackinac Island, Michigan: 8, 97, 97-n.ii, 102, 178-n.19, 197-n.198.
Necessity, now Farmington, Pennsylvania: xi, 8, 28, 32, 47, 49, 56, 57, 60, 65, 68, 73, 74, 82, 83, 84, 85, 86, 92-n.i, 114, 127, 131, 132, 135, 137, 140, 145, 169, 175-n.1, 186-n.100, 189-n.126, 190-n.134, 201-n.236, 204-n.247 & n.248, 206-n.276.
Niagara, now Youngstown, New York: xi, 36, 52, 58, 59, 79, 80, 81, 146, 170, 183-n.72, 187-n.113, 194-n.173, 195-n.174.
of the Lake of the Two Mountains, Quebec: 189-n.130.
Presque Isle, now Erie, Pennsylvania: 58, 79, 115, 121, 189-n.130.
Saint-Frédéric, now Crown Point, New York: 50, 51, 58, 189-n.124.
Saint-Jean, Quebec: 171.
Shirley, now Shirleysburg, Pennsylvania: 76, 193-n.164.
St. Joseph, aka royal post at the St. Joseph River; now Niles, Michigan: 6, 16, 18, 22, 23, 24, 33, 49, 70, 72, 86, 176-n.9.
William Henry, now Lake George, New York: 60, 61, 191-n.142.
Fox: see Meskwaki.
Fox River: 98-n.i & n.ii, 105.
Frontenac, Louis de Buade de: 157, 158.

Galissonnière: see Barrin de La Galissonnière.
Gallifet de Lacour, Louis, viscount of Gallifet: 46, 186-n.97.
Gàlvez, Bernardo de: 142, 201-n.240.
José de: 142, 201-n.240.
Gaspé: see Aubert de Gaspé.
Gaspereau River: 28, 29.
Gaultier, Jean-François: 32, 182-n.59.
René: 182-n.59.
Gaultier de Varennes, Pierre, sieur de La Vérendrye: 164.
Madeleine: 164, 168.
Gauthier de Varennes, Marie-Marguerite: 167.
George II, George Augustus; King of England: 37, 84.
George Island, Halifax; Nova Scotia: 181-n.50.
Gerome; killed with Jumonville: 113.
Girardin; captured by Washington: 113.
Glasgow, Scotland: 190-n.135.
Godefroy de Tonnancour, Louise: 164.
René: 164.
Goldthwait, Benjamin: 109, 110, 111, 198-n.205.
Gosselin, Amédée Edmond: xi, xii, **2**, 11, 44, 63, 175-n.1, 176-n.5, 184-n.84, 186-n.95, 200-n.219, 201-n.229, 201-n.236; confusing François for Louis: 48, 49, 71, 72-73; introduction by: 1-2.
Grand Pré, battle of, aka battle of Les Mines, Minas, or battle of Saint-Charles-des-Mines; Acadia: xi, 25, 26, **27-29**, 31, 32, 34, 83, 132, 175-n.1, 179-n.30, 181-n.51, 203-n.243 & n.244, 197-n.203, 198-n.204, n205 & n.206; French report of: **108-111**.

Index

Grant, James; British major: 78, 145, 175-n.1, **194-n.170**, 204-n.251.
  William: 194-n.170.
Great Meadows, now Farmington, Pennsylvania: 38, 175-n.1, 184-n.81, 189-n.126, 199-n.209.
Green Bay, la baie des Puants: xi, 9, 98-n.i & n.ii, 105, 197-n.198.
Grenoble, France: 194-n.171.
Gribouillard de Gesse, Catherine: 159.
Griffon d'Anneville, Josephine Catherine: 149.
Grignon, Augustine: 99-n.i, 105, 197-n.197 & n.198; reminiscences of La Baye affair: 105-107.
Groston, Jean: 177-n.11.
Groston de Saint-Ange, Elizabeth; 1st wife of François Coulon de Villiers: 82-83, 170, 177-n.11.
  Robert: 82-83, **177-n.11**, 195-n.176, 197-n.193.
Guadeloupe: 20, 86, 174, 3-n.iv, 191-n.142.
Guerin: 150.
Guillemette, Marie-Anne: 186-n.100.
Guillendard or Guillemard, Arnould: 141, 149.
Guillimin, Charles: 170.
  Marie-Josephte: 170.
Guyon-Després, Jeanne-Josephte: 170.
  Joseph: 165.
  Marie-Josephte: 165.
Haincque de Puygibault, Louis: 167.
  Marguerite: 167.
Half-King: see Tanaghrisson.
Hardouineau, Pierre: 160.
Havana, Cuba: 83, 149.
Hertel de Saint-François, Agathe: 168.
  Joseph: 168, 183-n.68.
Hervieux, Jean-Baptiste: 170.
  Marie-Anne: 170.

Hocquart, Gilles: 9, 22, 30, 50, 70, 101, **178-n.18**, 187-n.104, 1992-n.149; 1733 letter: 97-100.
  Jean-Hyacinthe: 178-n.18.
Homnier; captured by Washington: 113.
How, Edward: 109, 197-n.203.
Huchet de Kerniou, Pierre: 150.
Hurault, Marie: 180-n.42.
Huron, Huronne: 9, 54, 119.
Île-Royale: 100, 117, 157, 167, 181-n.50, 182-n.59.
Illinois, Ilinois, Jlinois, Jllinois, Jllinoise: Indians: 24, 72, 74, 76, 92, 93, 94; region: xi, 6, 7, 18, 20, 22, 23, 33, 48, 49, 65, 72, 73, 75, 77, 78, 82, 86, 144, 145, 146, 148, 176-n.5, 177-n.11, 193-n.163; river: xi, 197-n.191.
Innerarity, Jean: 149.
Iroquois, Irokois, Iroquoise, Jolocais, Jroquois, Jrroquois, Yrocois, Yrocoisses: xi, 4-n.v, 9, 34, 37, 51, 54, 92, 93, 94, 119, 144, 183-n.68, 185-n.86, 203-n.246.
Jacrau, Joseph-André-Mathurin: 24, **180-n.45**.
Jarret de Verchères, Angélique; wife of Nicolas-Antoine Coulon de Villiers, the father: 4, 21, 24, 83, 163, 169, 170, 171, 177-n.10, 179-n.32, 180-n.36, 203-n.246.
  François: 4, 177-n.10.
  Jean-Baptiste: 177-n.10.
  Joseph, de Pouligny: 21, 33, 177-n.10, **179-n.32**, 182-n.61.
  Louis: 177-n.10.
  Marguerite-Gabrielle: 49, 177-n.10.
  Marie-Jeanne: 203-n.246.
  Marie-Madeleine; aka, Madeleine de Verchères: 4-n.v, 24, 163, 177-n.10, 180-n.44, 203-n.246.
Jefferys, Charles William: 111, 198-n.206.
Jobart, Marie: 160.
Johnson, Christopher: 195-n.174.

Coulon de Villiers

William; First Baronet: 79, **194-n.174**.
Johnstown, New York: 195-n.174.
Joliet, Claire: 162, 181-n.44.
Louis: 181-n.44.
Joly, Catherine: 172.
Joncaire Chaber: see Chabert de Joncaire.
Jonquière: see Taffanel de La Jonquière.
Jorts, Catherine-Madeleine: 186-n.91.
Gabriel; seigneur de Fribois: 186-n.91.
Joybert, Louise-Elisabeth: 158, 161.
Pierre de: 158.
Pierre-Jacques: 163.
Joybert de Soulanges, Marie-Geneviève: 163, 188-n.121.
Juchereau, Genevieve: 159.
Marie-Anne: 166.
Juchereau de Saint-Denys, Marie-Catherine: 167, 178-n.19.
Jumonville: see Coulon de Villiers, Joseph, sieur de Jumonville.
Jumonville Coulon de Villiers, Aimee; daughter of Charles-Philippe: 150.
Alexander; son of Charles-Philippe: 150.
Celestine; daughter of Charles-Philippe: 150.
Charles-Philippe; son of François Coulon de Villiers: 150.
Claire; daughter of Charles-Philippe: 150.
Francois-Coulon; son of Charles-Philippe: 150.
Gustave; son of Charles-Philippe: 150.
Louis; son of Charles-Philippe: 150.
Marie-Ursula-Amable; daughter of Charles-Philippe: 150.
Odile; daughter of Charles-Philippe: 150.
Kaministiquia, Ontario: 188-n.115.

Kaninguen, Denis: 124-n.i.
Kerlérec: see Billouart de Kerlérec.
Kickapoo, Kicapous, Kicapoux, Kickap8, Kickapoux, Kikapaux, Kikapou, Kikapous, Kikapoux, Kis, Kiskaplux, Quicapoue, Quicapoux, Quikapoux, Quickapoue, Quykapoue, Quykapoux: 7, 92, 93, 96.
Kiercereau, René, dit Renaud: 205-n.258.
Kittanning, aka Attiquer, Pennsylvania: 75, 193-n.165.
La Babiche, Wea Indian village: 24.
La Batterie; killed with Jumonville: 113.
La Baye, post of: see Fort La Baye.
La Bourdonnaye de Montluc, Louis-Charles-Marie de: 193-n.168.
La Corne, François Josué de, sieur Dubreuil: 53, **188-n.115**.
Louis de, Chevalier de La Corne: 26-n.iv, 27-n.ii, 29, 34, **164**, 181-n.55, 182-n.67, 197-n.201 & n.203.
Luc de, La Corne Saint-Luc: 60, **169**, 188-n.115, 190-n.136.
La Corne de Chaptes, Jean-Louis de: 164, 168, 169, 188-n.115.
La Corne la Colombière, Antoine de: 61, **168**, 191-n.140.
La Croix-Avranchin, Manche, France: 182-n.59.
La Fosse, Antoine de, sieur de Valpantant: 12.
Louise de; wife of Raoul-Guillaume Coulon: 12.
La Lande, Anne-Catherine de: 178-n.18.
La Perrière: see Marin de La Perrière.
La Rochefoucauld, Louis de, Marquis de Roye: 181-n.50.
Marie-Louise-Nicole: 181-n.50.
La Rochefoucauld de Roye, Jean-Baptiste-Louis-Frédéric de,

Marquis de Roucy, Duc d'Anville: 27, **181-n.50**.
La Rocher, aka Starved Rock, Illinois: 92, 196-n.191.
La Valette, Marie-Angelique de: 160.
La Vérendrye: see Gaultier de Varennes.
LaForce: see Pepin.
Lake Champlain: 191-n.142.
   Erie: xi, 40, 53-n.iii.
   George, Lac Saint-Sacrement: 191-n.142.
   Huron: 11, 200-n.222.
   Michigan: xi.
   of Two Mountains or Lac des Deux Montagnes, Quebec: 37, 53, 54, 54-n.ii, 189-n.130.
   Ontario: xi, 77.
   Superior: xi, 34.
Lambert Dumont, Madeleine: 165.
Lamech, Louis; killed at 1730 Fox siege: 96.
Lamy, Louise; wife of Charles-Paul Marin de Malgue: 196-n.186.
   Marie; wife of Michel Dagneau Douville: 179-n.36.
L'Ange-Gardien, Quebec: 180-n.42.
Langlade: see Mouet de Langlade.
Languedoc; killed with Jumonville: 113.
Lansulyen, Louise de: 192-n.162.
Laperriere: see Boucher de la Perrière.
Laperrière: see Marin de La Perrière.
Laporte de Louvigny, Louis de: 159.
   Marie-Anne: 159, 173.
Larabel, Joseph; captured by Washington: 113.
Laubois, Anne; wife of Philippe Le Courtier: 12.
Lauris de Castellane, Marie-Thérèse-Charlotte de: 190-n.133.
Lauzon, Marie Antoinette Catherine de: 162.
Lavigne; captured by Washington: 113.
Le Ber de Senneville, Jacques: 173.
   Marie-Louise: 173.
Le Boeuf River, aka French Creek: 36, 40, 115, 121.
Le Couturier, Elisabeth; wife of Guillaume Coulon: 12.
   Philippe: 12.
Le Gardeur de Beauvais, Marie-Renée: 170.
Le Gardeur de Tilly, Angélique: 171.
   Charles: 158-159.
   Marguerite: 158, 161.
Le Gay de Beaulieu, Marie-Madeleine: 187-n.113.
Le Gouès de Grais, Catherine-Charlotte: 161.
   Louis-Joseph: 161.
Le Grand, Louise; wife of Antoine de La Fosse: 12.
Le Marchand de Lignery, Constant: 194-n.172.
   François-Marie: 79, **194-n.172**.
Le Mercier, François-Marc-Antoine: 38, 41, 55, 56, 61, 118, 119, 121, 126, 127, 130, **168**, 184-n.80, 188-n.125, 199-n.214.
   Nicolas-François: 168.
Le Moyne de Longueuil, Paul-Joseph; Chevalier de Longueuil: 54, 119, 121, **163**, 188-n.119 & n.121, 199-n.217.
Le Neuf, Catherine: 159.
Le Neuf de la Vallière, Marie-Josephte: 164.
Le Rebours, Charlotte: 168.
Le Verrier de Rousson, François: 161.
League of Augsburg: 145.
Leber, Marie; wife of Nicolas Coulon: 12.
   Simon, sieur de Malassis: 12.
LeBorgne, Alexandre; governor of Acadia: 196-n.187.
   Paul: 51, **172**, 187-n.108.
Lefebvre, Catherine: 186-n.100.

Legardeur, Marie-Charlotte: 178-n.25.
LeGardeur de Croisille, Charles: 171.
LeGardeur de Croisille de Courtemanche, Jacques-François: 52, **171**, 187-n.111.
LeGardeur de Croisille et de Montesson, Joseph-Michel: 54, **171**, 188-n.120.
LeGardeur de Repentigny, Jean-Baptiste-René: 9, 22, 97, 98, 99, 103, 167, **178-n.19**.
   Louis: 167.
   Marguerite: 169.
   Pierre-Jean-Baptiste-François-Xavier: 28, 61, **167**, 181-n.53, 191-n.141.
LeGardeur de Saint-Pierre, Jacques: 8, **164**, 170, 178-n.17, 179-n.29, 184-n.79.
LeGardeur de Saint-Pierre, Jean-Paul: 164.
LeGardeur de Villiers, Charles-Pierre: 18, **178-n.25**.
Lemaitre La Morille, Françoise: 164, 170.
LeMoyne, Charles: 158, 159.
LeMoyne de Bienville, Jean-Baptiste: 72, **159**, 192-n.152, 193-n.163.
LeMoyne de Longueuil, Charles, Baron de Longueuil; the father: 3, **158**, 161, 163, 176-n.4.
   Charles, Baron de Longueuil; the son: 35, 133, **161**, 185-n.73, 201-n.234.
   Joseph-Dominique-Emmanuel: 54, **188-n.121**.
Lenape, Leni Lenape; branch of Delaware: 184-n.75, 193-n.165, 199-n.216.
L'Enfant; killed with Jumonville: 113.
Léry: see Chaussegros de Léry.
Les Mines, battle of; aka battle of Minas, battle of Grand-Pré,
Grand-Pré massacre: see Grand Pré, battle of.
L'Estenduère, Henri-François des Herbiers; Marquis de l'Estenduère: 160.
LeVerrier, Ursule; wife of Jean-Paschal Soumande: 42, 44.
Lévis, François de, Duc de Lévis: 25-n.iv, 42, 43-n.ii, 45, 60-n.i, 61, 62-n.i, 77-n.iii, 78-n.ii, 79-n.i, , 152, 157, 185-n.88 & n.90, 193-n.143.
   Jean de, Baron d'Ajac: 185-n.90.
Levrault de Langis, Léon: 177-n.10.
Licaouais, Meskwaki chief: 95.
Liénard de Beaujeu, Daniel-Hyacinthe-Marie: 19, 26, 29, 166, **179-n.30**, 181-n.49.
   Louis: 179-n.30.
Lignery: see Le Marchand de Lignery.
Lisieux, Normandy, France: 168.
Little Butte de Morts, now Butte Des Morts, Wisconsin: 99-n.ii, 105.
Loches, France: 168, 171.
Lombard, Marguerite: 182-n.59.
London, England: 41.
Longueuil: see LeMoyne de Longueuil.
Lorette, Huron village on east bank of St. Charles River: 53, 54.
Louis XIV, Louis Dieudonné; Louis the Great (Louis le Grand) or the Sun King (Roi Soleil): 3, 4, 5, 6, 11, 152, 153, 155, 158, 176-n.8, 182-n.62, 206-n.275.
   XV, Duke of Anjou; Louis the Beloved: xi, 6, 9, 10, 37, 53, 63, 72-n.iv, 75, 76, 81, 84, 101, 104, 112, 114, 115, 116, 120, 121, 127, 129, 132, 136, 155, 162, 164, 165, 166, 167, 168, 169, 171, 172, 177-n.15, 185-n.91, 204-n.253, 205-n.269, 206-n.270.

XVI, Louis-Auguste, Duke of Berry: 45, 46, 154, 155, 195-n.180.
Louisbourg, Île Royale: 181-n.50.
Loyalhanna, later named Fort Ligonier: see Royal Fort Annon.
Lusignan: see Dazemard de Lusignan.
Luxembourg, Marshal: see Montmorency-Bouteville.
Macard, Marie: 178-n.25.
Macarty Mactigue, Jean Jaques: 75, 78, **193-n.163**.
Mackay, James; British captain: 56, 68, 73, 129, 132, **188-n.126**, 192-n.159, 200-n.228.
Madrid, Spain: 147.
Magnan, Catherine: 170.
Maguelonne, Jeanne-Marie de: 185-n.90.
Mahé, Seychelles archipelago: 167.
Mailhot, Marie-Françoise: 167, 189-n.130.
Maillard, Pierre; priest: 28, 181-n.52.
Maintenon: see d'Aubigné.
Ma-kau-ta-pe-na-se, aka Black Bird; Sauk boy alleged by Grignon to have killed Nicholas-Antoine Coulon de Villiers in 1733: 106, 107.
Mantes, France: 3, 11-13.
Maray de la Chauvignerie, Louis: 172.
Maray de la Chauvignerie, Michel: 130, **172**, 201-n.230.
Mariauchau d'Esgly, Louise-Madeleine: 170.
Marin, Joseph: 87.
  Louise; wife of Louis Prudhomme: 64, 169.
  Marie-Charlotte: 86-87.
Marin de La Malgue, Charles: 165.
  Charles-Paul: 196-n.186.
  Madeleine; 2nd wife of François Coulon de Villiers: 83, 149, 170.
  Pierre-Paul: 33, 83, **165**, 171, 182-n.64, 188-n.115, 189-n.130, 195-n.177, 205-n.260.
Marin de La Perrière, Claude: 86, 87, 196-n.186.
Marot de La Garaye, Angélique-Sylvie: 181-n.56.
Marsolet, Marie: 159.
Martel de Brouage, François: 170.
  Louise: 170.
Martin; killed with Jumonville: 113.
Martinique: 165.
Mascouten, Mascoutin, Mascoutins, Mask8tins, Maskoutins: 7, 92, 93, 95, 96.
Maskinongé, Quebec: 88.
Matras, Jeanne de: 178-n.25.
Menominee, aka Folleavoines, Folles Avoines, Fols Avoines: 97, 99, 103.
Méolaki; now Milwaukee, Wisconsin: 23.
Mésaiger, Charles-Michel; Jesuit priest: 6.
Meskwaki, aka Fox, Foxes, Mesquakie, Outagamies, Renard, Renards, Renart, Renarts: xi, 7, 8, 9, 10, 16, 22, 24, 49, 50, 70, 71, 97, 98, 99, 101, 102, 103, 105, 106, 133, 144, 175-n.1, 177-n.11 & n.12, 203-n.243; seige of: 92-96.
Metz, France: 168.
Miami, Mis, Misamis, Myamis, Twightwee: 7, 52, 53, 93.
Michelet Du Cosnier, Marie-Françoise: 178-n.18.
Midorge, Rachelle; wife of Simon Leber: 12.
Migeon de Branssat, Thérèse-Denise: 179-n.30.
Mi'kmaq or Micmacs: 109.
Milles, Nicolas; captured by Washington: 113.
Minas, Acadia: 108, 110, 198-n.205.
Mingo, Iroquois in the Ohio valley: 114, 185-n.86.

227

Miray de l'Argenterie, Marie-Louise: 173.
Mississauga; a band of Algonquin from the Lake Huron area: 122.
Missouri Indians: 93.
Mohawk, Anniers, Anniés, Auniers: 34.
Monbrun, Catherine de: 196-n.187.
Monceau; escaped from Washington: 184-n.83.
Monongahela, battle of: 60, 140, 166, 188-n.124.
Monongahela River, la rivière Malengueulée, Mal-engueulée, or Manangaîlé: xi, 38, 41, 189-n.127, 200-n.219.
Montauban, France: 166.
Montcalm, Louis-Daniel de: 189-n.133.
   Louis-Joseph de, Marquis de Montcalm: 43-n.i, 45-n.i, 59, 60, 61, 62, 63, 77, 157, **189-n.133**, 191-n.142, 193-n.167 & n.168.
Montesson: see LeGardeur de Croisille et de Montesson.
Montigny: see Testard de Montigny.
Montmorency-Bouteville, François Henri de, Duke of Piney-Luxembourg: 152.
Montreal, Quebec: xi, 3, 4, 5, 8, 9, 10, 15, 18, 26, 31, 34, 35, 37, 38, 42, 44, 48, 50, 51, 53, 54, 55, 57, 58, 59, 60, 61, 62, 63, 64, 69, 71, 85, 86, 89, 98, 99-n.iii, 100, 113, 132, 133, 144, 157, 158, 159, 161, 162, 163, 164, 165, 166, 167, 168, 169, 170, 171, 172, 173, 179-n.30 & n.31, 181-n.56, 187-n.102 & n.113, 188-n.121 & n.124, 189-n.129, 190-n.134 & n.135, 194-n.172, 195-n.180, 196-n.186, 201-n.232.
Moras: see Peyrenc de Moras.
Moreau de Saint-Méry, Louis-Médéric: 199-n.211, 200-n.219.

Morisseau; captured by Washington: 113.
Mouet de Langlade, Augustin: 197-n.198.
   Charles: 197-n.198.
   Charles-Michel: 105, **197-n.198**.
Munsee; sub-tribe of the Lenape: 76, 193-n.165, 199-n.216.
Natchitoches, Texas province: xi, 143, 146, 147.
Neuchâtel, Switzerland: 182-n.59.
Neuilly, France: 182-n.62.
New Orleans, Louisiana colony: xi, 2, 66, 81, 83, 142, 143, 144, 146, 147, 170, 193-n.163, 201-n.240, 201-n.241, 204-n.253.
New York; city: 80, 81, 142; colony: 34-n.i, 53-n.iii, 182-n.66 & n.68, 188-n.124, 195-n.177.
Neyon de Villiers, Pierre-Joseph: **19-20**.
Niaoure, Bay of Niaoure; now Six Town Point near Sackets Harbor, New York: 59.
Niort, Poitou, France: 63, 64, 192-n.156.
Nipising, Nepissingues: 37, 54, 119, 125.
Niquet, Marie-Madeleine: 165.
Noble, Arthur; Massachusetts provincial lieutenant colonel: xi, 28, 29, 83, 109, **181-n.51**, 195-n.178, 197-n.202 & n.203, 198-n.205.
Nolan, Marie: 159.
Normandy, France: 157.
Noyelles, Joseph de: 164.
Noyelles de Fleurimont, Nicolas-Joseph de: 7, 95, **164**, 177-n.13.
O'Callaghan, Edmund B.: 19, 34, 108.
Ohio Company of Virginia: 184-n.77, 200-n.221.
   River: see Belle-Riviere.
   Valley: 36, 55, 86, 133, 134, 181-n.85, 188-n.115, 189-n.126 & n.130, 190-n.134.

Ojibwe: see Chippewa.
Okeia, Indian chief; killed at 1730 Fox siege: 92.
O'Reilly, Alexander; Bloody O'Reilly: 143, 147, 194-n.169, **203-n.242**.
Orleans, France: 46.
Ottawa, Ouataouas, 8ta8ais, 8ta8as, outa8as, Outaoues, 8ta8ois, outa8ois, Outaouois, Outa8oy, Outaüacs, Outavois, Outawacs, Outawaws: 22, 24, 97, 99, 103, 119, 179-n.28, 197-n.198.
Oüataouaségo, Indian chief; killed at 1730 Fox siege: 96.
Ouéfigué, Indian chief; killed at 1730 Fox siege: 96.
Ouimet, Albert; captured by Washington: 113.
Outagamies: see Meskwaki.
Ouyatanons or Oüyâtanons: 53, 93, 94, 133.
Oüyénamégousy, Indian chief; killed at 1730 Fox siege: 96.
Papissa, Potawatomi: 93.
Parent, Joachim; captured by Washington: 113.
Paris, France: 12, 20, 41, 46, 81, 113, 134, 158, 160, 161, 172, 173, 176-n.9, 178-n.18, 179-n.28 & n.31, 182-n.62, 185-n.91, 191-n.142, 192-n.146, 193-n.162, 206-n.275.
Paris; killed with Jumonville: 113.
Parkman, Francis: 8, 25, 54, 203-n.243.
Parsons, Catherine: 165.
Paul, Louis; captured by Washington: 113.
Pawnee, Pani, Panis: 201-n.229.
Payen de Noyan, Catherine-Angelique: 167.
  Pierre: 167.
Pays, Renée: 160.
Péan, Michel-Jean-Hugues: 55, 57, **166**, 188-n.122, 201-n.229.

Péan de Livaudière, Jacques-Hugues: 166.
Pécaudy de Contrecoeur, Charlotte: 189-n.129.
  Claude-Pierre: 36, 37, 38-39, 41, 42, 52, 53, 54, 55, 56, 57, 58, 73, **167**, 184-n.77 & n.83, 187-n.112, 189-n.129, 192-n.157, 199-n.212; order to Coulon de Villiers: 121-122; order to Jumonville: 115-116; mentioned by Coulon Villiers: 117, 118, 119, 121, 122, 130; mentioned by Léry: 124; summons borne by Jumonville: 38-39, 112-113.
  François-Antoine: 167, 189-n.129.
  Louise-Renée: 169.
  Marie: 160, 164, 169.
  Marie-Françoise: 166.
Pelletier, Geneviève-Catherine: 171.
Pensacola, Florida: 83, 141.
Peoria, Peôrias: 24, 93, 196.
Pepin, Michel; dit LaForce; capturé red by Washington: 113, 125-n.i.
Perrot, François-Marie: 157.
  Marie; wife of François Jarret de Verchères: 4, 7.
Petit de Livilliers, Charles: 164, 168.
  Marguerite: 168.
  Marie-Charlotte: 164.
Petit de Thoizy, Marie-Anne: 184-n.82.
Petit-Boismorel, Madeleine: 165.
Peyrenc de Moras, François Marie: 61, **190-n.138**.
Phélypeaux de Pontchartrain, Jean-Frédéric; Count of Pontchartrain and Maurepas: 8, **177-n.15**.
  Jérôme; Count of Pontchartrain: 6, **176-n.8**.
  Louis: 176-n.8.
Philadelphia, Pennsylvania: 171, 125-n.1.
Philibert, Jacquin: 167.
Philippe, Catherine: 168.

229

Pianguichias, Piankishaw, Peanguichia, Peanguicha, Peanquichia, Peanquicha, Pianquichia; a division of the Miami, and formerly inhabiting southern Illinois and southern Indiana.: 53, 133.

Picoté de Belestre, François-Louis: 148.
    Hélène: 162.

Piercot, Pierre de: 186-n.100.

Piercot de Bailleul, François Odet de; Bailleul-Canut: 48, 127, **172**, 186-n.98 & n.100, 200-n.225.

Pigiquit or Pegiguet, Acadia: 28, 108.

Pimitoui, Pemitéoy; now Peoria, Illinois: 24.

Pindigaché, Indian chief; wounded at 1730 Fox siege: 93, 96.

Piot de Langloiserie, Suzanne: 183-n.72.

Place de Pondicherry, India: 167.

Plains of Abraham, battle of: 44, 189-n.129, 190-n.133.

Pointe-du-Lac, Quebec: 16, 88.

Poissel, Ursule: 162.

Pommereau, Jean-Baptiste: 172.

Pontbriand: see Dubreil de Pontbriand.

Pontchartrain: see Phélypeaux, Jérôme.

Port-Louis, Morbihan, France: 163.

Potier de Courcy, Madeleine; wife of Jacques de Callières: 157.

Pottawatomi, Pouatouamis, Poute8atami, Poute8atamis, P8tet8atamis, Poutet8atamis, Poutouatami, Poutouatames, Poutouatamy, Poutououatamis, Poutoutatamis, Poutoutouatamis: 24, 72, 92, 93.

Pouchot de Maupas, Pierre: 79, 80, **194-n.171**.

Pournain, Marie: 159.

Presidio of Los Adaes, Texas province: 46.

Prideaux, John; British brigadier general: 79, **194-n.173**, 195-n.174.

Primot, Catherine: 158, 159.

Priory of Saint Mary Magdalene of Villarceaux, France: 46.

Prudhomme, Amable; wife of Louis Coulon de Villiers: **62-64**, 169.
    Louis: 64, 169.

Pyvart de Chastullé, Marguerite-Françoise: 160.

Quebec City: xi, 2, 8, 9, 11, 14, 15-n.i, 16, 22, 24, 25, 26, 27, 29, 44, 48, 51, 59, 61, 62, 67, 71-n.i, 72, 82, 85, 86, 87, 100, 104, 113, 157, 158, 159, 160, 161, 162, 163, 164, 165, 166, 169, 170, 171, 172, 176-n.9, 178-n.25, 179-n.28 & n.36, 180-n.42 & n.43, 181-n.56, 182-n.60, 183-n.72, 185-n.88, 186-n.100, 187-n.113, 188-n.115 & n.121, 189-n.129, 190-n.133, 191-n.144, 192-n.156.

Quimper, France: 193-n.162.

Quintallina, Fr. Louis de: 82.

Raimbault, Marguerite: 170.
    Marie-Josephte: 172.
    Paul-François; sieur de Saint-Blin: 7, 172.

Ramezay, Claude de: 5, **159**, 163, 165, 176-n.7.
    Elisabeth: 165.
    Jean-Baptiste-Nicolas-Roch de: 23, 25, 26, 27, 28, 34, **163**, 180-n.37, 181-n.48, 182-n.65, 197-n.200.
    Louise-Geneviève de: 169.
    Timothée: 159.

Rebourceau, Marie: 177-n.11.

Red River: xi, 143, 147.

Red Stone Creek: 200-n.221.

Renards: see Meskwaki.

Renaud de Avesnes des Méloizes, Angelique: 166.

Index

Nicolas-Marie: 166.
Repentigny: see LeGardeur de Repentigny.
Repentigny, Quebec: 113, 187-n.113.
Revel, Haute-Garonne; France: 158.
Richard, Edouard: 33.
Richardière: see Testu de La Richardière.
Richibouctou, New Brunswick: 27.
Ricord, Madeleine-Félicité; wife of Alexandre-René Dagneau Douville: 86, 172.
Rigaud de Vaudreuil, François-Pierre de: 60, 161, 190-n.137.
   Jean-Louis de: 158.
   Philippe de, Marquis de Vaudreuil: 5, **158**, 161, 176-n.6.
Rigaud de Vaudreuil de Cavagnial, Pierre de, Marquis de Vaudreuil: 42, 43, 43-n.iii, 45, 59, 60, 61, 62, 63, 73, 74, 77, 78, 159, **161**, 166, 167, 168, 169, 170, 185-n.88, 186-n.92, 189-n.132, 192-n.158.
Rigault, Geneviève: 180-n.42.
Rigauville: see Blaise Des Bergères de Rigauville.
Riviere au Boeuf, aka French Creek: 36, 40, 115, 121.
Robineau, Marie-Anne-Geneviève: 171.
Robutel de La Noue, Anne: 194-n.172.
Rocbert de la Morandière, Louis-Joseph-Marie: 168.
   Marguerite-Élisabeth-Ursule: 187-n.113.
Rochefort, France: 162, 164.
Rouen, France: 171-n.144.
Rouillé, Antoine Louis: 33, **182-n.62**.
Roy, Joseph Edmond: 5-n.i.
   Philbert: 4.
   Pierre-Georges: xii, 3-n.iv, 11, 44, 88-n.iii, 186-n.95, 203-n.246.
Royal and Military Order of Saint-Louis: iv, xi, 20, 30, 31, 46, 57, 59, 61, 62, 64, 70, 76, 77, 78, 81, 117, 132, 143, 144, 146, 188-n.115, 189-n.129, 191-n.142, 193-n.163 & n.169, 195-n.180; recipients: 20, **157-174**, 185-n.88, 193-n.163 & n.169 ; history of: **151-156**; Coulons de Villiers, François: 76, 77, 78, 81, 143, 144, 146, 170; Louis: 57, 58, 59, 61, 62, 132, 169; Nicolas-Antoine: 30-31, 163.
Royal Fort Annon, or Loyalhanna: 146, 204-n.251 & n.252..
Ruette d'Auteuil, François-Madeleine-Fortuné: 166.
   Louise-Geneviève: 166.
Sabrevois, Jacques-Charles de: 168.
Sabrevois de Sermonville, Christophe: 61, **168**, 191-n.139.
Saint-André, Bordeaux; France: 182-n.159.
Saint-Ange: see Groston de Saint-Ange.
Saint-Antoine de Tilly, Quebec: 171.
Saint-Barthélémy Island: 172.
Saint-Cyr, Royal House of Saint-Louis, Versailles; France: 181-n.56.
Sainte-Croix, Mortagne-au-Perche; France: 178-n.18.
Sainte-Foy: 86, 87, 169; battle of: 44, 185-n.88.
Saint-François-du-Lac, Quebec: 182-n.68.
Saint-Jean-Port-Joli, Quebec: 87, 171.
Saint-Malo, Brittany; France: 181-n.56.
Saint-Martin Island: 172.
Saint-Ours, Jeanne de: 167, 189-n.129.
   Marie-Louise: 171.
   Montreal (city): 113, 161, 166.
   Pierre de: 171.
Saint-Ours Deschaillons, Jean-Baptiste de: 169.

Coulon de Villiers

Pierre-Roch de: 25, **169**, 181-n.47.
Saint-Pierre: see Legardeur de Saint-Pierre.
Sauk, Sac, Sacs, Saki, Sakis, Saquis: 9, 16, 17, 22, 24, 49, 50, 70, 71, 84, 93, 94, 98, 99, 101, 102, 103, 104, 105, 106, 107, 144, 175-n.1, 178-n.19, 197-n.198.
Saulteaux: see Chippewa.
Scioto River: 200-n.220.
Seneca, Sonnonthouons; Sonontouan: 40, 185-n.86, 200-n.220.
Shawnees, Chaoenons, Chaouannons, Cha8anons, Chaouanons, Cha8oynons, Chaouynon, Chauanon, Chavanons, Chavouanons, Ch8anons: 74, 75, 126.
Shirley, William; British major general: 58, 181-n.51, **189-n.131**.
Sioux of the Lake of Two Mountains, Sault, Cyoux, Scioux: 24, 53, 95, 119.
Smithtown, Ireland: 195-n.174.
Sonnioto, Shawnee village; now Portsmouth, Ohio: 78.
Sonontouan, Seneca village on Scioto River (not Sonontoen, the Seneca capital); now Richmond, Ohio: 122, 200-n.220.
Sorel, Quebec: 179-n.36.
Souart, Armand: 158.
  Claude-Elisabeth: 1584, 161, 163.
Soulanges, Quebec: 188-n.121.
Soumande, Jean-Pascal: 42, 44.
  Marie-Anne-Marguerite; wife of Joseph Coulon de Villiers, sieur de Jumonville: 42, **44-46**.
St. Joseph River, Illinois: 7, 8; see also Fort St. Joseph.
St. Lawrence River: xi, 26-n.v.
St. Louisianandry Parish, Louisiana colony: 148.
St-Etienne de la Tour, Marie: 196-n.187.

Stobo, Robert; Virginia provincial captain: 60, 129, 175-n.1, **190-n.135**, 200-n.227.
Sutherland, Scotland: 188-n.126.
Taffanel de La Jonquière, Jacques-Pierre de; Marquis de La Jonquière: 31, 51, 52, 133, **160**, 162, 164, 165, 182-n.58, 187-n.110, 201-n.233.
  Jean: 160.
Tanaghrisson, Deanaghrison, Johonerissa, Tanacharison, Tanahisson, Thanayieson, Thaninhison; aka Half-King: 40, 125-n.1, **185-n.86**.
Tanguay, Cyprien; Monseigneur: 11, 14, 14-n.ii, 15, 21, 21-n.iv, 42-n.ii, 62, 63, 64, 69, 85, 86, 86-n.1, 88.
Tarieu de la Pérade, Marie-Anne; wife of Nicolas-Antoine Coulon de Villiers, the son: 24-25, 163, 177-n.10, 180-n.42.
  Pierre-Thomas; aka Tarieu de Lanaudière, Sieur de la Pérade: 24, 159, 173-n.10, **180-n.44**.
Terrebonne, Quebec: 164.
Testard de la Forêt, Jacques: 159.
Testard de Montigny, Jacques: 8, **159**, 173, 178-n.16.
  Jean-Baptiste-Philippe: 73, **173**, 192-n.155.
Teste Plate: see Catawba.
Testu de La Richardière, Richard: 24, 163, 180-n.42.
Testu Du Tilly, Pierre: 180-n.42.
Thomas, Antoine Léonard: 39, 44, 134, 135.
Three Rivers, aka Trois-Rivières; Quebec: xi, 5, 30, 31, 48, 88, 158, 159, 161, 163, 164.
Toulon, France: 162.
Touraine, France: 163.
Trent, William: 200-n.221.
Trépaginer, Françoise: 192-n.163.
Trevet, Françoise de: 173.
Trottier, Marie-Anne: 186-n.100.

Index

Marie-Anne: 172.
Trottier des Ruisseaux, Antoine: 186-n.100.
Trouin; captured by Washington: 113.
Ulloa, Antonio de: 142, 143, 145, 203-n.242.
Upper country, Pays de Haute, or Great Lakes region: xi, 7, 24, 26, 48, 49, 51, 52, 54, 59, 72, 89, 101, 102.
Ursulines of Quebec: 15-n.i, 82, 85, 87.
Valfons, Charles de Mathei; Marquis de Valfons: 154.
Van Braam, Jacob; Virginia provincial captain: 60, 129, **190-n.134**, 200-n.226.
Vannes, France: 181-n.56.
Varin de La Marre, Jean-Victor: 73, **192-n.156**.
Varin de La Sablonnière, Jean: 192-n.156.
Vaudreuil: see Rigaud de Vaudreuil.
Vela, Delia: 150.
Verchères, Quebec: xi, 4, 5, 6, 7, 15, 21, 33, 49, 69, 169, 172, **176-n.10**, 180-n.36, 187-n.100, 203-n.246.
Verger d'Aubusson, Antoine du: 144, **203-n.246**.
Versailles, France: 11, 45, 46, 73, 81, 154, 158, 186-n.91, 191-n.142.

Viennay-Pachot, Marie-Françoise: 183-n.72.
Villedonné, Étienne de: 6, **176-n.9**.
Villeré, George: 141.
Villiers: see Coulon de Villiers.
Villiers du Terrage, Marc: 19, 30-n.iv, 70, 80.
Volsey, Pierre-François d'Haute-Mer de: 148, 205-n.258.
Vougny, Catherine Marguerite de: 186-n.91.
Warren, Anne: 195-n.174.
Washington, George; Virginia provincial colonel: xi, 8, 28, 36, 38, 41, 42, 44, 73, 83, 85, 92-n.i, 115, 169, 176-n.i, 184-n.82, 184-n.84, 189-n.126, 190-n.137 & n.135, 204-n.247, n.240 & n.241; Articles of Capitulation: 56, 68, 127-129, **131**; assassination of Jumonville: 39-40, 114; construction of Fort Necessity: 38, 184-n.81, 199-n.209; defeat at Fort Necessity: 126-130, 131; Jumonville poem mentions: 132, 135, 140; signature: 68.
  Lawrence: 190-n.134.
Wea; a division of the Miami on the waters of the Wabash: see Ouyatanons.
Winnebago, Pians, Piants, Puans, Puants: 72.
Youghiogheny River: 200-n.219.

CPSIA information can be obtained
at www.ICGtesting.com
Printed in the USA
FSHW010511010520
69821FS

9 781546 388463